Water Safety Plans: Book 3
Risk Assessment of
Contaminant Intrusion into
Water Distribution Systems

Water Safety Plans: Book 3

Risk Assessment of Contaminant Intrusion into Water Distribution Systems

*Kalanithy Vairavamoorthy, Sunil D. Gorantiwar,
Jimin Yan, Harshal M. Galgale,
M.A. Mohamed-Mansoor & S. Mohan*

Water, Engineering and Development Centre
Loughborough University
2006

Water, Engineering and Development Centre,
Loughborough University,
Leicestershire, LE11 3TU, UK

© WEDC, Loughborough University, 2006

ISBN 13 Paperback: 978 1 84380 102 3
ISBN Ebook: 9781788533737
Book DOI: http://dx.doi.org/10.3362/9781788533737

A catalogue record for this book is available from the British Library.

A reference copy of this publication is also available online at:
http://www.lboro.ac.uk/wedc/publications/

Vairavamoorthy, K., Gorantiwar, S. D.,
Yan, J. M., Galgale, H. M.,
Mohamed-Mansoor, M. A., and Mohan, S. (2006)
Water Safety Plans: Book 3
Risk Assessment of Contaminant Intrusion into
Water Distribution Systems
WEDC, Loughborough University, UK.

WEDC (The Water, Engineering and Development Centre) at Loughborough University in the UK is one of the world's leading institutions concerned with education, training, research and consultancy for the planning, provision and management of physical infrastructure for development in low- and middleincome countries.

This edition is reprinted and distributed by Practical Action Publishing.
Since 1974, Practical Action Publishing has published and disseminated books and information in support of international development work throughout the world. Practical Action Publishing trades only in support of its parent charity objectives and any profits are covenanted back to Practical Action (Charity Reg. No. 247257, Group VAT Registration No. 880 9924 76).

This document is an output from a project funded by the UK
Department for International Development (DFID)
for the benefit of low-income countries.
The views expressed are not necessarily those of DFID.

Designed at WEDC

About the authors

Kalanithy Vairavamoorthy

(k.vairavamoorthy@unesco-ihe.org) Currently chair for Sustainable Urban Infrastructure Systems in UNESCO, IHE, Delft, the Netherlands and previously a senior lecturer in the Water Engineering Development Centre (WEDC) at Loughborough University. He worked for South Bank University, London, from 1993 to 2002 and was head of the Water Development Research Unit within the Faculty of the Built Environment. He has an MSc degree and PhD in civil engineering from Imperial College, London. He has expertise in the design, operation and maintenance of urban water distribution systems. In particular, he has experience in researching and developing innovative solutions to water supply systems that operate under water shortage scenarios. He has also acted as a consultant on many projects for both UK water companies and overseas clients. More recently he has advised Indian water authorities on the management of intermittent water supplies, implementation of unaccounted for water action plans, leak detection and other related issues.

Sunil D. Gorantiwar

(sdgorantiwar@rediffmail.com) Associate professor and research engineer at the All India Co-ordinated Research Project on Optimisation of Groundwater Utilisation (ICAR) in the Department of Irrigation and Drainage Engineering, Mahatma Phule Agricultural University, Rahuri, India since 1985. Currently he is an academic visitor to the Water Engineering and Development Centre (WEDC), Loughborough University. He has an MTech degree in water resources development and management from IIT, Kharagpur, India and a PhD in civil engineering from Loughborough University, Loughborough, UK. He has expertise in water management of irrigation schemes in developing counties, micro-irrigation methods, optimum utilization of surface and groundwater, urban water related infrastructures and risk-based modelling.

Jimin Yan

(j.yan@lboro.ac.uk) A research scholar in the Water Engineering and Development Centre, Department of Civil Engineering, Loughborough University. He has an MSc degree in civil engineering from Harbin Institute of Technology (HIT), China. He has expertise in hydraulic and water quality modelling of water distribution systems, underground water asset management and unaccounted for water (UFW) management.

Harshal Galgale

(H.Galgale@lboro.ac.uk) A research scholar in the Water Engineering Development Centre, Department of Civil Engineering, Loughborough University. He has completed a MTech degree specializing in irrigation and drainage engineering at Mahatma Phule Agricultural University, Rahuri, India. After his masters he worked for a year at the National Environmental Engineering Research Institute (NEERI), Nagpur, India and Indian Agricultural Research Institute (IARI), New Delhi, India for six months. He was involved in environmental impact assessment studies using Remote Sensing and Geographical Information Systems (GIS) techniques at NEERI and in the design and development of a model for spatial prediction of crop yields on regional scales at IARI. He has expertise in the field of GIS, Remote Sensing and hydrological modelling.

M.A. Mohamed-Mansoor

(M.A.Mohamed-Mansoor@lboro.ac.uk) A research scholar in Water Engineering and Development Centre, Department of Civil Engineering, Loughborough University. He has completed Master of Science in Civil Engineering from South Bank University, London. After this, he worked with the Water Development Research Unit at South Bank. His areas of specialization are water supply management, water distribution system modelling and performance assessment of water distribution systems.

Professor S. Mohan

(smohan@iitm.ac.in) The Head, Department of Civil Engineering at Indian Institute of Technology Madras, Chennai, India. He has an ME degree and a PhD in Civil Engineering from Indian Institute of Sciences, Bangalore, India. His research interests include Environmental System Analysis, Water Quality Modelling, Water and Waste Water Treatment, Water Resources System Analysis, Irrigation Water Management, Evolutionary Computation. He has led and participated in several research and consultancy projects in these areas both nationally (in India) and internationally.

Acknowledgements

The financial support of the UK Department for International Development (DFID) is gratefully acknowledged. The authors would also like to thank those who have contributed to the development of these guidelines.

KAKTOS Consult, Hyderabad, India
India Institute of Technology (IIT), Chennai, India
Guntur Municipal Corporation, Municipal Corporation of Hyderabad, India
Public Health Engineering Department of Guntur, India

Finally, the authors wish to acknowledge Dr Guy Howard, DFID, Bangladesh and Dr Sam Godfrey, UNICEF, India for their intellectual input; Ian Smout, Director, WEDC for his constructive suggestions and Rod Shaw, Sue Plummer and Karen Betts of the WEDC Publications Office.

Who should read this book

This book has been written specifically for practitioners involved in the operation, maintenance and management of piped water distribution systems in urban areas of developing countries. These practitioners include engineers, planners, managers, and water professionals involved in the monitoring, control and rehabilitation of water distribution networks.

The book explains in detail how to evaluate the risk of deterioration of the water distribution network of a water supply system. It begins with the conceptualization of risk evaluation and its three different components (hazard, vulnerability and risk). The book further elaborates on each of these three components, explains the methodologies used to estimate the components, and presents the background to the mathematical models. Finally, the book explains how these components are integrated to form a GIS-based decision support system for risk evaluation. The book is designed to help practitioners understand the concept of risk evaluation and supports the 'Manual' of the IRA-WDS software, a GIS-based decision support system for risk evaluation.

How to use this book

The IRA-WDS software is developed for the evaluation of risk to piped water distribution systems in urban areas of developing countries. The user of this software needs to know about the consideration of different factors, data type and requirement, which may vary from one region to another. The user can understand the concept of evaluation from this book and decide upon the importance of the different factors involved and associated data collection.

It should be noted that combining this book with Book 1 provides the decisionmaker with a valuable tool to assess the overall risk of contaminant intrusion into a water supply system. It is also important to consider this book in relation to Book 2, as it is imperative that the institutions and authorities responsible for water management have the capacity to use and implement IRA-WDS, and also to recognize the importance of developing an integrated approach to water management.

How does this book fit into the overall guidelines?

This book is Document 3 in the guidelines series developed for Project KaR R8029 *Improved Risk Assessment and Management for Piped Urban Water Supplies*. This book presents the background to the mathematical models used in the development of IRA-WDS software. IRA-WDS is a GIS-based software that estimates the risk of contaminant intrusion into water distribution systems from sewers and surface foul water bodies. It should be noted that combining this book with Book 1 provides the decision-maker with a valuable tool for assessing the overall risk of contaminant intrusion into a water supply system. It is also important to consider this book in relation to Book 2, as it is imperative that the institutions and authorities responsible for water management have the capacity to use and implement IRA-WDS, and also to recognize the importance of developing an integrated approach to water management.

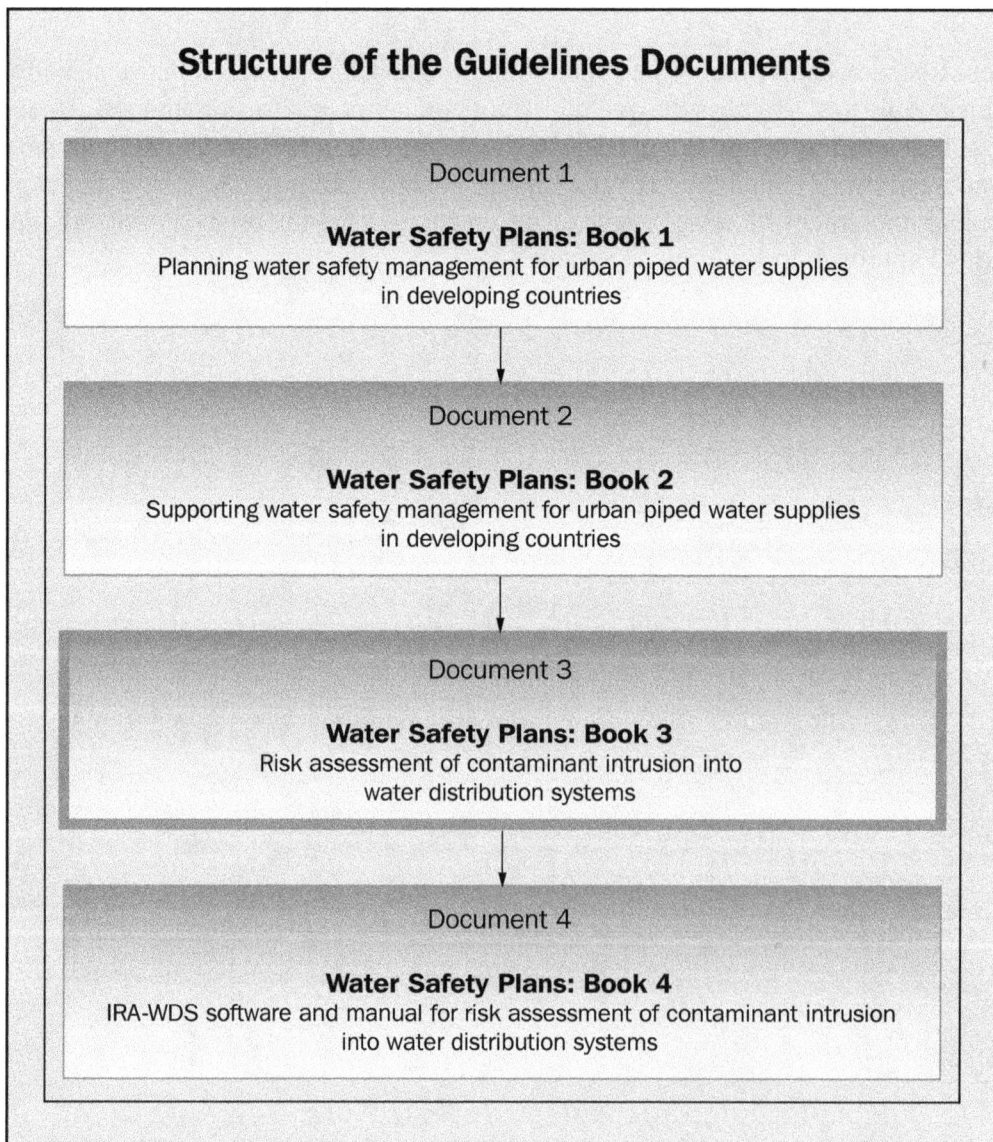

Structure of the Guidelines Documents

Document 1

Water Safety Plans: Book 1
Planning water safety management for urban piped water supplies
in developing countries

Document 2

Water Safety Plans: Book 2
Supporting water safety management for urban piped water supplies
in developing countries

Document 3

Water Safety Plans: Book 3
Risk assessment of contaminant intrusion into
water distribution systems

Document 4

Water Safety Plans: Book 4
IRA-WDS software and manual for risk assessment of contaminant intrusion
into water distribution systems

CONTENTS

Chapter 4: Risk Assessment Model   91

Chapter 5: Integration of the Model with GIS   101

Chapter 6: Example Application of Model (IRA-WDS)   125

List of boxes

List of tables

List of figures

CHAPTER ONE

Overview

Risk Assessment of Contaminant Intrusion into Water Distribution Systems

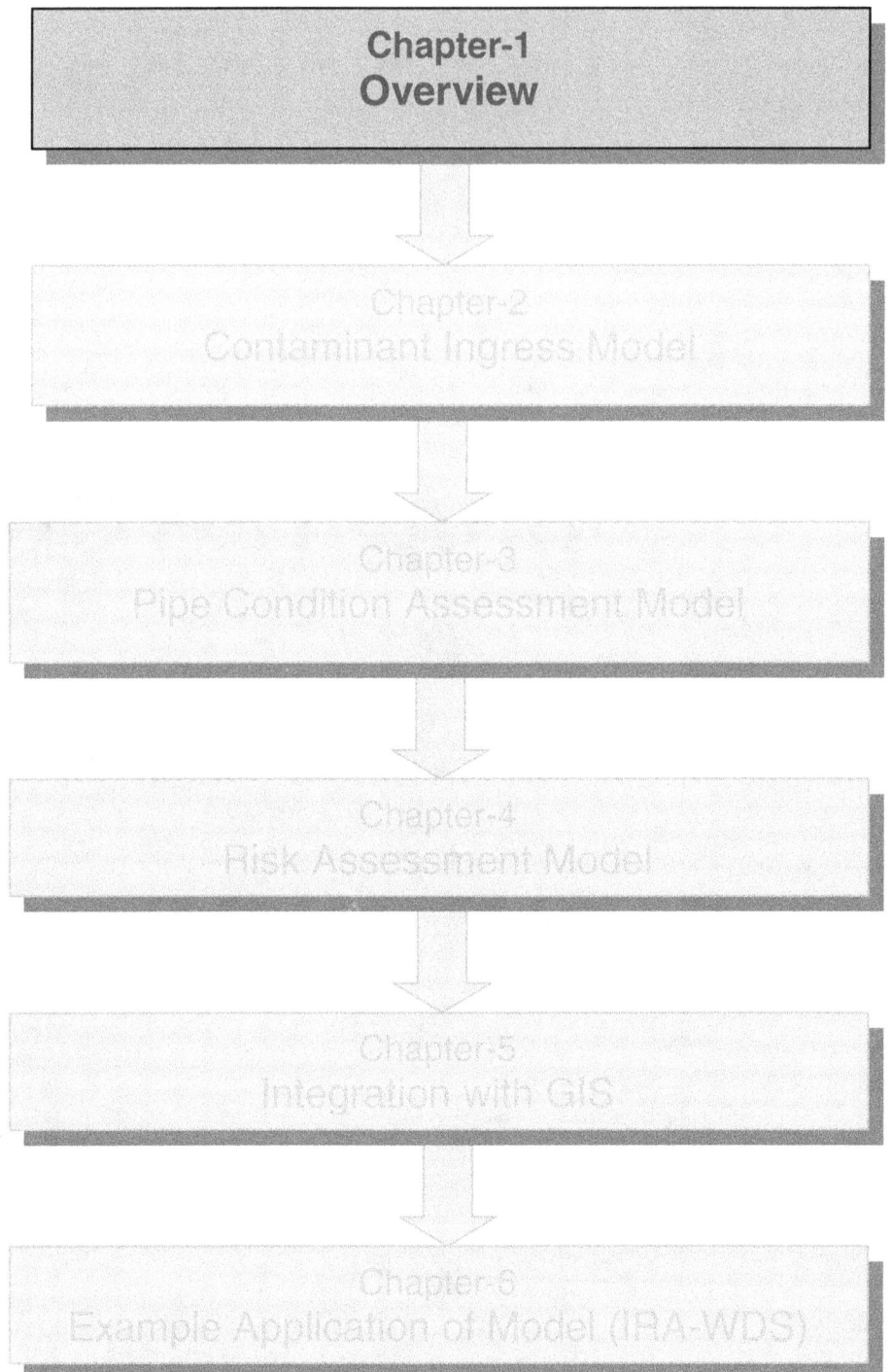

Chapter-1
Overview

Chapter-2
Contaminant Ingress Model

Chapter-3
Pipe Condition Assessment Model

Chapter-4
Risk Assessment Model

Chapter-5
Integration with GIS

Chapter-6
Example Application of Model (IRA-WDS)

Chapter 1: Overview

1.1 Introduction

In most developing countries water supplies are intermittent due to the prevailing water scarcity that results from depletion of existing water sources. Intermittent systems are those in which there are no supplies for long periods of time. In addition to the inadequate supply of water, other major shortcomings of such systems are the inequitable distribution of supply and the risk of contamination resulting from insufficient pressures when the distribution system is empty.

The importance of water supply with sufficient quantity and acceptable quality has been emphasized in the Millennium Development Goals (MDGs), drawn from the United Nations Millennium Declaration. Goal 7 of the MDGs says, 'Ensure environmental sustainability,' and Target 10 of Goal 7 says: 'Halve, by 2015, the proportion of the people without sustainable access to safe drinking water and basic sanitation' (United Nations 2005).

The quality of water received by the consumer is determined by the quality of water at source, water treatment and condition of water distribution system (WDS). Until recently, water quality was generally considered a treatment issue and not a distribution issue. As a result, distribution factors are often overlooked (Smith et al. 2000). Due to the ignorance of the influence of the deteriorating condition of WDS on water quality, several cases in which distribution pipes contributed to water quality problems were reported (Danon-Schaffer 2001; Geldreich 1996; Kirmeyer et al. 2001; Wyatt et al. 1998). Hence there is a growing concern about water quality variability within the distribution system (Galbraith et al. 1987; Payment et al. 1991; Payment et al. 1997).

Distribution systems with intermittent water supplies are prevalent among countries where rapid urbanization is taking place. It has been reported that around 50 per cent of utilities in 50 Asian cities supplied water for less than 24 hours a day in 1995. Supplies in six of the 50 cities were found to be a mere six hours a day (McIntosh and Yniguez 1997). More than 90 per cent of the population with a piped supply in South Asia receive water for less than 24 hours (McIntosh 2003). Similar situations exist in Africa and Latin America. In Zaria, Nigeria, in 1995, only 11 per cent of the consumers with a piped supply received water one day in two. It has also been reported that in Mombasa the average duration of the service is 2.9 hours per day (Hardoy et al. 2001). In Latin America, 10 of its major cities receive rationed supplies (Choe and Varley 1997).

A serious problem arising from intermittent supplies, which is generally ignored, is the associated high levels of contamination. This occurs in networks where there are prolonged periods of interruption of supply due to negligible or zero pressures in the system and when the pipes of the water distribution system criss-cross with the pollution sources, which is often a case in developing countries.

Boxes 1.1, 1.2 and 1.3 present the typical water distribution system, pollution sources and interaction of pollution sources with the water distribution system that deteriorate the water quality. Water distribution pipes lie below the pollution sources (surface foul water bodies, leaky sewers, open drains and canals) from which the contaminants seep into the surrounding soil and move towards the water pipes. Low dissolved oxygen, high nutrient loads, fecal matter, pathogens, objectionable floatable material, toxins, and solids are all found in abundance in these contaminants (Moffa 1990). These contaminants enter the deteriorated pipes through joints and cracks developed due to ageing, physical stresses and chemical processes (corrosion) and pollute the water in the distribution system. Such problems lead to increased health risks as water becomes contaminated with pathogens.

Thus the contamination risk is high when prolonged periods of interruption of supply due to negligible or zero pressures (loss of system integrity) in water distribution system are coupled with the movement of contaminated water from various pollution sources (surface foul water bodies, sewers, open drains and canals etc.). Figure 1.1 (a) shows the process of contaminant intrusion into the distribution system.

Box 1.1. Characteristics of typical water distribution systems in developing countries

The water distribution systems in the developing countries are at risk of contaminant intrusion for the following reasons.

1. *Pipe deterioration:* The pipes of water distribution system are deteriorated due to physical, environmental and operational factors. These deteriorated pipes develop cracks and leaks and pollutants surrounding the pipes can find entry into the pipes.
2. *Intermittent water supply:* The design of water distribution systems in the cities of developing countries assumes continuous water supply. However, in these cities the actual water supply is not continuous but intermittent, mostly because of the shortage of water. In intermittent systems, the pipes are empty for many hours of the day, during which time the pollutants surrounding the pipes can enter into the pipes through cracks and leaks.

4

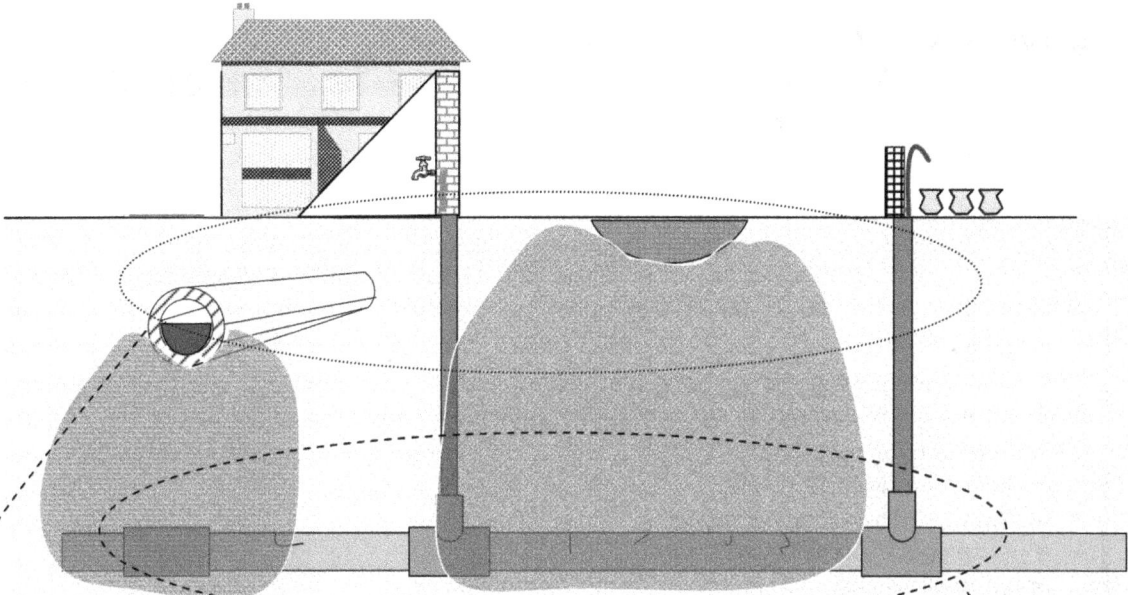

Figure 1.1 (a). Contaminant intrusion process into water distribution network

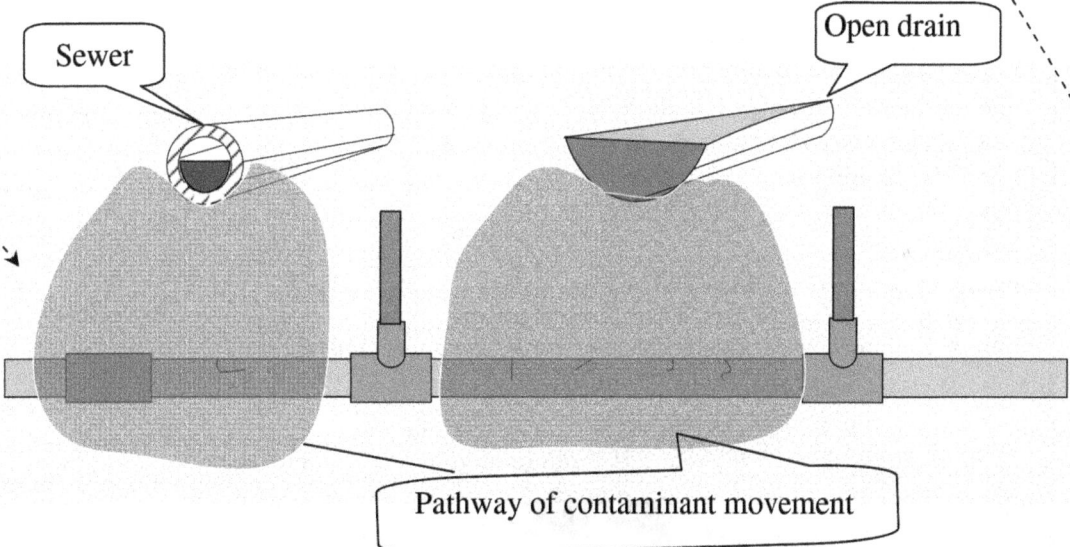

Sewer

Open drain

Pathway of contaminant movement

Figure 1.1 (b). Contaminant ingress process

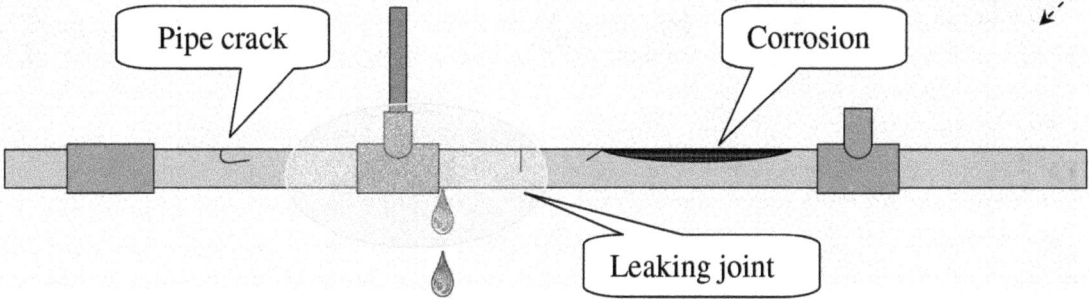

Pipe crack

Corrosion

Leaking joint

Figure 1.1 (c). Water distribution pipe deterioration

Box 1.2. Pollution sources

The pollution sources are the sewerage system and open surface foul water bodies. The sewerage system collects the wastewater or sewage from the homes through sewers. The sewers of sewerage systems in developing countries consist of closed pipes/conduits and open drains/canals. These conduits and drains are often the source of pollution to soil and groundwater. The wastewater carried through these conduits and drains contains pollutants which can be hazardous to health. The pollutants find their way out to the surrounding soil and groundwater through cracks and leaks that develop in damaged pipes/conduits and seep through the unlined open drains/canals into the soil.

Damaged conduits/pipes in the sewerage system cause leakage of contaminants into the soil. *These conduits/pipes can be damaged in different ways at various locations.* The primary causes are:

- Ground movement
- Ground erosion or soil loss
- Material deterioration of sewers
- Improper layout and installation
- Natural damage, such as minor earthquakes or proximity of trees.

For these reasons, *the most common defects which might give rise to the sewage leakage* from conduits/pipes are:

- Cracks and fractures
- Joint displacement
- Deformation and collapse
- Reverse gradients
- Siltation, blockage
- Poorly constructed connections
- Abandoned laterals left unsealed
- Root intrusion.

Apart from sewer pipes and open drains, there are other pollution sources from which water distribution system may be contaminated, the major one being the open surface water bodies such as wastewater disposal ponds. Thus the three important sources of pollution are:

- Sewer pipes/conduits (Figure 1.2 (a))
- Open drains/canals (Figure 1.2 (b))
- Open surface foul water bodies (Figure 1.2 (c))

(a) Sewer pipe   (b) Open drain   (c) Foul water body

Figure 1.2. The sources of pollution

Box 1.3. Interaction of water distribution systems and pollution sources

Water distribution and sewerage systems are two important components of the infrastructures in a city. However, in many cities these are not considered as a unit. Often these systems are planned individually rather than as a unit. This happens mainly because of the expansion of the city area and uncontrolled growth in population. Design, construction and operation of these systems are very important and they require a high degree of skill and judgement, both because of the nature of the work and because each phase of the problem involves the health of the citizens. In the absence of a proper decision support tool for the design, construction and operation, these systems can deteriorate quickly.

According to pipeline installation practices (Smith et al. 2000), the water distribution pipe should be located a minimum of about 3 metres away from a sewer pipe. If conditions require these pipes to be located close together (e.g. a narrow throughway or perpendicular crossing), the water distribution pipe should be located at least half a metre above the sewer pipe. However, in developing countries, the pipes of water distribution system and sewerage system often criss-cross each other. On many occasions, the pipes of the water distribution system are laid below the pipes of sewerage system. The contaminants from the leaky sewerage lines, open drains and surface foul-water bodies seep into the soil and subsequently enter the water distribution pipes and reach the groundwater. The contamination of water supply systems and groundwater by these pollution sources is increasingly a serious matter of public and regulatory concerns. Polluted water affects public health and even poisons people (Lerner 1994). Eiswirth and Hotzl (1994) reported that in the Federal Republic of Germany several 100 million m^3 of wastewater leak every year from partly damaged sewer systems into soil and groundwater. In developing and underdeveloped countries, the extent may be much greater as the piped sewer system is combined with open drains and surface foul water bodies. Such a situation is potentially dangerous for public health, as any further lapses in operation and maintenance of these systems will lead to intrusion of hazardous elements in the water distribution system and poses a risk to human life.

Causes of damage

In the present study, seepage of contaminants from the surface foul water bodies, open drains and sewer conduits are considered as the main pollution sources and that the drinking water distribution system is likely to be influenced by the movement of the contaminants through the soil from these pollution sources. Water distribution pipes are vulnerable to contaminant intrusion when they are below a sewer, surface foul water body or open drain. Under such circumstances, contaminants may enter water distribution pipes if:

- The contaminant flows out of pollution sources e.g. through cracks in a sewer pipe
- The water distribution pipe is within the contaminant zone of the pollution sources (Figure 1.3)
- The water distribution pipe has cracks where a pollutant might enter.

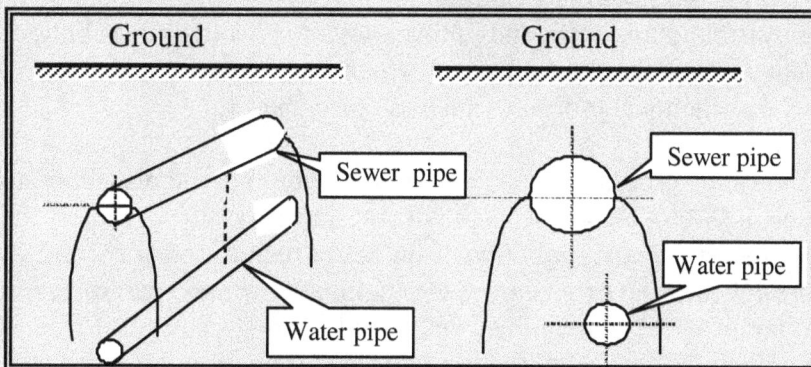

Figure 1.3. Water pipes in potentially polluted area

7

1.2 Why IRA-WDS?

In intermittent systems the loss of system integrity due to the prolonged periods of interruption of supply, coupled with the unique conditions of pollution sources interfering with the water distribution network, has meant that such systems pose a very serious contamination problem. Thus in developing countries where intermittent supplies are the norm, the water distribution network has become a point at which contamination frequently occurs to unacceptably high levels, posing a threat to public health. Hence, in developing countries there is a need to develop control measures to minimize the risks associated with contamination of drinking water, and improve management of water quality in drinking water distribution systems.

By identifying the relative risks associated with contaminant intrusion into water distribution systems, it may be possible for decision-makers to prioritize their operational maintenance strategies in order to achieve maximum benefits from their investments in terms of improvements to water quality. Hence Integrated Risk Assessment-Water Distribution System (IRA-WDS), a GIS-based spatial decision support system (SDSS), has been developed to assist the authorities in improving water quality.

The next section of this chapter presents an introduction to the development of IRA-WDS. The remaining chapters of this book present the details of the mathematical models that form the basis of the enclosed IRA-WDS software (Book 4), followed by a case study. The manual for use of IRA-WDS is presented in Book 4.

It should be noted that in order to use IRA-WDS, one does not require a detailed understanding of the models presented in this book. The information provided in the book is to give the user an insight into the basis of the model, the significance of the data required to drive the model and assistance in interpreting the results.

1.3 IRA-WDS and its components

Water distribution pipes lie below the pollution sources from which the contaminants seep into the surrounding soil and move towards water distribution pipes. Contaminants enter water distribution pipes which have deteriorated due to ageing, physical stresses and chemical processes such as corrosion.

Figure 1.1 (a) shows the process of contaminant intrusion into the distribution system. Three conditions need to exist for contaminant intrusion to occur in the water distribution system. These are: pollution sources, intrusion pathway, and intrusion condition. Figure 1.1 (b) is an extension of the 'pollution sources' part of Figure 1.1 (a) and shows the 'pathway' of contaminant movement through soil until it reaches the water distribution pipe. Figure 1.1 (c) expands the water distribution section of Figure 1.1 (a) and shows the deterioration of the water distribution pipe that provides the opportunity for contaminant intrusion to occur during non-supply hours or when low or negative pressure occurs.

In previous studies, pollution sources have not been taken into account when considering contaminant intrusion into the water distribution system. The contaminant source is either assumed to exist around the water distribution pipes or considered through simple spatial analysis (e.g. cross-connections between sewer conduits and distribution pipes). Neither the type of pollution sources nor their interaction with the distribution system has been addressed before. Most work has focused on hydraulic transients; however, many networks in the world (particularly in developing countries) have many hours of non-supply. This factor has not been considered previously.

IRA-WDS is based on a risk-based modelling approach that assesses the risk associated with contaminant intrusion into the water distribution system during non-supply hours (especially for intermittent water supplies). IRA-WDS overcomes many of the limitations of previous approaches. IRA-WDS is a GIS-based decision support system that predicts the risks associated with contaminated water entering the water distribution system from surrounding surface foul water bodies, sewer pipes, drains and ditches. Several modelling tools are included in IRA-WDS that simulate and predict the susceptibility conditions for contaminant intrusion (contamination sources, intrusion pathway) and obtain the risk of contaminant intrusion into the water distribution. The IRA-WDS also develops a risk map that highlights the risk areas of the water distribution system to display the risk spatially.

The IRA-WDS model consists of following three main components (Figure 1.4):

- Contaminant ingress model
- Pipe condition assessment model
- Risk assessment model.

The next three sections will give brief details of these components of the model.

1.3.1 Contaminant ingress model

This model simulates the movement of contaminated water from different pollution sources (surface foul water bodies, sewers, drains etc.) through typical soils and towards drinking water distribution pipes (see Figure 1.1 (b)). Table 1.1 shows the data required to implement the contaminant ingress model component of IRA-WDS.

The contaminant ingress model is divided into two components.

- Contaminant zone model: This model predicts the zone or envelope of contaminant (contaminant zone-CZ) emanating from a pollution source and the section of pipes in a water distribution system in the contaminant zone (SPCZ).
- Contaminant seepage model: This model simulates the variable concentration of the contaminants within the contaminant zone and predicts the contaminant loading on the SPCZ.

Thus, by considering the route of a drinking water distribution pipe and how it intersects with the contaminant zone of pollution sources (surface foul water body, sewer or ditches etc.), it is possible to estimate the potential contaminant load that might enter the water distribution pipe from the pollution sources. This is considered as 'hazard' in the risk assessment model.

9

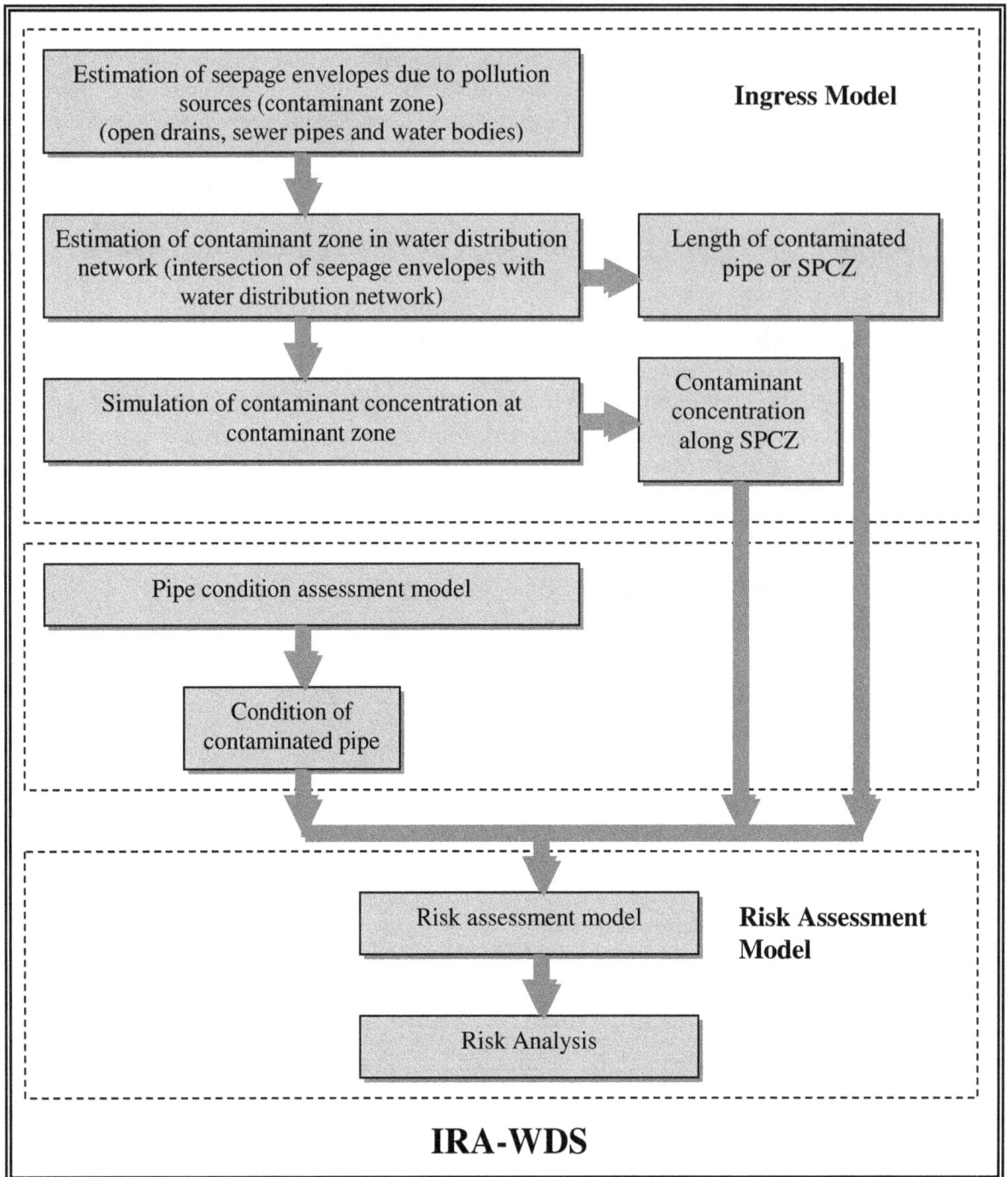

Figure 1.4. Main components of IRA-WDS

The output from the model is the prediction of the contaminant zone, SPCZ, variable concentration of contaminant in CZ, and contaminant loading along the SPCZ due to different pollution sources. Figure 1.5 shows contaminated pipes in the water distribution system.

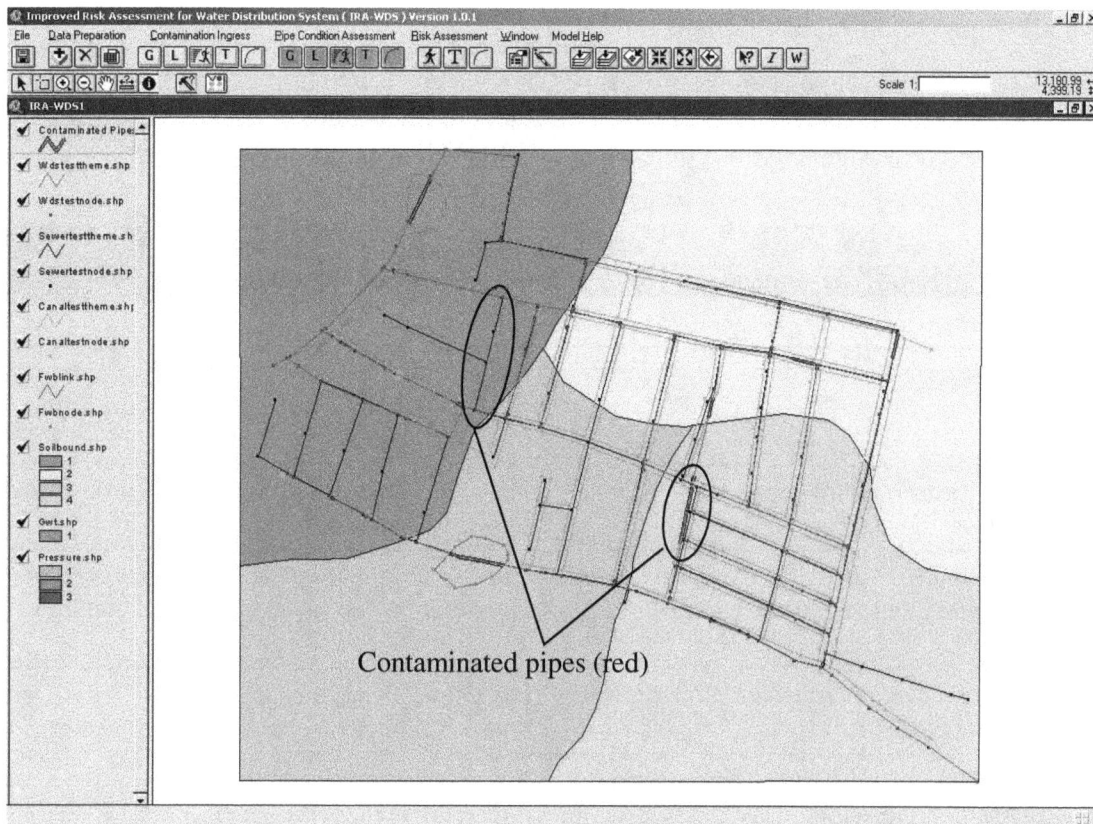

Figure 1.5. Example output from IRA-WDS that shows contaminated pipes or SPCZ in a water distribution system

The contaminant ingress model is discussed in detail in Chapter 2 of this book and the implementation of IRA-WDS is given in Chapter 3 of Book 4 (IRA-WDS user manual).

Table 1.1. Data requirement for contaminant ingress model	
Properties	**Purpose**
Sources of pollution	For estimating the contaminant zone or potentially polluted area
Spatial location of different pollution sources	
Properties of pollution sources	
Spatial location of water distribution network	For identifying the section of water distribution pipe in contaminant zone or potentially polluted area developed due to pollution sources (SPCZ)
Types of soils	For estimating the relative contaminant concentration in the contaminant zone
Characteristics of different soils	
Characteristics of contaminants/pollutants	

1.3.2 Pipe condition assessment model

This model assesses the condition of pipes in a water distribution network (see Figure 1.1 (c)) and identifies the pipes which are subject to the most risk. Table 1.2 shows the data required to complete this component of IRA-WDS.

Table 1.2. Data requirement for pipe condition assessment model	
Properties	**Purpose**
Spatial location of water distribution network	For identifying the sections of distribution system that are vulnerable to contaminant intrusion
Physical properties of pipes in the water distribution network	For pipe condition assessment based on physical condition
Environmental data such as soil, groundwater, surface characteristics, traffic load etc.	For pipe condition assessment based on deterioration due to environmental condition
Operational data such as duration of water supply, breakage history etc.	For pipe condition assessment based on deterioration due to operational parameters
Weightings for different pipe condition assessment indicators and groups of indicators	For indicating the relative importance of indicators in the same group
Balance factors for different groups of pipe condition indicators	For indicating the degree of compromise between indicators of the same group

The model considers each pipe in a water distribution system and estimates their relative condition. The condition of each pipe is assessed by means of numerous factors related to physical, environmental and operational aspects of the water distribution system. These factors are grouped into different indicators at three levels, depending on the nature of influence of each factor on the deterioration process of the pipe. These indicators are combined to give a single measure of the relative condition of each pipe. The outputs from the model are therefore a measure of the relative condition of each pipe in the water distribution system being studied. This is considered as 'vulnerability' in the risk assessment model. Figure 1.6 shows the relative pipe conditions in a water distribution system.

The relative condition of each pipe (vulnerability) (output from this section), coupled with the contaminant loading along the SPCZ (hazard) (outputs from contaminant ingress model presented in Section 1.2.1), provides an estimate of the potential pollutant load entering each pipe (risk of contaminant intrusion).

The pipe condition assessment model is discussed in detail in Chapter 3 of this book and the implementation of IRA-WDS is given in Chapter 4 of Book 4 (IRA-WDS user manual).

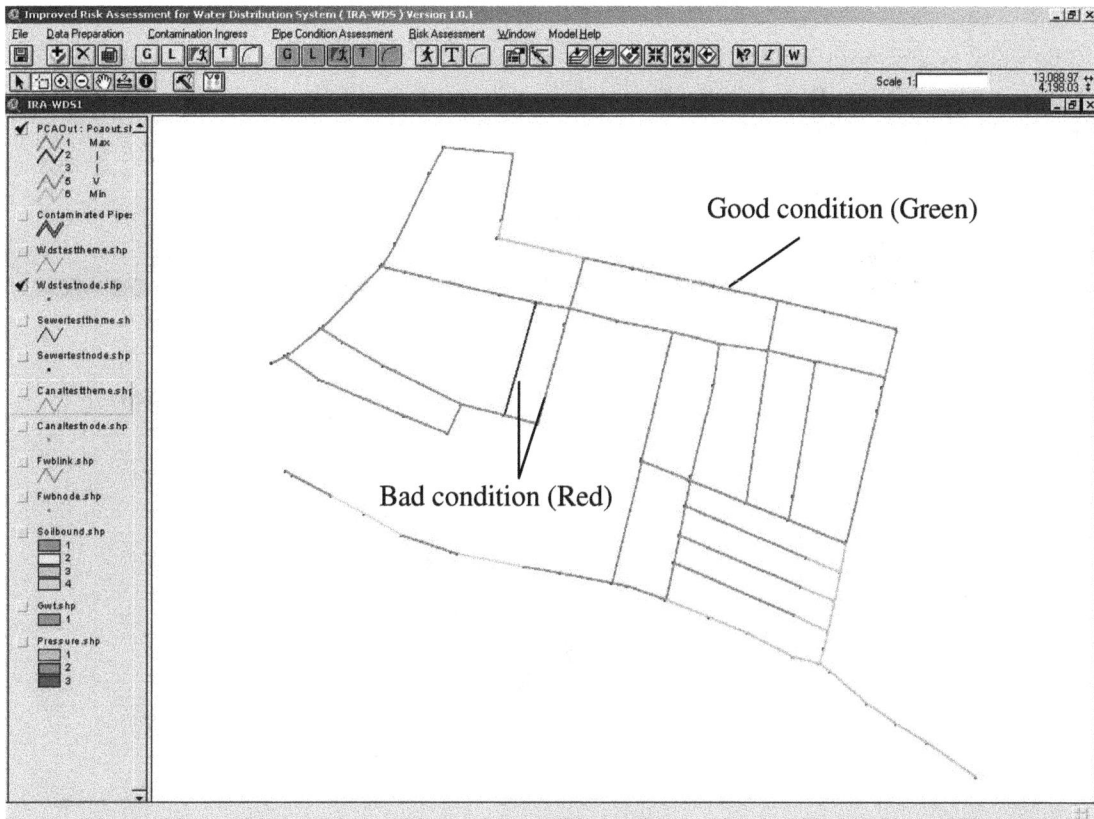

Figure 1.6. Example output from IRA-WDS that shows the relative condition of different pipes in a water distribution system

1.3.3 Risk assessment model

The risk assessment model estimates the risk of contaminant intrusion into the pipes of water distribution system. This model uses the outputs from the contaminant ingress model (hazard) and pipe condition assessment model (vulnerability). The model combines these outputs by using appropriate weightings to hazard and vulnerability and generate relative risk of contaminant intrusion due to each pipe of WDS. Table 1.3 shows the data required to implement this component of IRA-WDS.

The outputs from the model are relative risk maps showing the relative risk of contaminant intrusion into the entire water distribution system. Figure 1.7 shows an example of a relative risk map.

Table 1.3. Data requirement for risk assessment model	
Properties	**Purpose**
Spatial location of water distribution network	For identifying sections of the distribution system that are most vulnerable to risk
Weightings for SPCZ or potential polluted area and contaminant concentration	For indicating the relative importance of SPCZ or potential polluted area and contaminant concentration for hazard
Weightings for hazard and vulnerability	For indicating the relative importance of hazard and vulnerability for risk.

13

The risk assessment model is discussed in detail in Chapter 4 of this book and the implementation of IRA-WDS is given in Chapter 5 of Book 4 (IRA-WDS user manual).

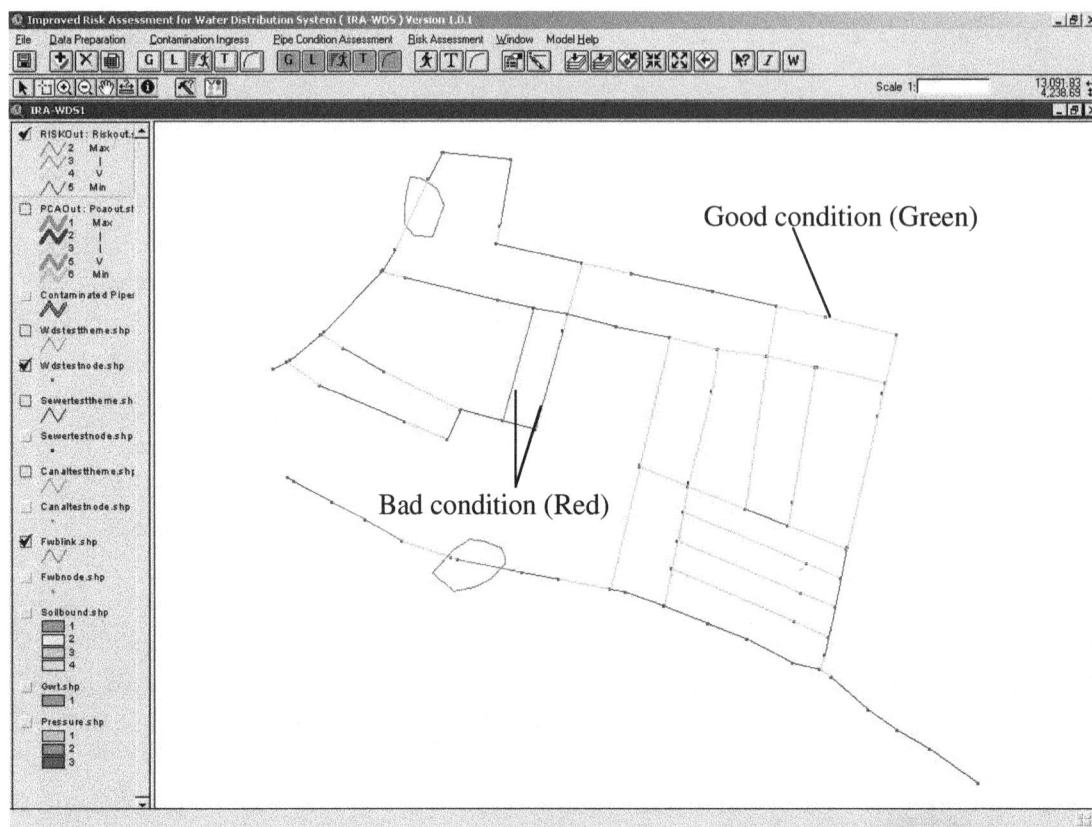

Figure 1.7. Example output from IRA-WDS that shows a relative risk map

It should be noted that the outputs from the risk assessment model can then be coupled with a water network quality model (e.g. EPANET (Rossman 1994)) to show the movement of contamination within the distribution system and to identify those areas and consumers most at risk. Note that this is beyond the scope of this study (although an example is given in Appendix F).

1.3.4 GIS integration

All the models are integrated into a GIS platform to produce SDSS. The results of all three models can be displayed through the GIS and appropriate thematic maps generated. The final outputs from the IRA-WDS will be risk maps indicating the relative risks associated with contaminant intrusion for different parts of water distribution systems. The integration with the GIS is discussed in detail in Chapter 5 of this book and the implementation of IRA-WDS is given in Book 4 (IRA-WDS user manual).

1.4 How to Interpret the Results

The output from IRA-WDS will be risk maps showing the risk of contaminant intrusion into the various parts of the water distribution system. These risk maps will be invaluable to the decision-makers/engineers in that they enable them to:

14

- Identify sections of a water distribution system that are most vulnerable to contaminant intrusion
- Prioritize operational maintenance strategies to have maximum impact in terms of improving water quality
- Investigate potential improvements in water quality with changes to operational maintenance (by simulating the models for various scenarios)
- Plan strategically rehabilitation programmes that will have maximum returns in terms of water quality for their investments.

1.5 Capacity of Institutions to Use IRA-WDS

1.5.1 Undertaking an organizational and institutional review

In order to successfully implement IRA-WDS, there needs to be sufficient capacity within the institutions and authorities responsible for water supply. The areas that need to be strengthened within an institution to effectively implement IRA-WDS include:

- *Appropriate staffing level:* Sufficient number of skilled competent staff who will carry out the tasks.

- *Staff education and training:* Delivered through awareness seminars (for senior staff), training workshops (for engineers and technical staff) and continuous practical training (for operations staff).

- *Operation and maintenance (O&M):* Important, as lack of O&M leads to inefficient practice, ineffective services and waste of resources.

- *Assessing and monitoring:* On-going monitoring to maintain water quality targets. This should be applied at three levels: *Strategic* (analysis of trends and projections); *Tactical* (maintenance and periodic inspections of facilities that have been established during the implementation of IRA-WDS); *Operational* (regular monitoring of systems performance).

Therefore it is important, when considering the use of IRA-WDS, to understand the institutional framework in which the water supply is currently being operated (i.e. who is involved). It is not only important to explore the institutional landscape in which IRA-WDS is to be used; it is also essential to understand the organizational set-up of each of the stakeholders, i.e. know who owns and operates the water treatment and distribution systems, and how they are operated, as well as who is responsible for quality control. Therefore it will be useful to review the current organizational and institutional structure of the water supplier and other sector stakeholders in order to establish which organizations have an interest in and/or responsibility for water quality in the distribution system. See Chapter 7 of Book 1 and Chapter 2 of Book 2 for further information.

A good starting point would be to analyse the management of water services including private and public roles. Box 1 in Chapter 2 of Book 2 gives a model of options for management of urban water supply, as far as private sector participation is concerned. The model provides several combinations of ownership and operation of assets. The analysis of these management models provides basic information on the operation and management of a water supply.

1.5.2 Commitment from managers and operational staff

Before the process of developing the IRA-WDS approach for authorities and institution responsible for water supply, it is imperative that all members of the water supplier agree on the benefits. Technical staff need a commitment to the IRA-WDS approach from all management level staff. Chapter 1 of Book 1 outlines examples of appropriate ways to achieve this agreement from different groups and emphasizes the importance of obtaining commitment from all levels of staff from field managers to the managing director. It further emphasizes that different tools and approaches are recommended for different groups of staff.

1.6 Summary

This chapter has provided an overview of the main components of IRA-WDS. The following three chapters will provide technical details of the mathematical model that underpins IRA-WDS. These chapters should be read in conjunction with Book 4, which outlines how to use the IRA-WDS software. It should be noted that the user is not required to understand all the technical details presented in Chapters 2, 3 and 4. The main purpose of these chapters is to provide an insight into the model, the data requirement and how to interpret the results.

CHAPTER TWO

Contaminant Ingress Model

Risk Assessment of Contaminant Intrusion into Water Distribution Systems

Chapter-1
Overview

Chapter-2
Contaminant Ingress Model

Chapter-3
Pipe Condition Assessment Model

Chapter-4
Risk Assessment Model

Chapter-5
Integration with GIS

Chapter-6
Example Application of Model (IRA-WDS)

Chapter 2: Contaminant Ingress Model

2.1 Introduction

This chapter presents details of the contaminant ingress model component of IRA-WDS. The contaminant ingress model simulates the movement of contaminated water from pollution sources such as open surface foul water bodies, sewers, drains etc. through typical soils, predicts the contaminant zone developed around these pollution sources, identifies the section of water distribution pipes in the contaminant zone (SPCZ) and estimates contaminant loading along SPCZ (see Figure 2.1).

The output from the model is the contaminant zone, SPCZ, variable concentration of contaminant in CZ and contaminant loading along the SPCZ due to different pollution sources (see Figure 2.24 at the end of this chapter).

The purpose of this chapter is to provide an insight into the background and the techniques that underpin the contaminant ingress model. This should enable the user of IRA-WDS to appreciate the significance of the data required and also aid in interpreting the results of the model. On completion of this chapter, the user should be able to complete Tables 2.1 to 2.4 that form the input data required to run the contaminant ingress model component of IRA-WDS.

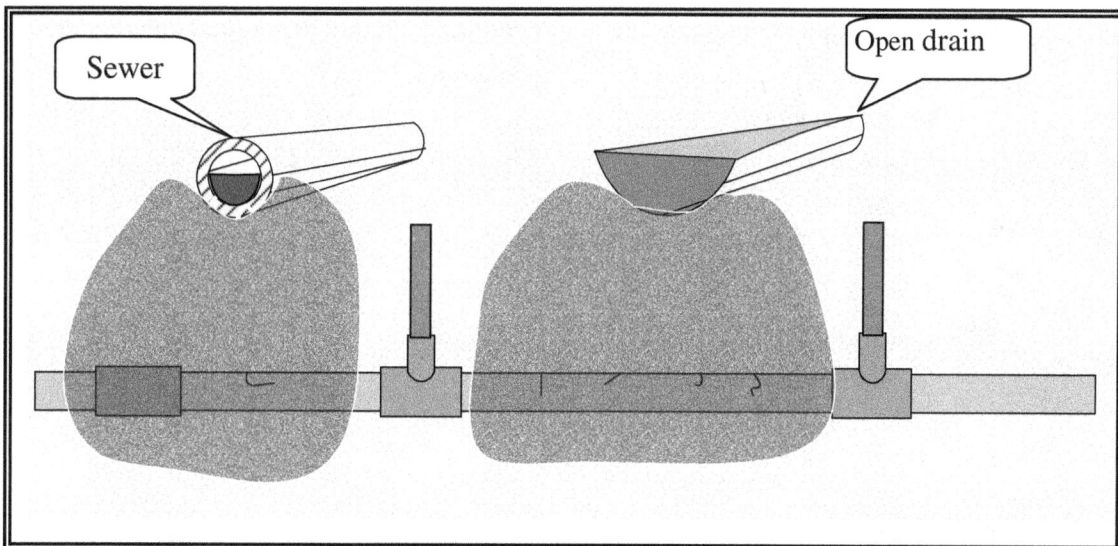

Figure 2.1. Movement of contaminated water (the shaded area) from pollution sources towards water distribution pipes

It should be noted, however, that to use IRA-WDS the user does not require a detailed understanding of technical components of the model presented in this chapter.

The contaminant ingress model is divided into two components.

- *Contaminant zone model* that predicts the zone or envelope of contamination (contaminant zone-CZ) emanating from a pollution source and the section of the water distribution pipes in the contaminant zone (SPCZ).

- *Contaminant seepage model* that simulates the variable concentration of the contaminants within the contaminant zone and predicts the contaminant loading along the SPCZ.

Table 2.1. Type of pollution source and its properties		
Properties of pollution source	**Unit**	**Value**
Underground sewer pipe		
Network map	*Shape file*	
For each pipe		
Length	*m*	
Bury depth	*m*	
Material		
Leakage rate	*cm/hr*	
Diameter	*cm*	
Lined open ditch/drain		
Network map	*Shape file*	
For each ditch/drain		
Length	*m*	
Material		
Leakage rate	*cm/hr*	
Depth	*cm*	
Unlined open ditch/drain		
Network map	*Shape file*	
For each ditch/drain		
Length	*m*	
Soil type		
Seepage rate	*cm/hr*	
Depth	*cm*	
Open surface foul water bodies		
Foul water body map	*Shape file*	
For each foul water body		
Area	m^2	
Soil type		
Seepage rate	*cm/hr*	
Depth	*cm*	

If the route of a drinking water supply pipe intersects the contaminant zone developed by the pollution source, there is a possibility that these contaminants might enter the water distribution pipes. It should be noted, however, that the potential contaminants that might enter the drinking water distribution pipe will also be a function of the condition of the water distribution pipe. Therefore, the outputs from the contaminant ingress model will be coupled with the pipe condition assessment model that is presented in the next chapter.

Table 2.2. Soil properties		
Soil map (shape file) and for each soil type:		
Soil property	**Unit**	**Value**
Saturated volumetric water content	cm^3/cm^3	
Initial volumetric water content	cm^3/cm^3	
Saturated hydraulic conductivity	$cm/hour$	
Soil characteristic curve coefficient	-	
Soil porosity	cm^3/cm^3	
Air entry head	cm	
Pore size index	-	
Bulk density	g/cc	
Fraction organic content	cc/g	

Table 2.3. Contaminant properties		
Contaminant property	**Unit**	**Value**
Liquid phase decay	$/hour$	
Diffusion coefficient	cm^2/day	
Organic carbon partition coefficient of the pollutant		

Table 2.4. Properties of pipes of water distribution network		
Parameter	**Unit**	**Value**
Network map	*Shape file*	
For each pipe of network		
Length	*m*	
Bury depth	*m*	

2.2 Background

In developing countries, water distribution systems often criss-cross with the pollution sources and in particular with the sewerage systems. If there is movement of contaminants from the pollution sources towards the water distribution system, the water distribution system might become polluted. The following two models are developed to identify the location and sections of polluted water distribution pipes and estimate contaminant concentration at these pipes:

- Contaminant zone model
- Contaminant seepage model

The contaminant zone model estimates the contaminant zone developed in a water distribution system due to pollution sources and thus identifies the location of polluted pipes in the water distribution system.

The contaminant seepage model estimates the relative contaminant concentration profile in the contaminant zone. The combination of these two models would give the relative contaminant concentration in polluted pipes of the water distribution system (Figure 2.2).

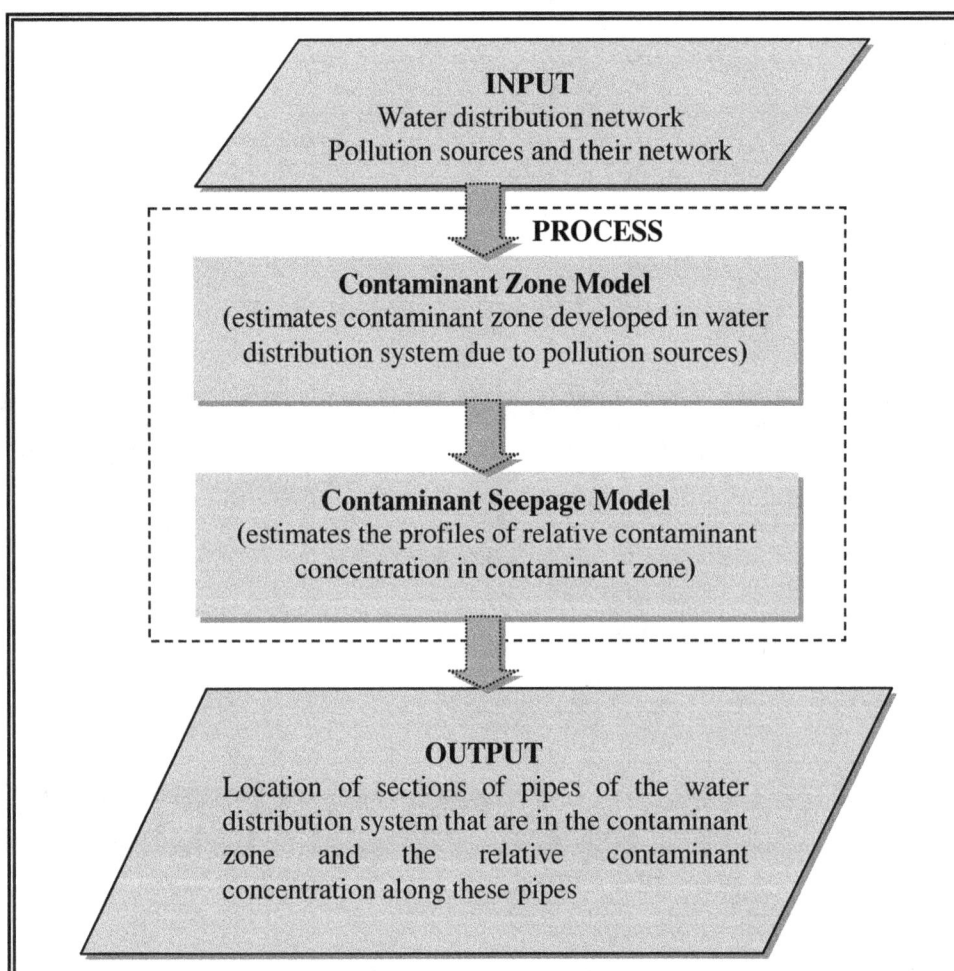

INPUT
Water distribution network
Pollution sources and their network

PROCESS

Contaminant Zone Model
(estimates contaminant zone developed in water distribution system due to pollution sources)

Contaminant Seepage Model
(estimates the profiles of relative contaminant concentration in contaminant zone)

OUTPUT
Location of sections of pipes of the water distribution system that are in the contaminant zone and the relative contaminant concentration along these pipes

Figure 2.2. Contaminant ingress model

2.3 Contaminant Zone Model

In this section a contaminant zone model is developed and presented, based on the seepage process of soil mechanical theory. This model makes it possible to identify the potential polluted area developed in a water distribution system due to pollution through contaminants intruding into water distribution pipes. Thus this model also allows design engineers to identify reasonable locations for laying new water pipes below sewers without the danger of contaminant intrusion. This model essentially consists of following two parts.

1. Estimation of the contaminant zone or potentially polluted area around pollution sources (sewer pipes, drains and foul water bodies).
2. Identification of sections of water distribution pipes that intersect with the contaminant zone (sections of the pipe that lie in the contaminant zone – SPCZ).

Figures 2.3 and 2.4 show typical scenarios that this model tries to simulate. The flowchart in Figure 2.5 summarizes the model.

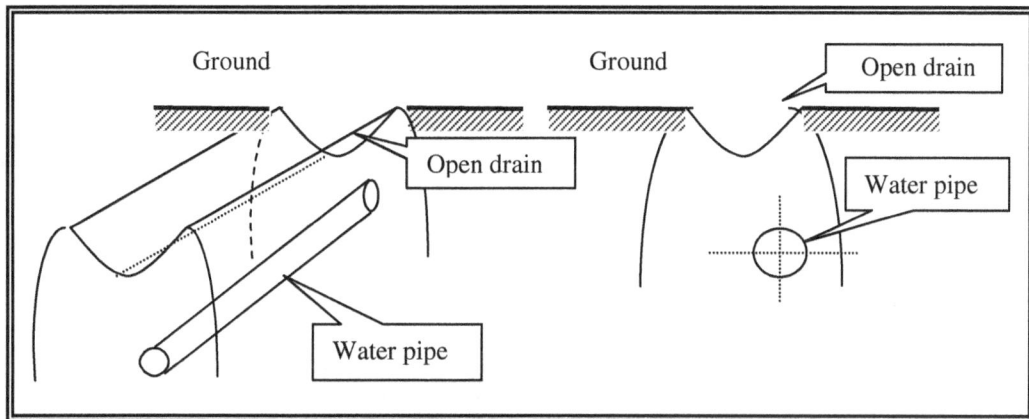

Figure 2.3. A typical scenario in which the model tries to simulate a water distribution network being influenced by a ditch/canal

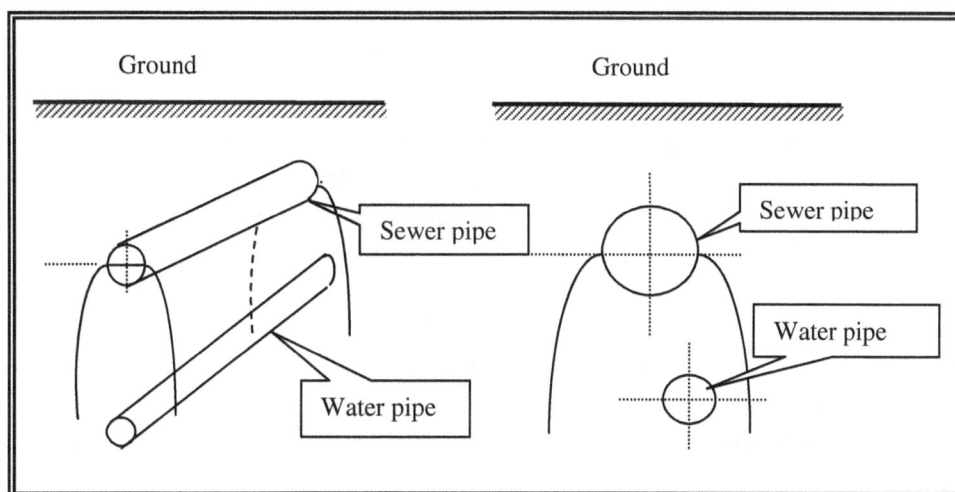

Figure 2.4. A typical scenario in which the model tries to simulate a water distribution network being influenced by a sewer pipe

23

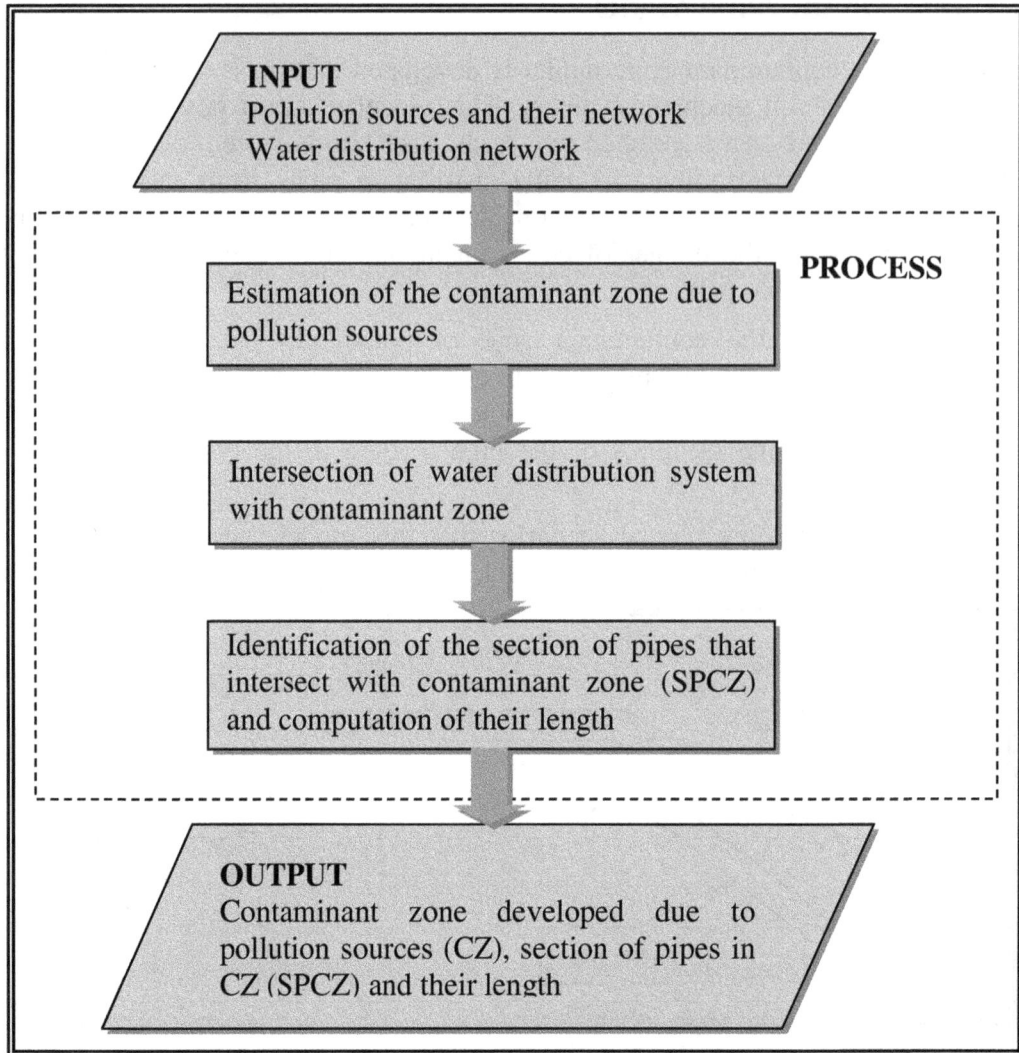

Figure 2.5. Contaminant zone model

2.3.1 Estimation of the contaminant zone due to pollution sources (CZ)

When contaminated water seeps from the pollution sources, it creates a seepage zone underneath. This zone is called a contamination zone (CZ). It is essential to know the shape of the contamination zone, as this zone determines the sections of water distribution pipe that may be subjected to contaminant intrusion. This zone is based on the seepage of the contaminated water from the pollution source into the soil. When considering seepage, important parameters include dimensions and shapes of the boundaries of pollution sources. The procedure for estimating the contaminant zone due to different pollution sources is described in this section. The different pollution sources are:

1. Unlined ditch/canal
2. Lined ditch/canal
3. Sewer pipe
4. Open surface foul water bodies

The procedure is described in the flowchart in Figure 2.6.

24

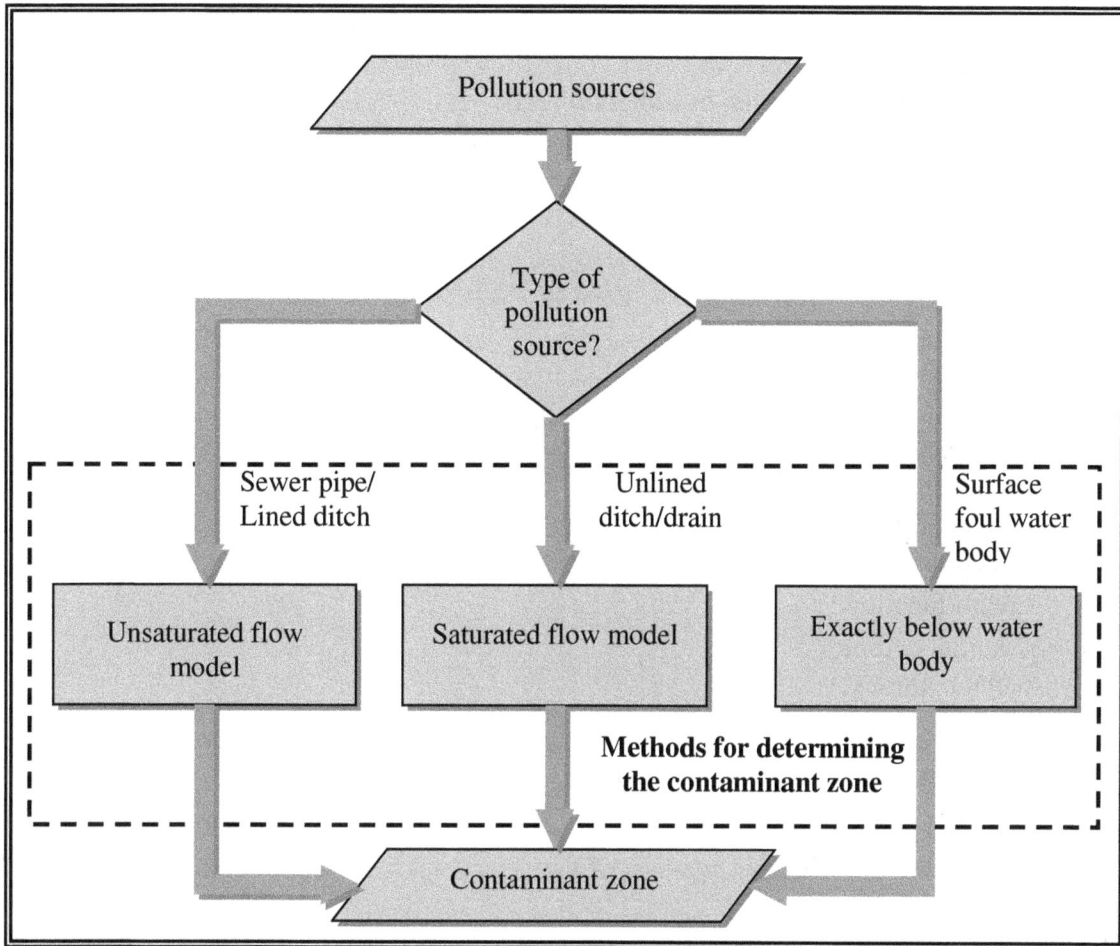

Figure 2.6. Estimation of contaminant zone due to different pollution sources

2.3.1.1 *Contaminant zone due to unlined ditch/canal*

Figure 2.7 shows the typical scenario in the canal or ditch. The width and depth of the contaminated water in the ditch are B and H respectively. Contaminated water in the ditch seeps into soil from the bottom of the ditch, forming the contaminant zone or envelope as shown in the figure. As the depth (z) increases, the distance (x) will increase, which means that the seepage envelope will enlarge during the process of seepage. The procedure used to establish the shape of this seepage envelope is elaborated below.

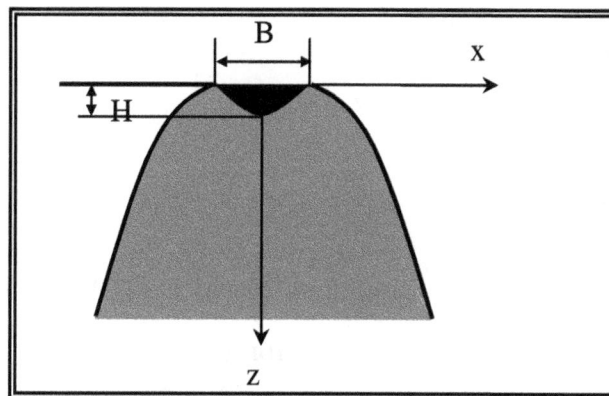

Figure 2.7. Seepage of contaminated water from ditch

Seepage equations: The flow of water in soil due to seepage from unlined ditch/canal is saturated flow. In order to solve this flow problem, Harr (1962) examined Zhukovsky's function as given by equation (2.1).

$$\theta = ip + \frac{w}{k} = Ae^{\frac{w}{\alpha}} \tag{2.1}$$

$$p = x + z\,i$$

$$w = \varphi + \psi i$$

where

α - a parameter

A - a real constant

k - permeability of soil

φ - potential function

ψ - stream function

w - potential complex

p - spatial complex.

Separating this expression into real and imaginary parts gives equation (2.2).

$$\frac{\varphi}{k} - z = Ae^{\frac{\varphi}{\alpha}} \cos(\frac{\psi}{a})$$

$$\frac{\psi}{k} + x = Ae^{\frac{\varphi}{a}} \sin(\frac{\psi}{a}) \tag{2.2}$$

Substituting $-\psi$ for ψ and $-x$ for x in equation (2.2), we see that the system of streamlines defined by ψ in these equations is symmetrical about the y-axis. Hence, the y-axis can be taken as the streamline $\psi = 0$. The free surface must satisfy the condition $-z + \frac{\varphi}{k} = 0$, and $\psi = -\frac{q}{2}$, and hence from the first of equation (2.2) we find

$$\cos(-\frac{q}{2\alpha}) = 0$$

$$q = -(2n+1)\alpha\pi \tag{2.3}$$

where

q - flow rate

In particular, taking $n = 0$ and substituting equation (2.3) with $\psi = -\frac{q}{2}$ and $\varphi = kz$ into the second of equation (2.2), we obtain for the free surface

$$x - \frac{q}{2k} = -Ae^{-\frac{k\pi}{q}z} \tag{2.4}$$

Letting $z = 0$ in equation (2.4), we obtain for the half width of the ditch

$$x_{z=0} = \frac{B}{2} = \frac{q}{2k} - A \qquad (2.5)$$

Now taking $\varphi = 0$ in equation (2.2), as $\psi = 0$ at the bottom of the ditch, from the parametric equation for the perimeter of the ditch, we find $z = -A = H$, where H is the maximum depth of water in the ditch. Hence, the quantity of seepage from the ditch section is found from equation (2.5) to be $q = k(B + 2H)$. Rearranging equation (2.4), we can find the seepage free surface equation:

$$x = \frac{1}{2}(2H + B) - He^{-\frac{\pi}{2H+B}z} \qquad (2.6)$$

For practical purposes, the seepage free surface of the flow net can be considered to approach its vertical asymptote, and the equipotential lines can be taken as horizontal at a depth of $z = 3(B + 2H)/2$ (Harr 1962). From equation (2.6), when $z > 3(B+2H)/2$, $x = (B+2H)/2$, and the width between the two vertical asymptotes is $B + 2H$. Thus the characteristics of the seepage envelope for an unlined ditch/canal are (see Figure 2.8):

1. The depth at which flow lines become vertical $(z) = 3(B+2H)/2$
2. The width of the vertical seepage envelope $= B + 2H$
3. The equation of the curved seepage envelope: $x = \frac{1}{2}(2H + B) - He^{-\frac{\pi}{2H+B}z}$

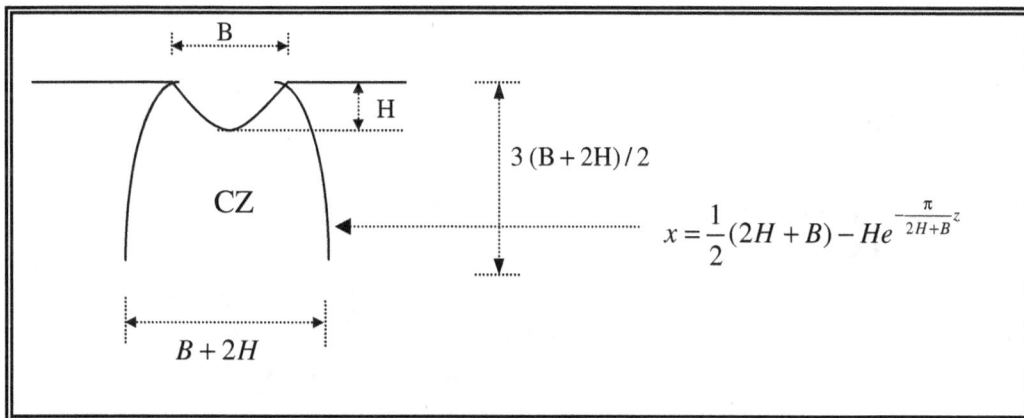

Figure 2.8. Characteristics of the seepage envelope for an unlined ditch/canal

2.3.1.2 Contaminant zone due to sewer pipe and lined ditch/canal

The flow of water in soil due to seepage from a sewer pipe or lined ditch/canal is unsaturated flow. Therefore the seepage envelope is not governed by the equation (2.6). However, for the purpose of simplicity, it is assumed that the maximum width of the seepage envelope at any depth below the sewer pipe and lined ditch/canal is half the width obtained for unlined ditch/canal (saturated flow). Thus the characteristics of the seepage envelope due to sewer pipe and lined ditch/canal are (see Figure 2.9):

1. The depth at which flow lines become vertical $(z) = 3(B+2H)/2$

2. The width of the vertical seepage envelope $= (B+2H)/2$

3. The equation of the curved seepage envelope: $x = \dfrac{\frac{1}{2}(2H+B) - He^{-\frac{\pi}{2H+B}z}}{2}$

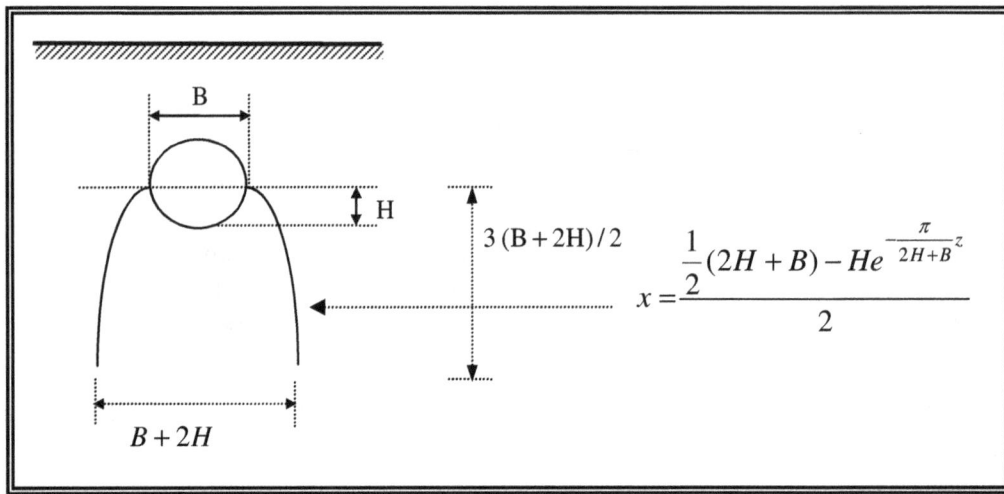

Figure 2.9. Characteristics of the seepage envelope for a sewer pipe and a lined ditch/canal

2.3.1.3 *Contaminant zone due to open surface foul water bodies*

The width of the open surface foul water bodies is usually large compared to sewer pipes or drains. The flow of water in soil due to seepage from the foul water bodies is saturated flow. Therefore it is assumed that the seepage envelope due to a surface foul water body lies exactly below it. Thus the width and breadth of seepage envelope due to a foul water body are the width and breadth of foul water body itself.

2.3.2 Identification of the section of water distribution pipes in contaminant zone – SPCZ

In order to identify the section of water distribution pipes in a contaminant zone (SPCZ) or the potential polluted area in the water distribution system due to pollution sources (open ditch, sewer pipe and foul water bodies), it is necessary to establish the intersection of the contaminant zone developed by pollution sources, with the paths of the water pipe. The procedure used to establish the intersection is described in this section for line pollution sources (sewer pipes, ditches, canals etc.) and surface foul water bodies.

2.3.2.1 *Open ditch/canals (lined and unlined) and sewer pipes*

Identification of the intersection of contaminant zone due to open drains and sewer pipes with the water distribution network requires extensive computational efforts, as the envelope of the potential polluted area or contaminant zone is three-dimensional in nature (see Figure 2.10).

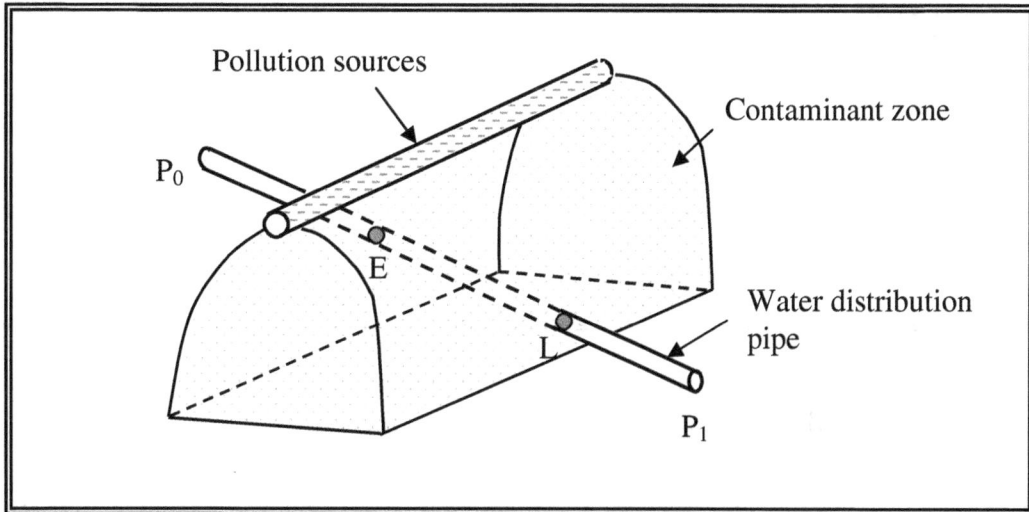

Figure 2.10. Three-dimensional view of the intersection of a water distribution pipe with a contaminant zone

The boundary of the contaminant zone approximates to the parabola. The portion of the water distribution pipe which intersects with the parabola of contaminant zone formed by the pollution sources is SPCZ (Figures 2.11 (a) and 2.11 (b)).

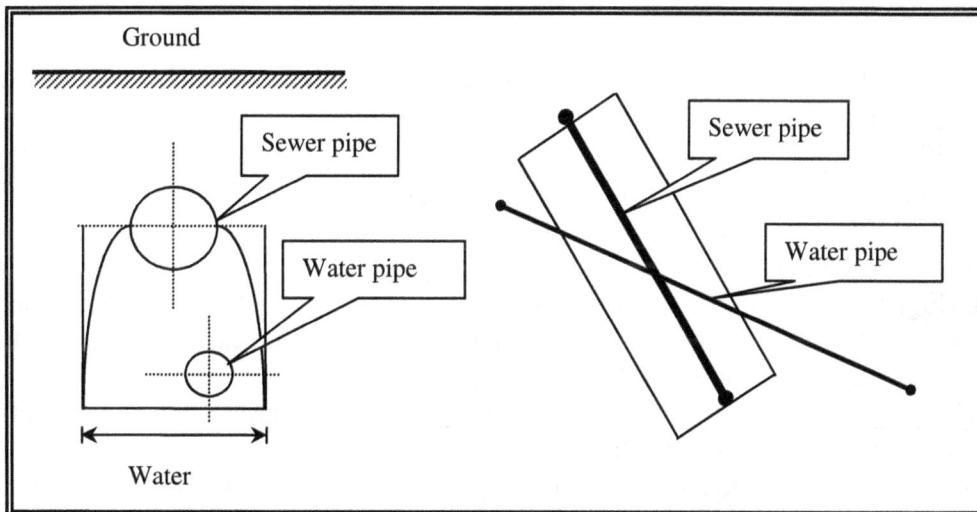

Figure 2.11 (a). Identification of SPCZ due to the intersection of water distribution pipe and contaminant zone formed by sewer pipe

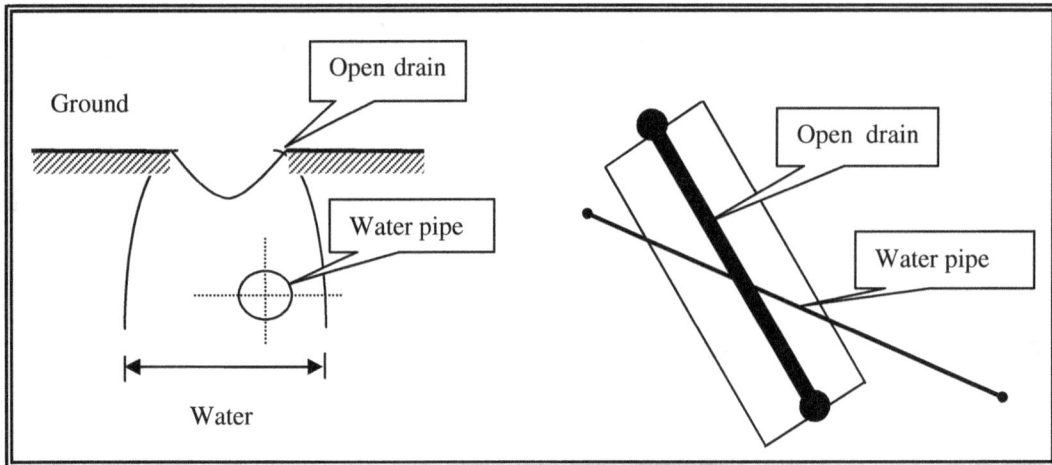

Figure 2.11 (b). Identification of SPCZ due to the intersection of water distribution pipe and contaminant zone formed by an open drain

The methodology used for obtaining the segment of intersection of water distribution pipe with the contaminant zone is described below.

Procedure: The intersection points of the water distribution pipe with the contaminant zone are required to be obtained by three-dimensional (3D) spatial geometry analysis. However the 3D spatial geometry analysis can be projected into a 2D space by projecting both water distribution pipe and contaminant zone on to the same horizontal plane. The 2D solutions are then substituted into the water distribution pipe segment equation to obtain a 3D solution of intersection point. The procedures used are as follows.

1) Establish the coordinates of contaminant zone: Figure 2.10 shows a 3D contaminant zone. This contamination zone is simplified as a polyhedron (3D) to simplify the geometry calculation. Figures 2.12 (a) and (b) show a two-dimensional (2D) front view and top view respectively. The top view transfers a spatial 3D problem into a 2D problem on a horizontal plane. Thus in 2D the contaminant zone is represented as a rectangle with four vertices, V1, V2, V3 and V4. (Figure 2.12 (b)). The coordinates of these vertices are obtained with the help of coordinates at start and end nodes of sewer pipe/drain and their dimensions (diameter for sewer, width and length for open drain).

2) Establish the coordinates of water distribution pipe: The top view of water distribution pipe (Figure 2.12) transfers a spatial three-dimensional problem into a two-dimensional problem on a horizontal plane. In 2D, the water distribution pipe is thus simplified to a segment between start and end nodes of the pipe, P_0P_1. The 3D coordinates for the start and end nodes of the water distribution pipe are obtained from the geo-database.

3) Calculate the intersection: The intersection of water distribution pipe with contaminant zone is performed on a horizontal projection (2D). The intersection points are E (enter or upstream) and L (leave or downstream), as shown in Figure 2.12. The 2D coordinates for the intersection points are then entered into the segment equation of water distribution pipe to obtain its 3D coordinates.

4) Length of pipe segment in contaminant zone: The length of water distribution pipe in the contaminant zone (LC) is calculated using the upstream and downstream intersection points:

$$LC_k = \left| \overrightarrow{up_k dp_k} \right| \qquad k = 1, 2, \ldots NC \qquad (2.7)$$

where

LC_k - the length of pipe k in the contaminant zone (m)

up_k and dp_k - the upstream and downstream intersection points of pipe k with the contaminant zone

NC - the number of water distribution pipes within contaminant zone

Projecting a 3D problem to 2D simplifies the computational process involved in determining the intersection of water distribution pipe with the contaminant zone. The resulting contamination zone is usually larger than the actual one shown in Figure 2.12 (a), where the solid points indicate the result after simplification whereas the hollow points represent the true solution. However, as we are concerned about the risk of contaminant intrusion into water distribution pipes, considering these overestimated scenarios adds a factor of safety. The complete procedure is presented in the flowchart in Figure 2.13.

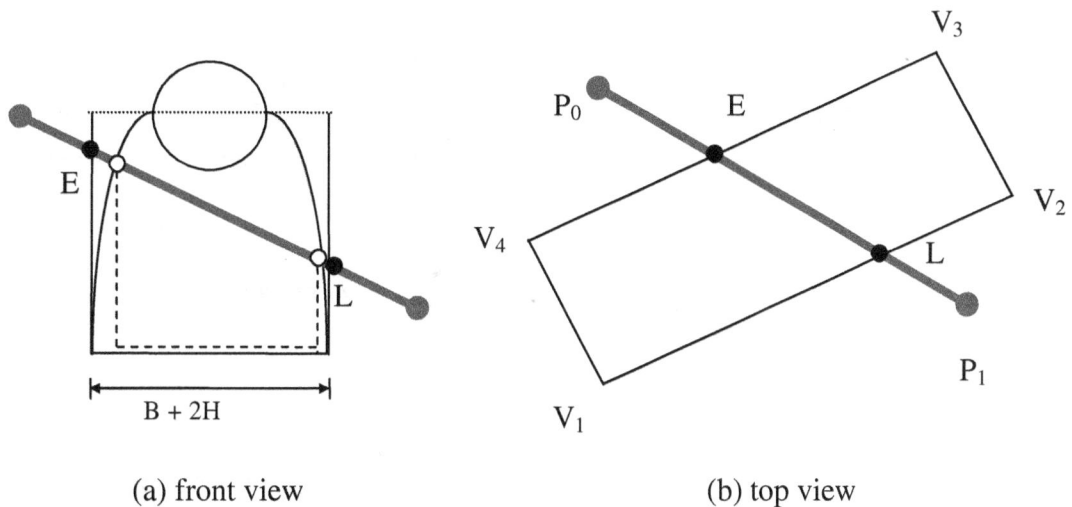

(a) front view   (b) top view

Figure 2.12. Two-dimensional simplification of intersection of the contaminant zone with the water distribution pipe

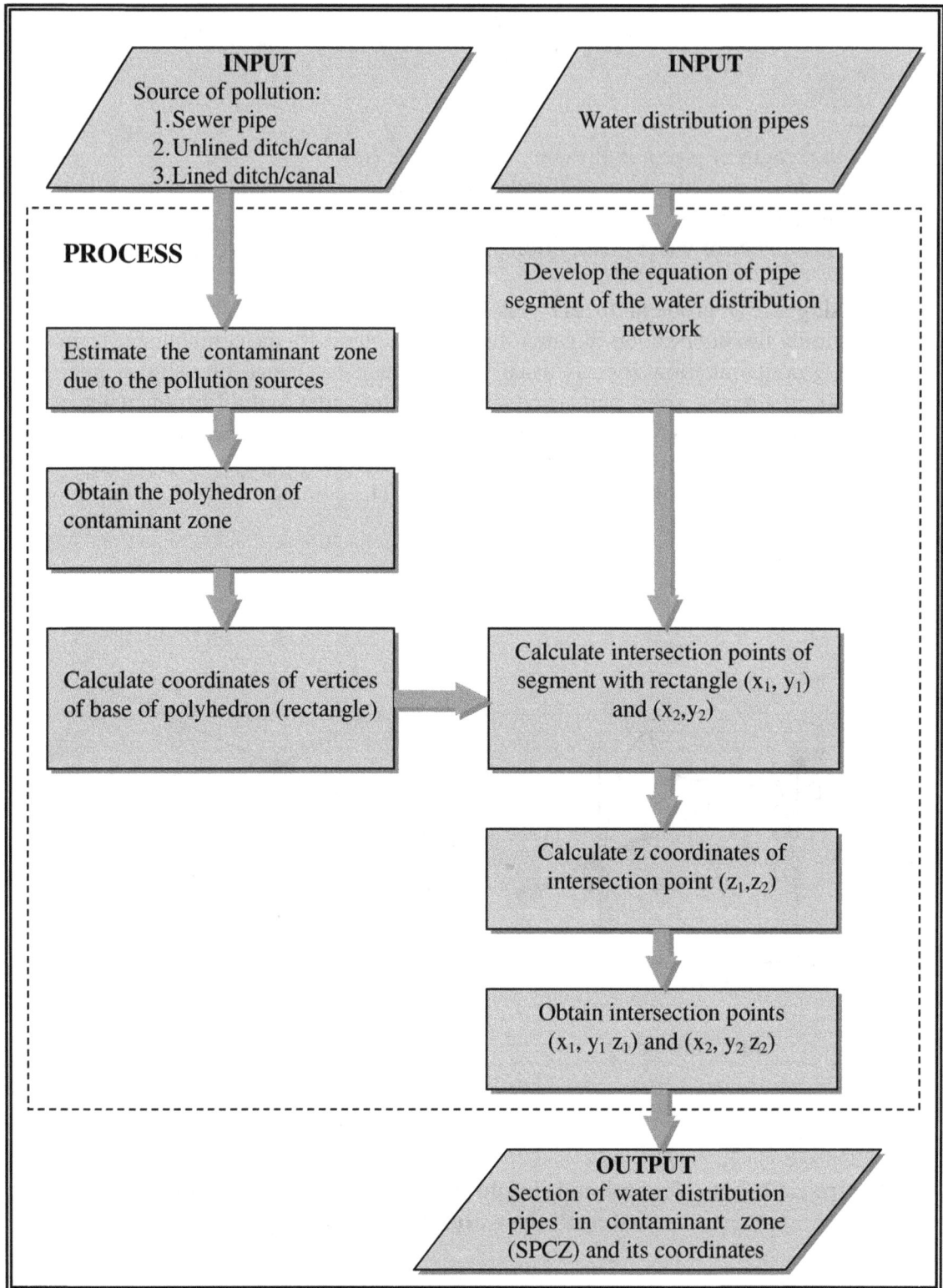

```
┌─────────────────────────┐         ┌─────────────────────────┐
│         INPUT           │         │         INPUT           │
│   Source of pollution:  │         │                         │
│    1. Sewer pipe        │         │ Water distribution pipes│
│    2. Unlined ditch/canal│        │                         │
│    3. Lined ditch/canal │         │                         │
└─────────────────────────┘         └─────────────────────────┘
```

PROGRESS

Develop the equation of pipe segment of the water distribution network

Estimate the contaminant zone due to the pollution sources

Obtain the polyhedron of contaminant zone

Calculate coordinates of vertices of base of polyhedron (rectangle)

Calculate intersection points of segment with rectangle (x_1, y_1) and (x_2, y_2)

Calculate z coordinates of intersection point (z_1, z_2)

Obtain intersection points $(x_1, y_1\ z_1)$ and $(x_2, y_2\ z_2)$

OUTPUT
Section of water distribution pipes in contaminant zone (SPCZ) and its coordinates

Figure 2.13. The methodology for obtaining coordinates for the section of water distribution pipes in a contaminant zone (SPCZ)

32

2.3.2.2 Foul water bodies

Apart from sewer pipes and drains/ditches, there are other pollution sources such as a wastewater disposal pond, buried waste, spills or landfills etc., from which a water distribution system may become contaminated. The boundaries of these water bodies can be simplified to polygons. When considering such water bodies, whose area is vast but which are shallow in depth, the seepage boundary can be assumed to be uniform during the movement of contaminant through the soil. This assumption simplifies the computational process involved in determining the potential polluted area in the water distribution system. Otherwise, numerical methods such as Finite Element Method (FEM) need to be employed. The 2D projection of the contaminant zone developed by these large surface foul water bodies is a polygon instead of a rectangle as in the case of contaminant zone developed by sewer pipes and ditches. The procedure described above (in Section 2.3.2.1) is followed to obtain the coordinates of the SPCZ, i.e. the intersection of polygon and water distribution pipe. If the polygon is convex, it is divided into several concave polygons (as shown on the right of Figure 2.14) and the SPCZ arising from each individual polygon is identified.

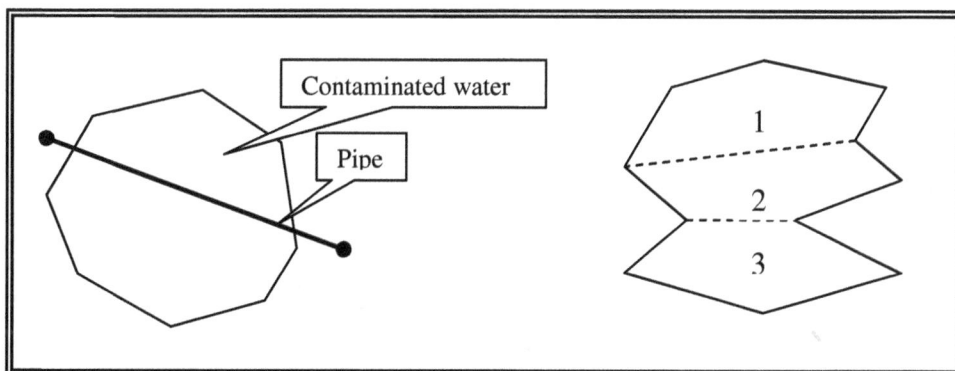

Figure 2.14. Water distribution network as influenced by the pollution source of surface water body

2.4 Contaminant Seepage Model

The procedure developed for the prediction of the contaminant zone due to different pollution sources and identification of the section of water distribution pipe in the contaminant zone (SPCZ) is described in the preceding sections. It is now required to estimate the contaminant loading along the SPCZ. This can be estimated by simulating the variable contaminant concentration in the contaminant zone.

Simulation of the contaminant concentration requires knowledge of the movement of contaminants through the soil due to seepage from open drains/canals, sewer pipes and surface foul water bodies. A mathematical model has been developed for this purpose. The concentration of contaminant is changed during seepage due to filtration by the soil. Therefore the model consists of two components, the first modelling the seepage process and the second modelling the variable concentration of contaminant migration through the soil. The output of this model in terms of variable contaminant concentration from the pollution sources is used to evaluate the magnitude of pollution when contaminants intrude into water distribution systems.

Three sources of contaminant seepage are grouped into two for the purpose of modelling the movement or transport of contaminants through the soil. These are:

1. Sewer pipes and open ditch/canal (lined): The seepage in soil due to water flowing in pipes and lined ditch/canal is considered as unsaturated flow. The contaminant transport model (CTM) for unsaturated flow is developed.
2. Surface foul water bodies and open ditch/canal (unlined): The seepage in soil due to water ponding or flowing over the surface and in unlined ditches/canals is considered as saturated flow. The contaminant transport model (CTM) for saturated flow is developed.

The procedure is described in Figure 2.15.

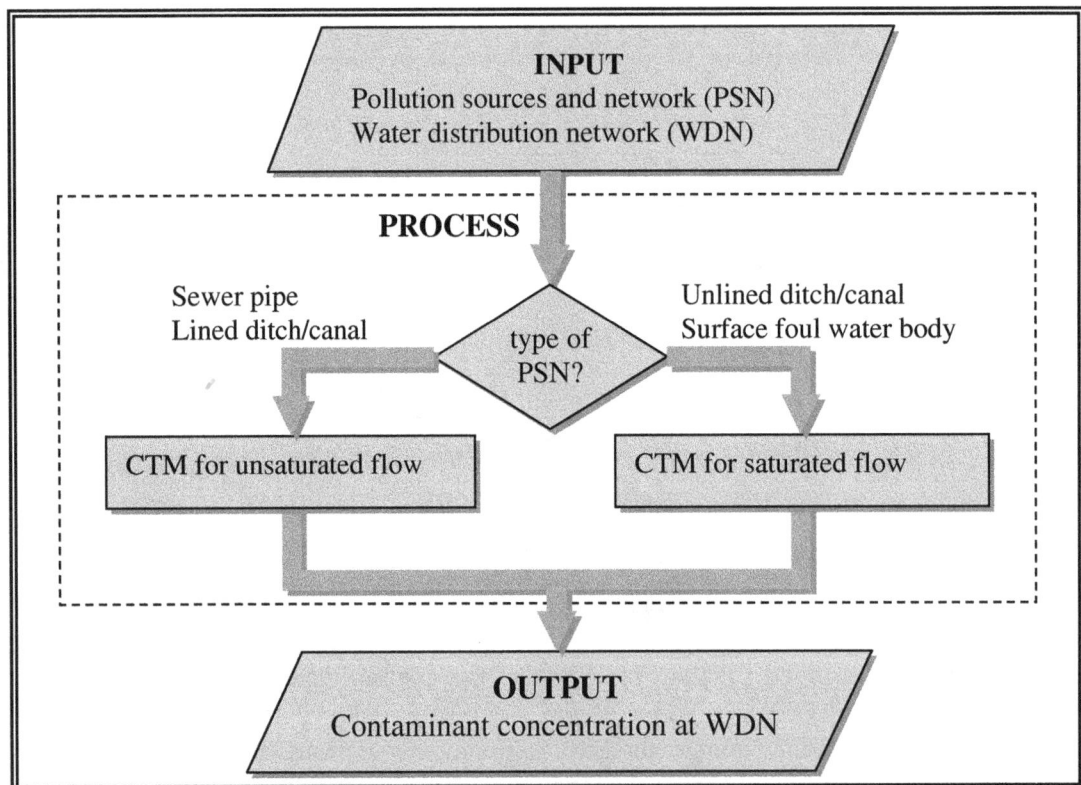

Figure 2.15. The contaminant seepage model

2.4.1 The contaminant transport model for unsaturated flow

The contaminant transport model (CTM) for unsaturated flow consists of the following two parts:

1. Modelling of seepage from sewer pipes and open drains/canals (lined)
2. Modelling of contaminant transport.

2.4.1.1 Modelling of seepage from sewer pipes and open drains/canals (lined)

Water flow into unsaturated soil is a very complex process due to various climatic conditions, the soil's physical and hydraulic properties, and geological conditions. Therefore, the appropriate model should be selected for the different boundary conditions of the modelling scenario. In this study, water flow and contaminant transport under surface ponding conditions were considered. Several infiltration models for ponding conditions have been developed, including those by Parlange et al. (1985), Haverkamp et al. (1990; 1994) and Salvucci and Entekhabi (1994).

The Green-Ampt model (Green and Ampt 1911) is the first physically based equation describing water flow into soil. The Green-Ampt model has been subject to considerable developments in applied soil physics and hydrology. This model can be applied to a great variety of hydrological problems such as homogeneous and non-homogeneous soils, ponding and non-ponding conditions. The use of a more sophisticated approach (e.g. the models based on the non-linear Richards equation), is both impractical and inefficient as more information on soil hydraulic parameters (e.g. water retention and hydraulic conductivity functions) is required (USEPA 1998a). The Explicit Green-Ampt model (Salvucci and Entekhabi 1994) was chosen as a quick and easy method of modelling water flow into unsaturated soil under surface ponding conditions. In this section, the mathematical formulation of the Explicit Green-Ampt model is presented. First the terminologies used in the model are explained, and then the equations.

- Air entry head, or bubbling pressure head (ψ_b): The point where desaturation commences in the soil located above the water table is referred to as the air-entry point. The hydraulic head associated with this point is referred to as the air-entry head.

- Air exit head (h_e): The air exit head may be taken as equal to one half of the air entry head.

- Capillary pressure head at the wetting front (h_f): The capillary pressure is the suction of water in the pore space due to surface tension or capillary force. This parameter is a function of soil water content, and can be determined from experimental measurements (Hillel 1982) or from the following equation $h = 2L/r$, where L is the surface tension of water and r is the radius of capillary.

- Exponent of the Brooks-Corey conductivity model (η_b): This is the exponent of the Brook-Corey conductivity model.

- Initial volumetric water content (θ_0): Initial volumetric water content present in the soil (see Table 2.5 for the residual volumetric contents for different types of soils).

- Ponding depth or capillary pressure at the surface (h_s): This parameter defines the thickness of water accumulated at the soil surface during water infiltration. The extent of ponding depth depends on soil types and is thus site-specific (see hs in Figure 2.16).

- Saturated hydraulic conductivity (K_s): This parameter is a coefficient of proportionality that describes the rate at which water can move through a soil at saturation. It should be noted that the density and kinematic viscosity of the water are considered in the measurement. The standard value of hydraulic conductivity is defined for pure water at a temperature of 15.6°C. The values for different soil textures are given in Table 2.5.

- Saturated volumetric water content (θ_s,): The saturated water content of the soil is the volume of water at saturation relative to the bulk volume density. Typical values for saturated water content for different soil textures are given in Table 2.5.

- Pore size index (λ_b): This is the exponent of the Brook-Corey water retention model.

- Van Genuchten soil parameter (*m*): This is the parameter for Genuchten soil model.

- Water flux (*q*): It is the seepage rate (Table 2.6)

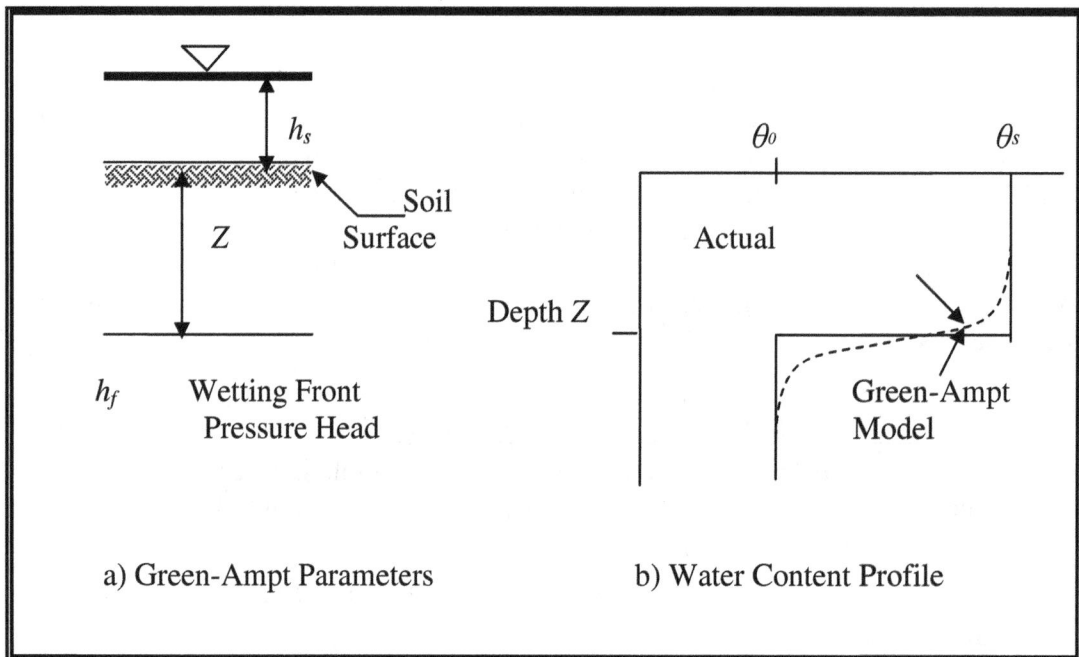

Figure 2.16. Illustration of Green-Ampt parameters and the conceptualized water content profile, which demonstrates the sharp wetting front (USEPA 1998b)

The mathematical formulations for this model are given in equations (2.8) to (2.12):

$$\frac{q}{K(\theta)} = \frac{\sqrt{2}}{2}\left(\frac{t}{\chi+t}\right)^{-1/2} + \frac{2}{3} - \frac{\sqrt{2}}{6}\left(\frac{t}{\chi+t}\right)^{1/2} + \frac{1-\sqrt{2}}{3}\left(\frac{t}{\chi+t}\right) \quad (2.8)$$

$$\chi = \frac{\left(h_s - h_f\right)\left(\theta - \theta_0\right)}{K(\theta)}$$

where

q - water flux (L/T)

θ - volumetric water content at soil surface (L^3/L^3)

K(θ) - hydraulic conductivity (L/T) at water content equals to θ

t - elapsed time (T)

h_s - ponding depth or capillary pressure at the surface (L)

h_f - is capillary pressure head at the wetting front (L)

θ_0 - initial volumetric water content (L^3/L^3)

$K(\theta)$ is estimated by van Genuchten (1980) and is given by equation (2.9).

$$K(\theta) = K_s S_e^{1/2} \left[1 - \left(1 - S_e^{1/m}\right)^m\right]^2 \qquad (2.9)$$

where

$S_e = (\theta - \theta_o)/(\theta_s - \theta_o)$

K_s - saturated hydraulic conductivity (L/T)

θ_s - saturated volumetric water content (L^3/L^3)

m - van Genuchten soil parameter.

Among these parameters, θ_0 is assumed as residual volumetric water content, h_s is considered to be the constant surface ponding depth, while h_f is given by Brakensiek and Onstad (1977) as presented in equation (2.10):

$$h_f = \frac{\eta_b}{\eta_b - 1} h_e \qquad (2.10)$$

where

η_b - exponent of the Brooks-Corey conductivity model, as given in equation (2.11)

h_e - the air exit head, as given in equation (2.12):

$$\eta_b = 2 + 3\lambda_b \qquad (2.11)$$

$$h_e = \frac{\psi_b}{2} \qquad (2.12)$$

where

λ_b - pore size index

ψ_b - air entry head, or the bubbling pressure head.

2.4.1.2 *Modelling of contaminant transport*

The concentration of contaminant will vary during movement through soil. The mechanism of contaminant transport through soil is advection, hydrodynamic dispersion, and interactive processes between pollutant and soil surface (Harvey and Garabedian 1991). A simple one-dimensional equation for transport of pollutant dissolved in water through soil (Enfield et al. 1982) is used. The terminologies associated with the equation are described first and then the equation is given.

- Dispersion coefficient (D): The process by which a substance or chemical spreads and dilutes in flowing groundwater or soil gas. A measure of the spreading of a flowing substance as a result of the nature of the porous medium is known as dispersion coefficient.

- Pore-water velocity (v): Seepage velocity.

- Bulk density (ρ_b): This parameter defines the mass of dry soil relative to the bulk volume of soil. Ranges for bulk density with respect to different soil types are given in Table 2.5.

- Porosity (n): The ratio of the volume of pore spaces in a soil to the total volume of the soil. n is assumed as equivalent to θ_s.

- First-order decay coefficient in liquid phase (λ): This describes those processes where pollutant mass is lost within the soil system. In general, degradation occurs primarily by soil micro-organisms and may vary depending upon soil temperature and moisture. It depends on the interaction of chemical with soil and hence is site specific.

- Sorption constant (K_d): The sorption constant is the linear partition coefficient which describes the relative distribution of the pollutant between that which is sorbed to the solid phase and that which is dissolved in water. The higher the value of the partition coefficient the greater the tendency for sorption to the solid phase; in contrast, low partition values indicate most of pollutant distribution is retained in the water. The partition coefficient is a constant for a given set of conditions. As a result, it is a site specific value. In particular, it is a function of the fraction organic content of the soil and can be estimated as the product of the fraction organic content (f_{oc}) and the organic carbon partition coefficient of the pollutant (K_{oc}). Thus $Kd = f_{oc} K_{oc}$.

- Diffusion coefficient of the chemical in soil (D_p): The process by which molecules in a single phase equilibrate to a zero concentration gradient by random molecular motion (Brownian motion). The flux of molecules is from regions of high concentration to low concentration and is governed by Fick's Second Law. A parameter that measures how rapidly a constituent will diffuse in water is known as diffusion coefficient. It depends on the interaction of chemical with soil and hence is site specific.

- Characteristic curve coefficient for the soil (b): This parameter relates the relative saturation of the soil to the relative conductivity of the soil under steady-state conditions. If this constant cannot be determined, it can be obtained from Table 2.5. for different soil textures.

The mathematical formulation of this model is given below:

$$\frac{\partial C}{\partial t} = D\frac{\partial^2 C}{\partial^2 z} - v\frac{\partial C}{\partial z} - \frac{\rho_b}{n}\frac{\partial S}{\partial t} - \lambda C \qquad (2.13)$$

where
C - liquid-phase pollutant concentration (M/L^3)
t - time (T)
z - depth along the flow path (L)
D - dispersion coefficient (L^2/T)
v - pore-water velocity (L/T)
ρ_b - bulk density (M/L^3)

n - porosity
S - solid-phase concentration (M/L^3)
λ - first-order decay coefficient in liquid phase (1/T)

The term $\partial S/\partial t$ is the rate of loss of solute from liquid phase to solid phase due to sorption. Under the assumption of linear, instantaneous sorption, $\partial S/\partial t$ can be evaluated by equation (2.14):

$$\frac{\partial S}{\partial t} = K_d \frac{\partial C}{\partial t}$$

(2.14)

where
K_d - sorption constant

Two cases are considered in the model: Steady state and Unsteady state

Steady state

In steady state situations the contaminant concentration in the soil is not influenced by time. It varies only with depth. For a continuous steady flow with initial concentration c_0 seeping into the soil, the steady state outflow concentration is governed by equation (2.13) with $\partial C/\partial t = 0$ (Harter et al. 2000). The boundary condition of equation (2.13) are: $z = 0, C = C_0$ and $z = \infty, C = 0$. With the assumption of $\partial C/\partial t = 0$ and the above boundary conditions, we find the solution of equation (2.13) as:

$$\frac{C}{C_0} = e^{\frac{v - \sqrt{v^2 + 4D\lambda}}{2D} z}$$

(2.15)

where

C_0 - initial pollutant concentration (mg/l).

Unsteady state

In unsteady state situations the contaminant concentration in the soil varies with respect to time and depth. Substituting for $\partial S/\partial t$ from (2.14) into (2.13), one obtains

$$\frac{\partial RC}{\partial t} = D \frac{\partial^2 C}{\partial^2 z} - v \frac{\partial C}{\partial z} - \lambda C$$

(2.16)

where

$$R = 1 + \frac{\rho_b K_d}{n}$$

(2.17)

The dispersion coefficient can be calculated from the relationship developed by Biggar and Nielsen (1976), as given in equation (2.20):

$$D = D_p + 2.93(v)^{1.11}$$

(2.18)

where
D_p - diffusion coefficient of the chemical in soil (L^2/T)

The pore-water velocity may be determined from water flux (q) calculated from the water flow model given previously (equation 2.18) and projected water content (USEPA 1994) as shown in equation (2.19):

$$\theta = \theta_s \left(\frac{q}{K_s} \right)^{\frac{1}{2b+3}}, \qquad q \leq K_s$$
$$\theta = \theta_s, \qquad q > K_s \qquad\qquad (2.19)$$

where
θ - projected water content
b - characteristic curve coefficient for the soil.

Therefore, the pore-water velocity (seepage velocity) is:

$$v = \frac{q}{\theta} \qquad\qquad (2.20)$$

For a continuous source of infinite duration, the analytical solution subject to the following initial and boundary conditions may be found in literature

$$
\begin{aligned}
C(z, t=0) &= 0 & x \geq 0 \\
C(z=0, t) &= C_0 & t \geq 0 \\
C(z=\infty, t) &= 0 & t \geq 0
\end{aligned} \qquad\qquad (2.21)
$$

where
C_0 - initial pollutant concentration (M/L^3)

The analytical solution for no conservative solute ($\lambda \neq 0$) is presented by Bear (1972) and developed by O'Loughlin and Bowmer (1975) using Laplace transforms (Runkel 1996) as given in equation (2.22):

$$\frac{C}{C_0} = \frac{1}{2} \left\{ \exp\left[\frac{vz}{2D}(1-\Gamma) \right] \mathrm{erfc}\left(\frac{z - \frac{vt}{R}\Gamma}{2\sqrt{Dt/R}} \right) + \exp\left[\frac{vz}{2D}(1+\Gamma) \right] \mathrm{erfc}\left(\frac{z + \frac{vt}{R}\Gamma}{2\sqrt{Dt/R}} \right) \right\} \quad (2.22)$$

where

$$\Gamma = \sqrt{1 + 2H} \qquad\qquad (2.23)$$

$$H = 2\lambda D / v^2 \qquad\qquad (2.24)$$

erfc(z) is the complementary error function which is defined as

$$\mathrm{erfc}(z) = 1 - \frac{2}{\sqrt{\pi}} \int_0^z \exp(-z^2) dz \qquad\qquad (2.25)$$

Table 2.5. Typical values of different input parameters for different soil types (Meyer et al. 1997)   *Estimated

Soil type	Properties							
	Saturated volumetric content	Residual volumetric content	Saturated hydraulic conductivity	Soil characteristic curve coefficient	Air entry head	Pore size index	Bulk density	Fraction organic content of the soil
	θ_s (m³/m³)	θ_r (m³/m³)	K_s (cm/hr)	b	ψ_b (cm)	λ_b	ρ_b (g/cm³)	f_{oc}
Sand	0.430	0.0466	29.59	0.998	7.02	1.67	1.65	0.0071
Loamy sand	0.410	0.0569	14.36	1.40	9.58	1.27	1.6*	0.0061
Sandy loam	0.410	0.0644	4.212	1.96	17.7	0.892	1.50	0.0071
Sandy clay loam	0.39	0.101	1.163	4.27	26.2	0.479	1.45*	0.0019
Loam	0.43	0.0776	1.051	3.07	38.9	0.56	1.40	0.0052
Silt loam	0.45	0.067	0.3359	3.80	70.3	0.414	1.30	0.0058
Silt	0.456	0.0352	0.176	3.21	68.1	0.38	1.3*	0.0025*
Clay loam	0.410	0.0954	0.357	5.97	88.0	0.318	1.35	0.001
Silty clay loam	0.430	0.088	0.0554	7.13	132	0.230	1.35*	0.0013
Sandy clay	0.380	0.0993	0.1278	6.90	50.7	0.275	1.4*	0.0038
Silty clay	0.360	0.0706	0.0079	10.2	340	0.157	1.3*	0.002*
Clay	0.380	0.0685	0.1314	14.1	353	0.127	1.25	0.0038

Table 2.6. Typical values of seepage/leakage rate from canals of different types of lining		
Sr. No.	Type of canal lining	Seepage/leakage rate m^3/m^2/day
1	Clay	0.061119
2	Silt clay loam	0.09127
3	Clay loam	0.12183
4	Silt loam	0.182948
5	Loam	0.304778
6	Fine sandy loam	0.380973
7	Sandy loam	0.457167
8	Sand	0.586739
9	Plastic	0.077824
10	Concrete	0.066823
11	Gunite (spray applied concrete)	0.020373
12	Compacted earth	0.01365
13	One layer brick	0.05
14	Double layer brick	0.03

Note These values are derived from the following sources:
1. Texas Board of Water Engineers (1946)
2. Fipps and Pope (2004)
3. USBR (1963)
4. Nofziger (1979)

2.4.2 Contaminant transport model for saturated flow

The contaminant transport model (CTM) for saturated flow consists of the following two parts:

1. Modelling of seepage from open drains/canals (unlined) and surface foul water bodies
2. Modelling of contaminant transport.

2.4.2.1 Modelling of seepage from open drains/canals (unlined) and surface foul water bodies

The seepage of water into the soil through open drains/canals (unlined) and surface foul water bodies is considered as saturated flow. Hence the water flux is estimated using Darcy's law. The following procedure is used for simulating water flow from these pollution sources.

The seepage flow nets with different stream functions and potential functions are calculated using the equation (2.26).

$$\frac{\varphi}{k} - z = Ae^{\frac{\varphi}{\alpha}} \cos(\frac{\psi}{a})$$

$$\frac{\psi}{k} + x = Ae^{\frac{\varphi}{a}} \sin(\frac{\psi}{a})$$

(2.26)

where
α - a parameter
A - a real constant
k - permeability of soil
φ - potential function
ψ - stream function
w - potential complex
p - spatial complex.

Equation (2.15), which is developed for estimation of contaminant concentration for steady state flow, is a one-dimensional problem with the relationship of concentration (C) and depth (z). But another parameter, pore velocity, is a function of both depth (z) and distance (x), because the streamline and equipotential line is curved as shown in Figure 2.17. Therefore, equation (2.15) needs to be extended to a two-dimensional problem for accurate calculation. Therefore the flow region is divided into many flow pathways, consisting of streamlines, and then each flow pathway is subdivided into elements by equipotential lines. Thus the plane flow region is made into elements of flow lines and equipotential lines of curvilinear cells, as shown in Figure 2.17. The figure also illustrates that as depth increases, the streamlines approach the vertical asymptote, and equipotential lines approach straight lines.

In each cell, i, the velocity v_i is estimated by equation (2.29) obtained by combining equation (2.27) for velocity potential and equation (2.28), Darcy's law.

Velocity potential φ is defined as

$$\varphi = -K_s h + C \tag{2.27}$$

Darcy's law of could be written as

$$v = -K_s \frac{dh}{ds} \tag{2.28}$$

$$v_i = \frac{d\varphi_i}{ds_i} \tag{2.29}$$

$$v_i = \frac{\varphi_i - \varphi_{i-1}}{\dfrac{s_{ri} + s_{li}}{2}}$$

Figure 2.18 illustrates the seepage process in a single flow pathway. The distance Sr_i and Sl_i of the element is calculated using the coordinate of flow pathway. The equation (2.29) is solved in a loop from $i=0$ (the flow at the bottom of the ditch) to $i=n$ where n is the number of elements in the flow pathway. Equation (2.29) yields the flow at each element by knowing the change in flow along the selected flow pathway. The process in repeated for each flow pathway across the flow net, to yield the flow profile across the entire seepage envelope.

2.4.2.2 Modelling of contaminant transport

The relative concentration (C/C_0) distribution in all the flow nets is then estimated by using equation (2.15); parts of these are shown in the bottom and right of Figure 2.19. The contaminant concentration is then estimated at the desired depth. Using the calculated flow profile, we can find the concentration profile at the bottom and centre of the flow region. Figure 2.19 shows the change in relative concentration in both the x and y directions.

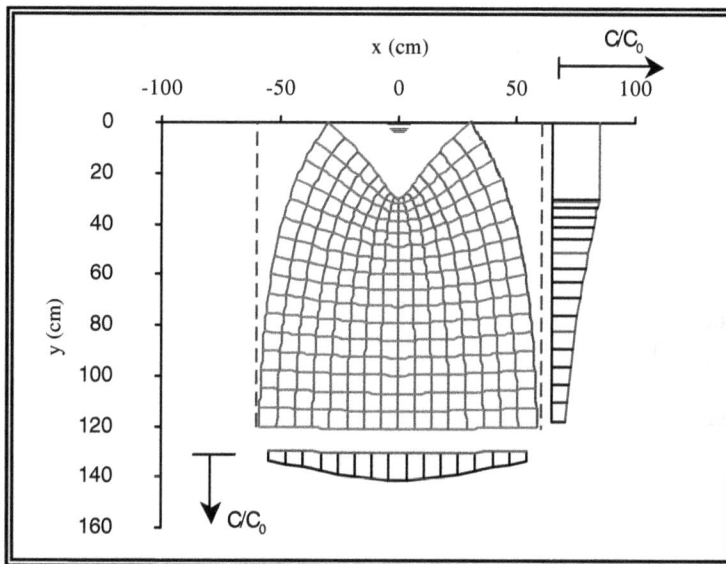

Figure 2.17. Flow net for the seepage beneath the unlined drain/canal and surface foul water bodies

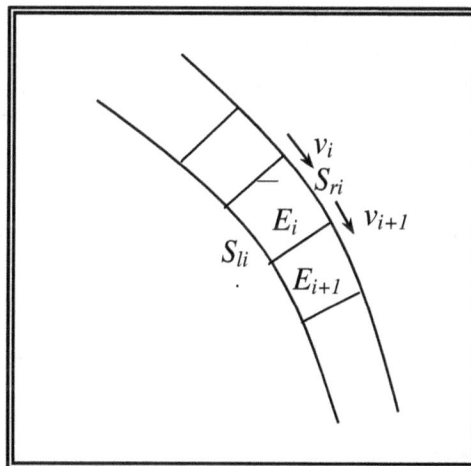

Figure 2.18. A flow channel of flow net

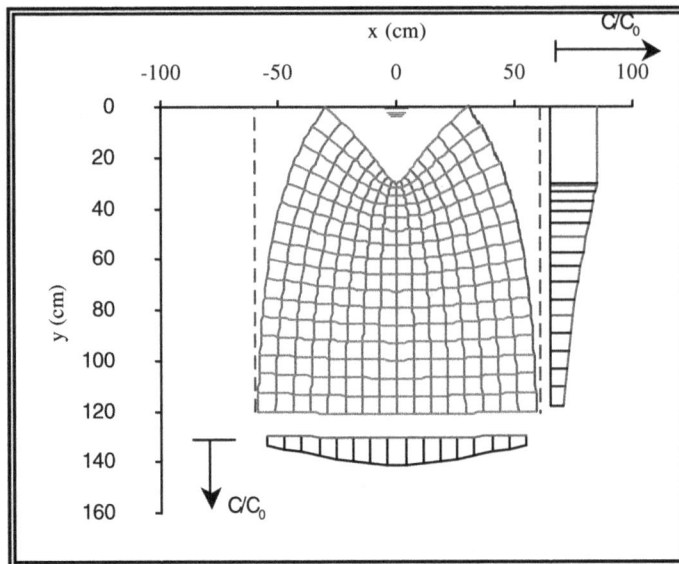

Figure 2.19. The concentration profile

2.5 Contaminant Loading

The output from contaminant zone model (Section 2.3) is the length of water distribution pipe in a contaminant zone calculated with the coordinates of upstream and downstream intersection points of the segment that represents the intersection of water distribution pipes with the contaminant zone (SPCZ). The concentration of contaminant at these intersection points can be obtained from the contaminant seepage model (Section 2.4). The concentration along SPCZ is assumed as the average of concentration of the upstream and downstream intersection points, as shown in Figure 2.20.

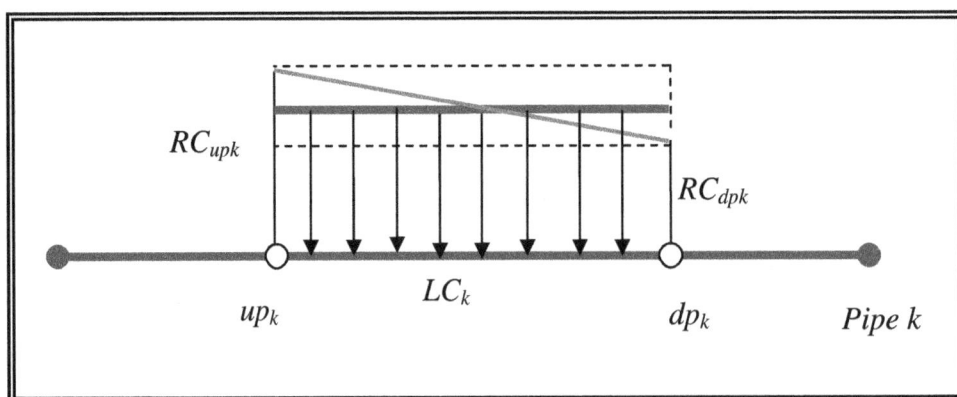

Figure 2.20. Contaminant loading along SPCZ

The contaminant seepage model simulates the contaminant concentration at upstream and downstream ends of SPCZ. The contaminant concentration along SPCZ is then determined by taking the average of the concentrations at its upstream and downstream ends (equation 2.30):

$$CC_k = \frac{RC_{upk} + RC_{dpk}}{2} \qquad k = 1, 2, ...NC \qquad (2.30)$$

where
CC_k - average contaminant concentration along SPCZ of pipe k (mg/l)
$RCup_k$ - contaminant concentration at upstream intersection point (mg/l)
$RCdp_k$ - contaminant concentration at downstream intersection point of pipe k (mg/l)

$RCup_k$ and $RCdp_k$ are estimated by equation (2.22) by knowing the value of contaminant concentration at source (C_0).

The contaminant load is then estimated by equation (2.30) that combines the section of pipe in the contaminant zone (SPCZ) and contaminant concentration along this section.

$$CL_k = LC_k \times \pi \times r_k \times CC_k \qquad k=1, 2, ...NC \qquad (2.31)$$

where
CL_k - estimation of contaminant load for pipe k (mg/m)
r_k - radius of pipe k (mm)

2.6 Implementation of the Contaminant Ingress Model in IRA-WDS

The IRA-WDS software has a default database for the characteristics of different soils. These default values are given in Table 2.5. These values of soil characteristics can be used if the soils are known. Alternatively, values of soil characteristics from other sources or measurements can be used. The different soil and contaminant parameters described in this chapter, required for the contaminant seepage model and data presented in Table 2.5, enable the user to decide upon the values of these parameters and complete Tables 2.2 and 2.4. The information provided in these tables is required for the contaminant ingress model of IRA-WDS for predicting the variable concentration of contaminants within the contaminant zone and obtaining results of the contaminant ingress model (see Chapter 3 of Book 4 (IRA-WDS user manual)).

Three examples are presented in this book (one example in this section and two in Appendix A) to illustrate the modelling of contaminant seepage from the pollution sources of sewer pipe, open drain and surface foul water body. Each example is presented in two parts: the model input data and the output in the form of a relative contaminant concentration profile along depth.

Figure 2.21 shows a water distribution pipe that lies below a leaky sewer pipe. The leaky sewer pipe develops a contaminant zone in which contaminant will seep down to the water distribution pipe. The contaminant concentration is modelled using the unsaturated flow model (Section 2.4.1). The properties of sewer pipe, soil and contaminant are given in Table 2.7. This shows the input for the contaminant ingress model. The profile of relative concentration is presented in Table 2.8 and Figure 2.22. It should be noted that the contaminant concentration at the upstream and downstream ends of the segment of water distribution pipe that lies in the contaminant zone can be estimated from these contaminant concentration profiles by knowing the location of the water distribution pipe in relation to pollution source.

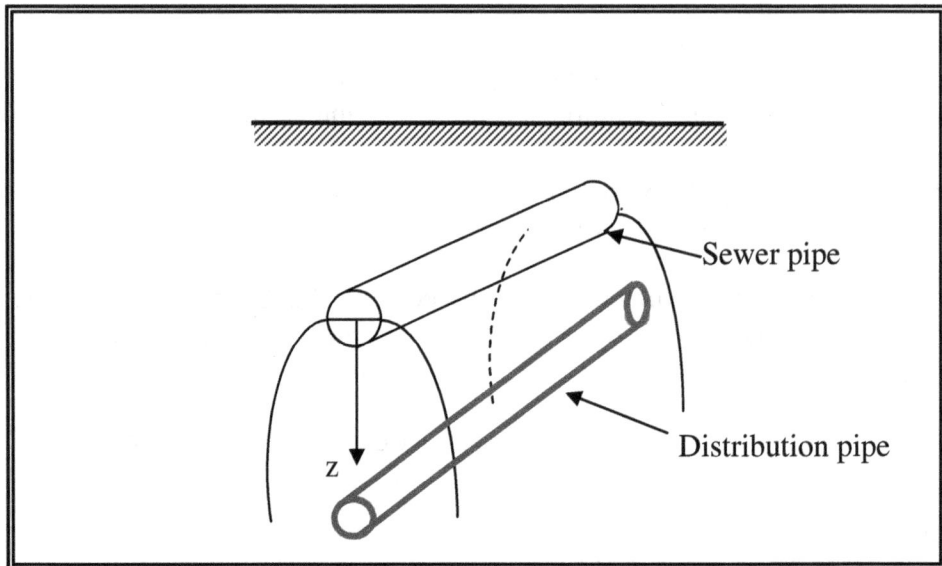

Figure 2.21. Contaminant seepage from leaky sewer pipe

Table 2.7. Example to demonstrate the estimation of contaminant concentration at water distribution pipe due to sewer pipe

Sewer pipe

Property	Symbol	Value	Units
Material	Concrete		
Leakage rate	r	0.066823	*m/day*
Diameter	h_s	10	*cm*
Soil properties			
Saturated volumetric content	θ_s	0.43	cm^3/cm^3
Initial volumetric water content	θ_0	0.0776	cm^3/cm^3
Saturated hydraulic conductivity	K_s	1.05	*cm/hour*
Soil characteristic curve coefficient	b	3.07	-
Soil porosity	n	0.43	cm^3/cm^3
Air entry head	ψ_b	-38.9	*cm*
Pore size index	λ_b	0.56	-
Bulk density	ρ_b	1.4	*g/cc*
Sorption constant	K_d	7.3×10^{-2}	*cc/g*
Contaminant properties			
Liquid phase decay	λ	2.22×10^{-4}	*/hour*
Diffusion coefficient	D_p	0.72	cm^2/day
Procedure used			
See Sections 2.3.1.2 and 2.4.1			
Results			
See Table 2.8 and Figure 2.22 for profile of relative contaminant concentration			

Table 2.8. Relative contaminant concentration in soil due to sewer pipe (for data presented in Table 2.7)	
Depth z (m)	**Relative concentration C/C_0**
0.0	1.000
0.5	0.938
1.0	0.880
1.5	0.826
2.0	0.775
2.5	0.727
3.0	0.682
3.5	0.639
4.0	0.600
4.5	0.563
5.0	0.528
5.5	0.495
6.0	0.465
6.5	0.436
7.0	0.409
7.5	0.384
8.0	0.360
8.5	0.338
9.0	0.317
9.5	0.297
10.0	0.279

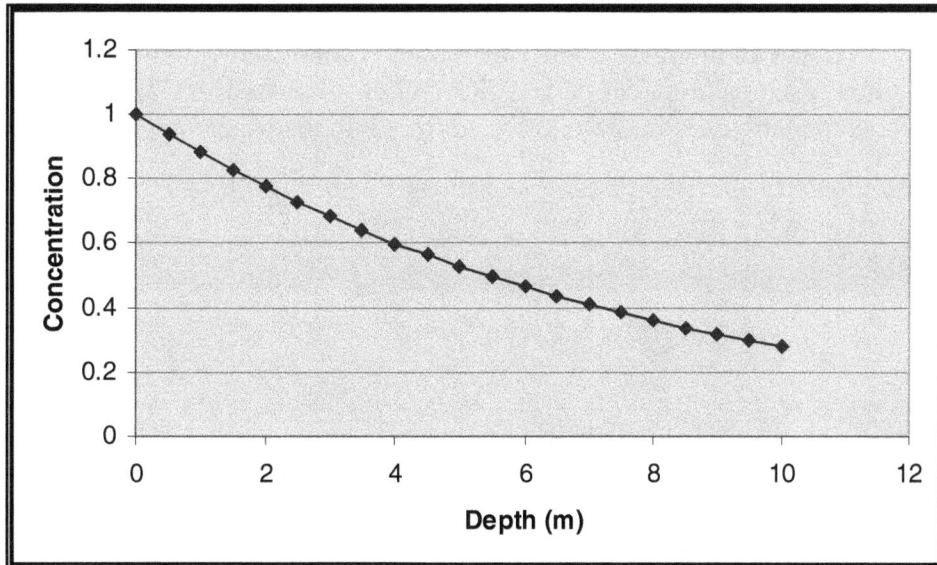

Figure 2.22. Relative contaminant concentration in soil due to sewer pipe (for data presented in Table 2.7)

2.7 Conclusions

At this stage of the chapter the reader should be able to complete Tables 2.1 to 2.4 for their particular area of study. These tables form the basis of the input data for the contaminant ingress model part of IRA-WDS. The data contained in Tables 2.1 to 2.4 are entered into IRA-WDS by means of the several input dialog windows within the software. Figure 2.23 shows an example of these input dialog windows and more details of this can be found in Chapter 3 of Book 4 (IRA-WDS user manual).

Figure 2.23. Example of input dialog window used for contaminant ingress model of IRA-WDS

An example of the output from a successful run of the contaminant ingress model part of IRA-WDS is shown in Figure 2.24. This output is combined with the outputs of the pipe condition assessment model part of IRA-WDS (discussed in Chapter 3), to give potential contaminant loads from pollution sources into the water supply pipes.

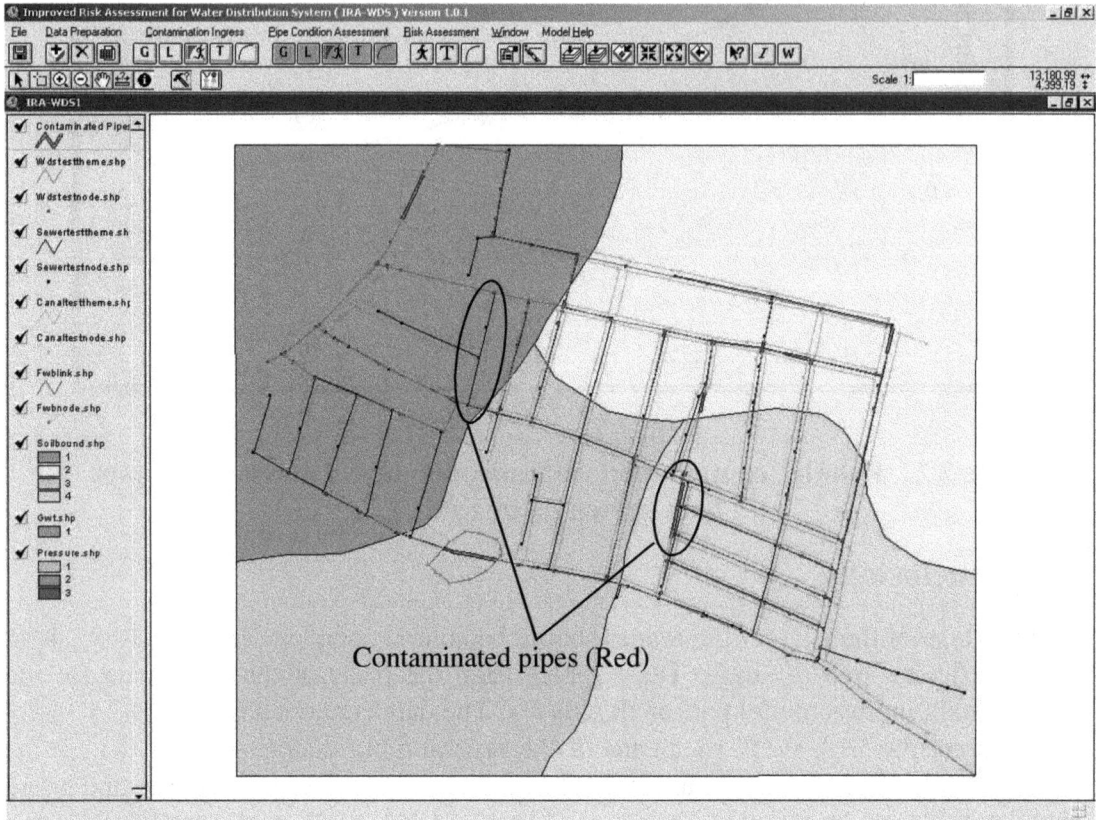

Figure 2.24. An example of the output from a successful run of the contaminant ingress model part of IRA-WDS

CHAPTER THREE

Pipe Condition Assessment Model

Risk Assessment of Contaminant Intrusion into Water Distribution Systems

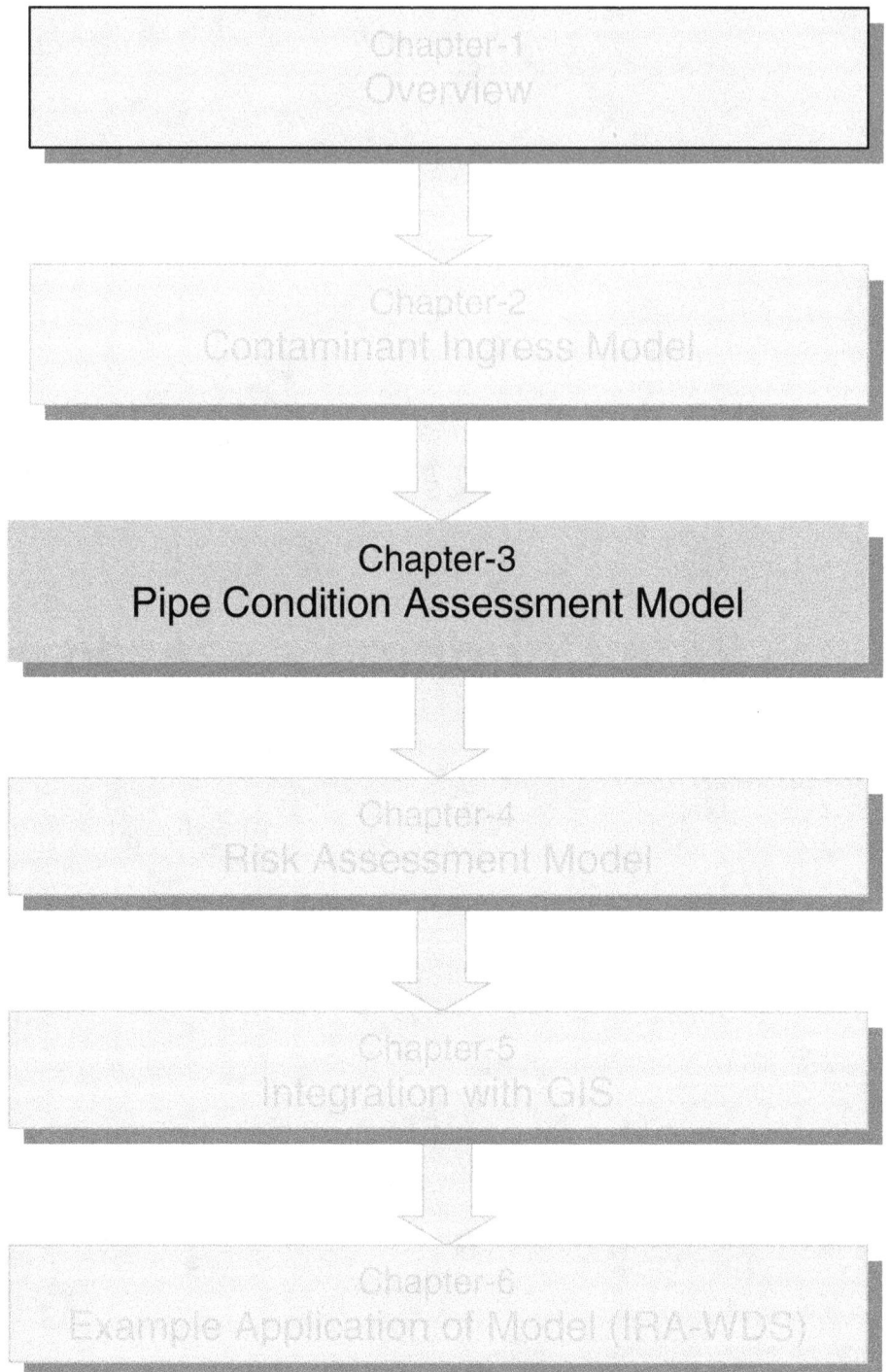

Chapter-1
Overview

Chapter-2
Contaminant Ingress Model

Chapter-3
Pipe Condition Assessment Model

Chapter-4
Risk Assessment Model

Chapter-5
Integration with GIS

Chapter-6
Example Application of Model (IRA-WDS)

Chapter 3: Pipe Condition Assessment Model

3.1 Introduction

This chapter presents details of the pipe condition assessment model component of IRA-WDS. As the name implies, this model considers all pipes in a water distribution system and estimates their relative condition (see Figure 3.1).

The outputs from the model presented in this chapter are therefore a measure of relative condition of each pipe in the water distribution system being studied. Figure 3.12 and Table 3.17 at the end of this chapter give a typical example of the outputs.

The purpose of this chapter is to provide an insight into the background and the techniques that underpin the pipe condition model. This should enable the user of IRA-WDS to appreciate the significance of the data required and also aid in interpreting the results of the model. On completion of this chapter, the user should be able to complete Tables 3.1 to 3.8, which form the input data required to run the pipe condition assessment model of IRA-WDS. Information on the data that needs to be developed in order to complete Tables 3.1–3.8 is given in this chapter.

It should be noted, however, that to use IRA-WDS the user is not required to have a detailed understanding of the technical component of the model presented in this chapter.

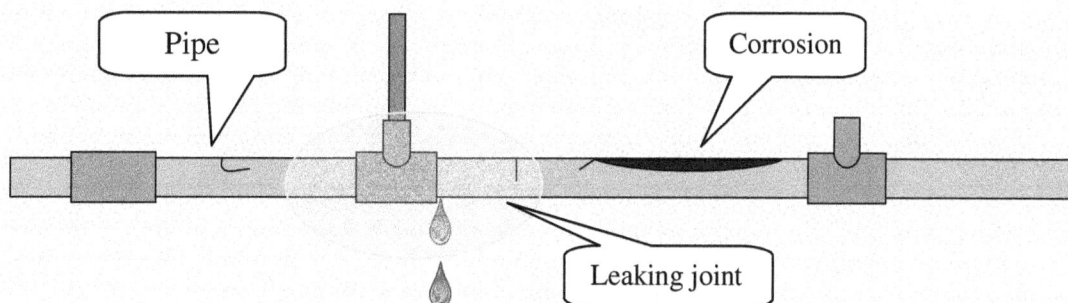

Figure 3.1. Water distribution pipe deterioration

The condition of each pipe is assessed by means of numerous indicators related to physical, environmental and operational aspects of water distribution system. These indicators are combined to give a single measure of the relative condition of each pipe. The relative condition of each pipe, coupled with its section in the contaminant zone and the contaminant loading along this section (outputs from the contaminant ingress model presented in Chapter 2), provides an estimate of the potential pollutant load entering each pipe.

Table 3.1. Properties of water distribution network		
Parameter	**Unit**	**Value**
Network map **For each pipe of network**	*Shape file*	
Length of pipe	*m*	
Joint method	Linguistic *(rubber, leadite …)*	
Material type	Linguistic *(CI, DI, RCC, PVC …)*	
Traffic load	Linguistic *(busy, medium, quiet…)*	
Surface type	Linguistic *(hard, grassed, water body…)*	
Internal protection	Linguistic *(good, medium, bad…)*	
External protection	Linguistic *(good, medium, bad…)*	
Bedding condition	Linguistic *(good, medium, bad…)*	
Workmanship	Linguistic *(good, medium, bad…)*	
Diameter of pipe	*mm*	
Installation year	*(year)*	
Bury depth of start node	*m*	
Bury depth of start node	*m*	
No. of connections	-	
No. of breaks per year	-	
Leakage rate	*lps*	
No. of valves	-	
Duration of water supply per day	*hrs*	
No. of times water supplied per day	-	

Table 3.2. Properties of different pipe materials			
Property	**Unit**	**value**	
Pipe material: _____			
Corrosion index	Linguistic *(good, medium, bad...)*		
Maximum pressure	kg/cm^2		
Maximum load	*m-kg/m*		
Design life	*years*		
Maximum diameter	*mm*		
Minimum diameter	*mm*		
Hazen-William Roughness Coefficient, C		Age, years	Value
		0-10	
		11-20	
		21-30	
		31-40	
		41-50	
		51-60	
		61-70	
		71-80	
		81-90	
		91-100	

Table 3.3. Membership Functions

Sample of membership functions

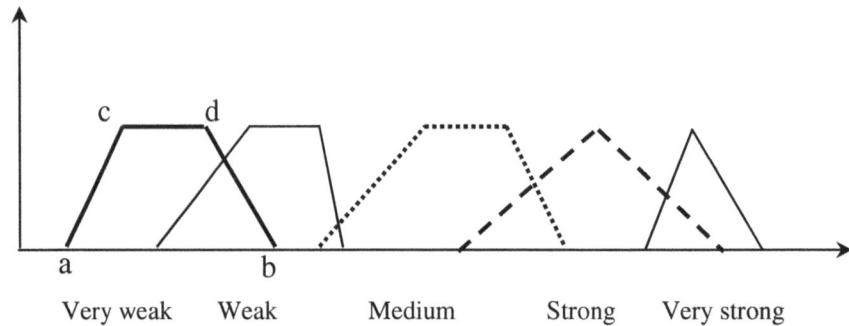

Very weak   Weak   Medium   Strong   Very strong

Corrosive Index (normalized values)				
	a	b	c	d
Very weak				
Weak				
Medium				
Strong				
Very strong				

Internal Protection (normalized values)				
	a	b	c	d
Very bad				
Bad				
Medium				
Good				
Very good				

External Protection (normalized values)				
	a	b	c	d
Very bad				
Bad				
Medium				
Good				
Very good				

58

Soil Corrosivity (ohm-m)				
	a	b	c	d
Non-corrosive				
Mildly corrosive				
Corrosive				
Highly corrosive				
Extremely corrosive				
Surface Permeability (normalized values)				
	a	b	c	d
Very hard				
Hard				
Grassed				
Open land				
Water body				
Groundwater Fluctuations (normalized values)				
	a	b	c	d
Very bad				
Bad				
Medium				
Good				
Very good				
Joint Method (normalized values)				
	a	b	c	d
Very bad				
Bad				
Medium				
Good				
Very good				
Bedding condition (normalized values)				
	a	b	c	d
Very bad				
Bad				
Medium				
Good				
Very good				

Workmanship (normalized values)				
	a	b	c	d
Very bad				
Bad				
Medium				
Good				
Very good				
Traffic density (Vehicles/hr)				
	a	b	c	d
Very busy				
Busy				
Medium				
Quiet				
Very quiet				
Maximum pressure (m)				
	a	b	c	d
Very high				
High				
Medium				
Low				
Very low				

Table 3.4. Soil data		
Soil type: _____		
Property	Unit	Value
Soil corrosivity	*ohm-m*	

Table 3.5. Groundwater table		
Groundwater zone: _____		
Property	Unit	Value
Average groundwater table depth	*m*	
Average groundwater fluctuation	*m*	

Table 3.6. Pressure		
Pressure zone: _____		
Property	**Unit**	**Value**
Pressure	kg/cm^2	

Table 3.7. Balance factors for different groups of indicators	
Group	**Balance Factor**
Pipe	
Installation	
Corrosion	
Load/strength	
Intermittency	
Failure	
Physical	
Environmental	
Operational	
Pipe condition assessment	

Table 3.8. Weights for different indicators					
Indicator	**Weight**	**Indicator**	**Weight**	**Indicator**	**Weight**
Level 3 indicators		*Level 2 Indicators*		*Level 1 Indicators*	
		Group 1		*Group 1*	
Physical		Pipe		Material decay	
Environmental		Installation		Diameter	
Operational		*Group 2*		Length	
		Corrosion		Int. protection	
		Load/strength		Ext. protection	
		Group 3		*Group 2*	
		Intermittency		Bedding condition	
		Failure		Workmanship	
				Joint method	
				No. of joints	
				Group 3	
				Year of install.	
				Soil corrosivity	
				Surface permeability	
				GW condition	
				Group 4	
				Buried depth	
				Traffic load	
				Hydraulic pressure	
				Group 5	
				No. of valves	
				No. of water supply/day	
				Duration of water supply/day	
				Group 6	
				Breakage history	

3.2 Background

A water supply system consists of:

- Visible surface assets such as treatment plants and pumping stations
- Invisible assets – the buried infrastructure of the water distribution system.

The water distribution system (WDS) is the most important component of water supply system, conveying water from source to consumers' outlets. The distribution system constitutes a substantial proportion of the cost of a water supply system, in some cases as much as half the overall cost of the system.

Over 98 per cent of pipelines are buried. No matter how well these pipelines are designed, constructed and protected, once in place they deteriorate due to their physical condition, environmental abuse, external damage, soil movements/instability etc. Thus one of the problems faced by the water utilities around the world is the ageing and deterioration of the pipe network of the water distribution system. It is estimated that water networks serving the utilities in Western Europe and North America are up to 150 years old (Sægrov et al. 1999). Half of all large diameter water mains in the 50 largest US cities are more than 50 years old (Summers 2001). It is well documented in the literature (Yan and Vairavamoorthy 2003a) that structural and functional deterioration of water mains has the potential to cause health hazards. USEPA emphasizes that water pipes corrosion and ageing is one of the main concerns related to water distribution networks that may pose a threat to public health (AWWSC 2002).

As a result of the ageing and deterioration process taking place over the past few decades, it is estimated that over the next 20 years urban pipeline infrastructure rehabilitation is one of the main activities being undertaken by municipal water and wastewater authorities (McNeill and Edwards 2001). The estimated capital investment needed for the rehabilitation of these water supply pipes and sewers is more than $700 billion (McNeill and Edwards 2001; Summers 2001).

There may not be adequate budgetary provision for the huge investment to be made in the rehabilitation of the water supply pipes of many municipalities in developing and underdeveloped countries. Therefore there are chances that this important activity is overlooked and in that process the water distribution network is damaged completely. Over the years, water utilities have learnt from past experience that pro-active rehabilitation is much more cost-effective than a reactive one, since the reactive approach advocates the rule of 'do nothing until a system component fails', which increases cost and leads to customer dissatisfaction and potential environmental problems (Loganathan et al. 2002). However, pro-active rehabilitation requires the assessment of current pipe condition and predication of future pipe break rates.

As the investment needed for the rehabilitation of the entire water distribution system is huge, it is essential to prioritize the activities of rehabilitation of the water distribution systems in terms of the section of the pipe distribution network which needs to be considered first for the rehabilitation. However, inspection and replacement of underground assets will be time-consuming and costly, and the available funds for such rehabilitation activities are often limited. Therefore there is a need to prioritize investment based on an assessment of pipe condition. In general, while undertaking a pipe rehabilitation programme the following steps are performed:

- Predict condition of pipes using condition assessment model.
- Inspect pipes with the worst condition.
- Undertake pipe rehabilitation based on the above.

Therefore, before undertaking any pipe rehabilitation works, assessment of pipe condition and the identification of the worst pipes are important. The objective of this model is to provide guidelines which enable to assess the condition of pipes of water distribution network and identify the pipes which are subjected to the most risk, if not replaced.

As stated in Chapter 1, IRA-WDS assesses the risk associated with contaminant intrusion into the water distribution system during non-supply hours (especially for intermittent water supplies). The condition of water distribution pipes that determines the potential intrusion pathway is one of the 2 conditions for contaminant intrusion into water distribution systems that are intermittent (the other condition being a pollution source, as described in Chapter 2). The pipe condition, assessed by the PCA model presented below, is combined with the contaminant loading along the pipe estimated by contaminant ingress model (Chapter 2) to know the relative risk of contaminant intrusion due to the pipe (Chapter 4).

3.3 Pipe Condition Assessment

Pipe condition assessment is the process of assessing the status of the underground pipes based on their condition. Water pipe condition is affected by a deterioration process which is complex because of its dependency on many factors that interactively contribute to the process. These factors can be broadly categorized into three groups (AWWSC 2002):

- Physical factors (e.g. pipe age, diameter, length, material, etc.)
- Environmental factors (e.g. soil corrosivity, internal and external loads, pipe location, etc.) and
- Operational factors (e.g. break history, leak records, operation pressure, etc.).

The pipe condition is the cumulative effect of the different factors in these three categories.

The method for assessing pipe condition based on the above factors would obviously involve uncertainties, as in most cases it is not possible to obtain accurate asset information due to a lack of organized record-keeping by the water authorities. However, some of these factors, especially physical factors, may be available in inventory databases, which have deterministic values except for pipe material. Environmental and operational factors are difficult to quantify using deterministic values but are dealt with using the possibility approach to take account of the associated uncertainties.

Existing methods for predicting the conditions of buried pipes can be classified according to three models:

- Deterministic
- Probabilistic
- Cost.

Deterministic models use parameters like pipe age and breakage history, operational environments, pipe material etc. to predict the pipe failure (Shamir and Howard 1979), whereas probabilistic models predict the probabilities of the pipe failure based on survival rates, breakage rate etc. (Kleiner and Rajani 2001). Cost models on the other hand are based on both deterministic and probabilistic models and consider the economical life of the pipes along with the deterioration factors (Loganathan et al. 2002). These approaches appear to have difficulties in dealing with pipe deterioration. In case of deterministic approach, there are many factors that contribute to deterioration and only a few are considered in the development of models. In the probabilistic approach, due to the insufficiency and inaccuracy of breakage data, it is difficult to establish the probability distribution function for breakage. The insufficient knowledge about the complexity of the pipe deterioration process (for deterministic models), the lack of pipe breakage historical data (for probabilistic models) and a lack of pipe deterioration data (for cost models) cause difficulties when applying these models. Furthermore the validity of these methods is highly dependent on the availability of data and they also have the shortcoming of an inability to incorporate inherent uncertainties associated with data.

However, there is enough knowledge regarding the deterioration factors causing pipe breakage and understanding of their influence on pipe deterioration. It is therefore possible to develop a model to assess the condition of a water pipe using the available knowledge and understanding about these deterioration factors. Hence, a pipe condition assessment model which ranks different pipes based on their deterioration due to combined effect of different factors using a 'fuzzy' approach (to consider uncertainties associated with data) was developed and used for this study.

By using this model, the pipe condition can be evaluated with basic pipe condition indicators such as pipe age, pipe material, pipe diameter, soil condition, traffic loads, etc (first level indicators). The uncertainties inherent in these pipe condition indicators are described with fuzzy set theory (Zadeh 1965). The first-level indicators are aggregated into groups based on their similarities to form the second-level indicators. Similarly, the second-level pipe condition indicators are grouped to form the final indicator (Figure 3.3). Based on the hierarchical pipe condition structure established from the above aggregation process, fuzzy composite programming is used to compute an 'indicator distance metric' for each indicator, and finally an 'overall distance metric' for each pipe is obtained. This final distance metric is used to evaluate and rank the conditions of pipes. The fuzzy composite programming used for the PCA model is described in the next section and the methodology used for estimating the final distance metric is described in Figure 3.3.

65

3.4 Fuzzy Composite Programming

The methodology used in pipe condition assessment is the multiple-criteria decision-making (MCDM) technique which combines the available, often completely different, pipe condition indicators into a final overall pipe condition indicators. The selected MCDM technique is fuzzy composite programming (FCP) which incorporates both fuzzy set theory and its arithmetic corollaries (Dubois and Prade 1988; Kaufmann and Gupta 1991). FCP has been applied in many instances in MCDM to problems related to water resource and environment engineering (Bardossy and Duckstein 1992; Hagemeister et al. 1996; Lee et al. 1991; Lee et al. 1992). Application of FCP methods to pipe condition assessment was more recently introduced by Yan and Vairavamoorthy (2003b). However, they stated that the application of FCP to pipe condition assessment may be sensitive to weights and balance factors used in the process.

Zeleny (1973) developed a mathematical programming technique that employs a single level normalized/non-normalized distance-based methodology to rank a discrete set of solutions according to their distances from an ideal solution. This is called *compromise programming*.

This technique forms the basis for *composite programming*, developed by Bardossy et al. (1985). This deals with problems of a hierarchical nature (i.e. when certain criteria contain a number of sub-criteria). Composite programming extends compromise programming to a normalized multi-level methodology. Composite programming generates composite distance metrics of each sub-criterion within the same group, and then combines the distance metrics of each sub-criterion to form a single composite distance metric. The process iterates with the successive levels until a final level composite distance metric is reached (one composite distance metric for each alternative).

The fuzzy set theory (Zadeh 1965) is used to include the inherent uncertainties. The addition of fuzzy set theory to compromise programming to represent uncertainties of indicators forms *fuzzy compromise programming*.

Similar to this, when fuzzy compromise programming is extended to a normalized multi-level distance-based methodology (composite programming) to account for uncertainties, *fuzzy composite programming* (FCP) is formed. Thus the combination of fuzzy set theory with composite programming forms fuzzy composite programming (FCP), which can cope with unavoidable vagueness, imprecision, and uncertainty associated with basic pipe condition indicator data. This FCP technique is used for the pipe condition assessment in the present study.

3.4.1 Method

Compromise programming uses equation (3.1) to rank a discrete set of solutions according to their distance from an ideal solution. Composite programming applies the compromise programming equation (3.1) to each sub-criterion, and then combines the compromise distance metrics of each sub-criterion to form a single composite distance metric (one composite distance metric for each objective or alternative of the problem; in this case different alternatives are pipes).

$$L_j = \left\{ \sum_{i=1}^{n} \left[w_i^p \left(\frac{f_i - f_i^w}{f_i^b - f_i^w} \right)^p \right] \right\}^{\frac{1}{p}}$$

(3.1)

where

L_j - distance metric of alternative

w_i - weight of indicator i

p - balance factor

f_i^b - best value for indicator i

f_i^w - worst value for indicator i

f_i - actual value for indicator i

n - number of indicators

The addition of fuzzy set theory (Zadeh 1965) to compromise programming is used to represent uncertainties of indicators and this is called fuzzy compromise programming, and when this is extended to a normalized multi-level distance-based methodology, fuzzy composite programming is formed. The normalization process is performed with the use of best and worst first-level indicator values (Hagemeister et al. 1996).

$$S_i = \frac{f_i - f_i^w}{f_i^b - f_i^w}$$

(3.2)

where

f_i - actual value of ith fuzzy indicator

f_i^w - the worst value of ith indicator

f_i^b - the best value of ith indicator

The normalization formula given above can have different forms depending on whether the maximum is the 'best' or 'worst' value.

$$S_i = \begin{cases} \dfrac{f_i - f_i^-}{f_i^+ - f_i^-} & f_i^+ = f_i^b \\[3mm] \dfrac{f_i^+ - f_i}{f_i^+ - f_i^-} & f_i^+ = f_i^w \end{cases}$$

(3.3)

where

f_i^+ - maximum possible value of ith fuzzy indicator

f_i^- - minimum possible value of ith indicator

It should be noted that this normalization process will result in the coordinate (1, 1) to be the ideal point. Substitution of equation (3.2) into equation (3.1), and ignoring the exponent p on the weight w (Bardossy and Duckstein 1992), yields the following composite distance for j^{th} group of indicators. The composite distance, L_j, is the distance between the actual point of indicator and the ideal one (Woldt and Bogardi 1992):

$$L_j = \left[\sum_{i=1}^{n_j} w_{j,i} S_{j,i}^{p_j} \right]^{1/p_j} \tag{3.4}$$

where

L_j - composite distance metric for B+1 level group j of B level indicators

$S_{j,i}$ - normalized value of the B level indicator i in the B+1 level group j of B level indicators

n_j - number of B level indicators in group j

$w_{j,i}$ - weights expressing the relative importance of B level indicators in group j such that their sum is 1

p_j - balancing factors among indicators for group j

For example, if we consider the composite structure presented in Figure 3.4, and let B=1: at B+1=2 level group, j=1 is pipe indicator which is obtained from combining the three indicators (material decay, diameter, length, internal protection and external protection) at B=1 level. Therefore equation (3.4) combines the normalized first-level indicators to obtain their respective second-level composite distance. The process of computing successive levels of composite distance is repeated with previous level composite distance, L_j, being substituted in place of variable $S_{j,i}$ until the final composite distance is reached for the system. In the case of pipe condition assessment, this final-level indicator illustrates the combination of physical, environment and environmental factors. The procedure is explained in Figure 3.5.

3.4.2 Fuzzy set theory

One of the main features of fuzzy set theory is its ability to deal with uncertain, imprecise and linguistic information, such as busy, very busy, good, excellent, etc. (Zadeh 1965). This theory uses fuzzy numbers to represent parameter uncertainty. In this study, therefore, fuzzy number is used to interpret the linguistic values and represent the uncertainties. The process to determine the fuzzy number to express linguistic value is subjective and could rely a great deal on experts' knowledge.

A fuzzy number is a quantity whose value is imprecise and is described by the possibility that the uncertain parameter, X, may take on a certain value x with the help of a membership function. A membership function, $\mu(X)$, is a curve or relationship that defines how each point in the input space or range of parameter, X, is mapped to a membership value (or degree of membership) between 0 and 1. Thus the degree to which a parameter belongs to a fuzzy set is denoted by a membership value between 0 and 1. The two common representations of fuzzy numbers are triangular and trapezoidal (see Figure 3.2).

A popular way to carry out fuzzy arithmetic operations is by way of interval arithmetic (Kaufmann and Gupta 1991). This is done by introducing an α-cut of the membership function $\mu(X)$, (denoted as α). α is the set of all X such that $\mu(X)$ is greater than or equal to α. Thus a set of α-cut of a fuzzy number (X_α) is always represented by an interval and hence fuzzy arithmetic operations are possible. For a fuzzy set, X, shown in Figure 3.2, the α-cut set of X is the set of all x such that membership value of X, $(\mu(X))$, is greater than or equal to α and is defined by equation (3.5).

$$X_\alpha = \{\alpha | \mu[X] \geq \alpha\}$$ (3.5)

Note that by virtue of the condition on $\mu(X)$ in equation (3.5), the set X_α is now a crisp set. In this way, a fuzzy set can be converted to an infinite number of cut-sets. For example, for a trapezoidal membership function of Figure 3.2 (b), when $\alpha = 0.5$, $X_{0.5}$ =[a_1, a_2] or when $\alpha = 1.0$, $X_{1.0}$ = [b_1, b_2]. Therefore, any fuzzy number may be represented as a series of intervals (one interval for every α-cut). Thus the fuzzy number operation is converted into an intervals operation, the details of which can be found in Kaufmann and Gupta (1991).

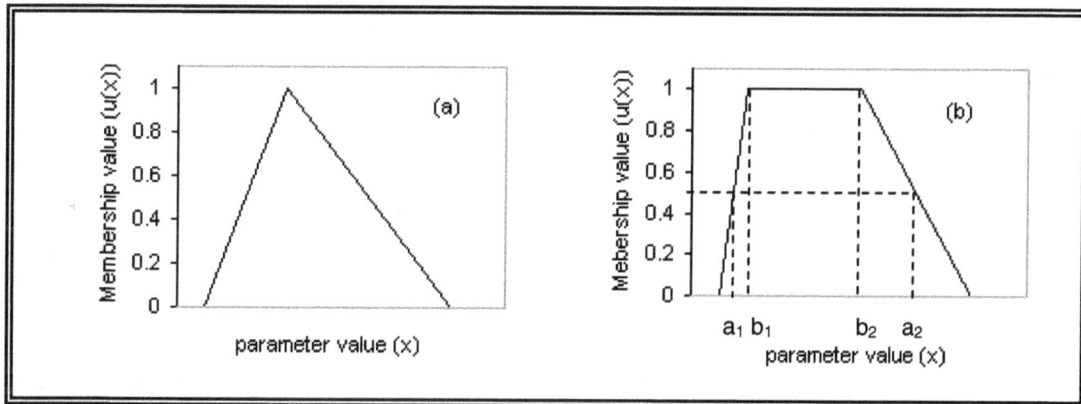

Figure 3.2. Two representations of fuzzy number (a) Triangular (b) Trapezoidal

3.4.3 Balance factors

The decision-maker is also required to determine balance factors when applying the pipe condition assessment model. Balance factor determines the degree of compromise between indicators of the same group. Low balance factors are used for a high level of compromise among indicators of the same group (Jones and Barnes 2000).

- A balance factor of 1 suggests that there is a perfect compromise between indicators of that group.
- A balance factor of 2 suggests that the level of compromise is moderate.
- A balance factor greater than 3 indicates that there is minimal compromise.

69

3.4.4 Weights

Prior to examining alternatives, decision-makers must assign weights to indicate their preferences to the relative importance of the various pipe indicators in a particular group. Most of the applications of the FCP method mentioned above use crisp numbers to express weights according to the judgement of decision-maker. However, Lee et al. (1991; 1992) proposed the use of the *analytic hierarchy process* (AHP).

In this study the following three methods are used:

- 'Equal weights' method assigns an equal weight to all the indicators of a particular group. The weights are assigned such that their sum equals 1.
- 'Variable weights' method gives the user flexibility to assign different weights to different indicators of a particular group. The different weights will be based on the user's perception of the relative importance of one indicator over another. Again the sum of the weights assigned must be equal to one.
- The AHP method can also be used to calculate and assign weights. Details of this method are given in Appendix B (Appendix D provides a questionnaire that can be completed by several respondents to aid in the AHP process.).

3.5 Application to Pipe Condition Assessment

The procedure for assessment of pipe condition used in the model involves the following steps.

1. Identify the indicators influencing the pipe condition and their types (fuzzy or crisp).
2. Prepare the composite structure of the pipe condition indicators.
3. Obtain the weightings for each indicator in each group and decide balance factor for the group.
4. Normalize all the indicators into a scale of [0, 1].
5. Obtain a fuzzy number by using the FCP-based hierarchical aggregation process for each pipe (i.e. for a pipe network with n pipes, n fuzzy numbers are obtained)
6. Rank the fuzzy numbers.

The procedure is illustrated by the flowchart in Figure 3.3.

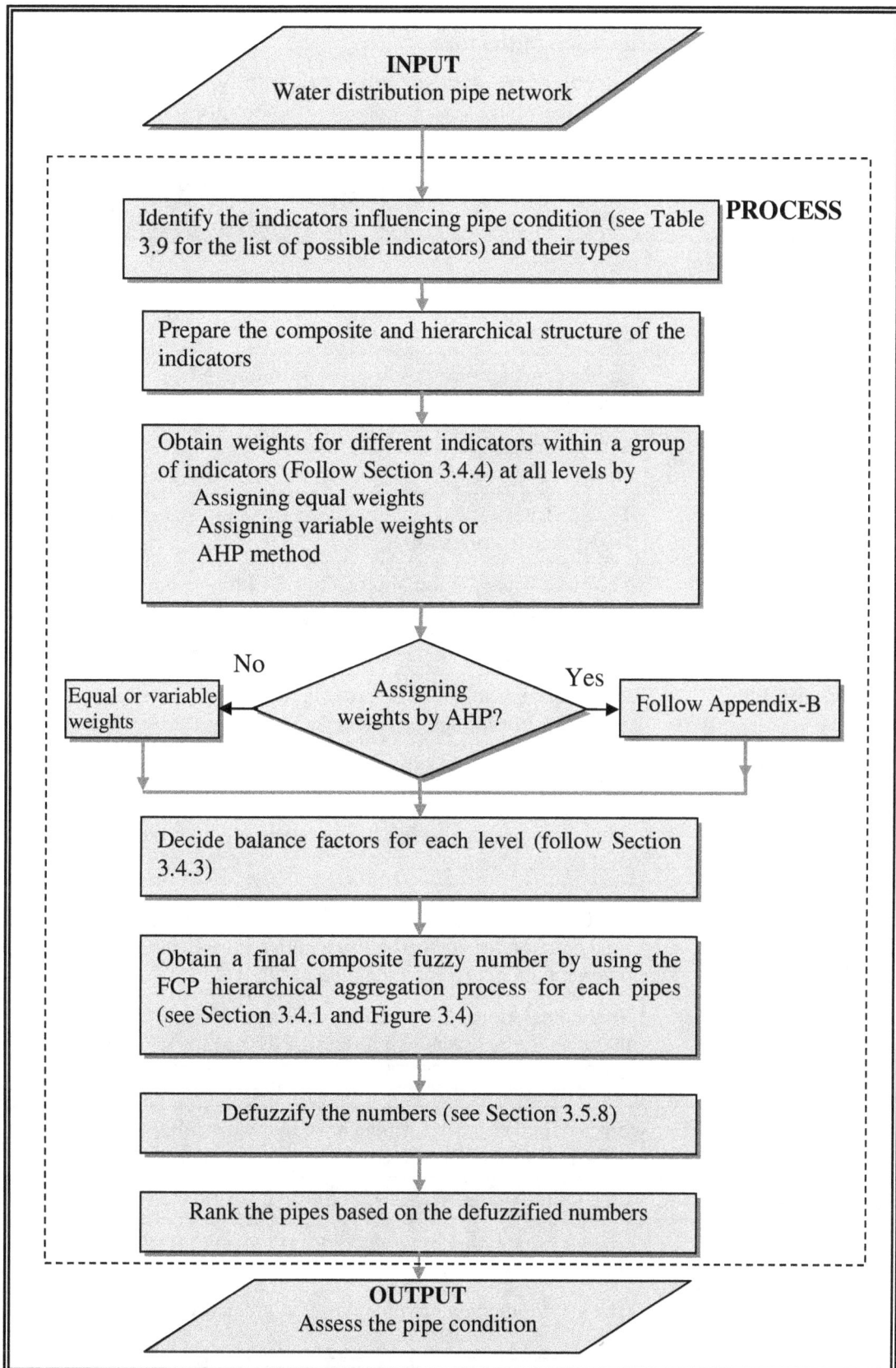

INPUT
Water distribution pipe network

PROCESS

Identify the indicators influencing pipe condition (see Table 3.9 for the list of possible indicators) and their types

Prepare the composite and hierarchical structure of the indicators

Obtain weights for different indicators within a group of indicators (Follow Section 3.4.4) at all levels by
    Assigning equal weights
    Assigning variable weights or
    AHP method

No ← Assigning weights by AHP? → Yes

Equal or variable weights

Follow Appendix-B

Decide balance factors for each level (follow Section 3.4.3)

Obtain a final composite fuzzy number by using the FCP hierarchical aggregation process for each pipes (see Section 3.4.1 and Figure 3.4)

Defuzzify the numbers (see Section 3.5.8)

Rank the pipes based on the defuzzified numbers

OUTPUT
Assess the pipe condition

Figure 3.3. The flowchart for pipe condition assessment

3.5.1 Basic pipe deterioration indicators

A number of indicators (Table 3.9) of water pipe susceptibity to deterioration have been identified. More detailed explanations are given in Appendix C.

Table 3.9. Pipe Condition Assessment Indicators	
Level 1 Indicators	**Description**
Material decay	Hazen-William coefficient of friction (C) is considered to characterize this influence
Diameter	Larger diameter pipes are less prone to failure than smaller diameter pipes
Length	Larger length pipes are more prone to failure than smaller length pipes
Int. protection	The pipes having internal protection by lining and/or coating are less susceptible to corrosion
Ext. protection	The pipes having external protection by lining and/or coating are less susceptible to deterioration
Bedding condition	Improper bedding may result in premature pipe failure
Workmanship	Poor workmanship may deteriorate the pipes and cause more risk regardless of pipe age and other factors
Joint method	Some types of joints experience premature failure (e.g. leadite joints)
No. of joints	The more joints a pipe has, the greater the risk of the pipe getting structurally worse
Year of installation	The effects of pipe degradation become more apparent over time
Soil corrosivity	Pipe deteriorates quicker in more corrosive soil and the degree of deterioration depends on the pipe material
Surface permeability	The more permeable surface allows more moisture to percolate to the pipe. Surface salts will be carried to the pipe with the moisture
GW condition	The water pipes are deteriorated by the groundwater table
Buried depth	Pipes buried at greater depths have more possibility of failure than those buried at shallower depths
Traffic load	Pipe failure rate increases with traffic loads on the surface
Maximum pressure	Changes to internal water pressure will change stresses acting on the pipe
No. of valves	The greater the number of valves, the greater the deterioration of the pipe
No. of water supply/day	The greater the number of water supplies the more the pipes will deteriorate
Duration of water supply/day	The longer the duration of water supply, the smaller the chances of pipe failure
Breakage history	The number of pipe breakages per year

3.5.2 Types of indicators

Among the twenty selected pipe condition indicators at the first level, many of them are difficult to express in crisp form; for example, soil corrosivity, pipe material, pipe bedding condition, and pipe joint method are a few which involve vague and imprecise information. In addition to the existing vagueness, some information such as traffic loads and pipe location are expressed linguistically. Such vague or imprecise and linguistic information can be dealt with fuzzy set theory (Zadeh 1965) (see Section 3.4.2) and hence used in this study to interpret the linguistic values and represent the uncertainties. Triangular or trapezoidal fuzzy membership functions are used to map the parameter to membership values between the interval (0,1). Interval operations are used as fuzzy number arithmetic in this research. Five intervals, i.e. 0, 0.25, 0.5, 0.75, 1.0 are used for fuzzy arithmetic operations.

3.5.3 Composite structure

The hierarchical structure of composite programming provides a process for integrating different types of information into a single indicator that can provide deeper understanding of the interrelationships between numerous pipe condition indicators. Figure 3.4 gives the composite hierarchical structure used in pipe condition ranking in this study. This structure is developed in a way that enables known or relatively easily obtained information to be used to produce the first level indicators. The composite programming hierarchical structure is used to combine first-level indicators based on their similarities into second-level indicators. The aggregation process continues until the final-level indicator is achieved.

The pipe condition can be evaluated with basic pipe condition indicators (first level indicators) that contribute to the deterioration. To illustrate the relationships between the pipe condition assessment indicator and deterioration, twenty first-level indicators (Figure 3.4) are proposed in this study. These are broadly divided into six groups (pipe indicators, installation indicators, corrosion indicators, load/strength indicators, intermittency and failure indicators) at second level. These are grouped into three third level indicators (physical, environmental and operational). These are further combined to obtain final indicator, pipe condition assessment.

It should be noted that more indicators could be added into this composite structure if more information were available (e.g. water quality) or indicators for which information/data are not available can be omitted (for example, hydraulic pressure).

Depending on the importance of each indicator and the availability of data, the user should select the indicators for pipe condition assessment and mark those in Table 3.1. The input dialog window of IRA-WDS (Chapter 4 of Book 4 (IRA-WDS user manual)) allows the user to select the specified indicators. When some indicators at the first level are treated as fuzzy numbers, the second level, third level and final level indicators are also fuzzy numbers. The different indicators with their type are presented in Table 3.4.

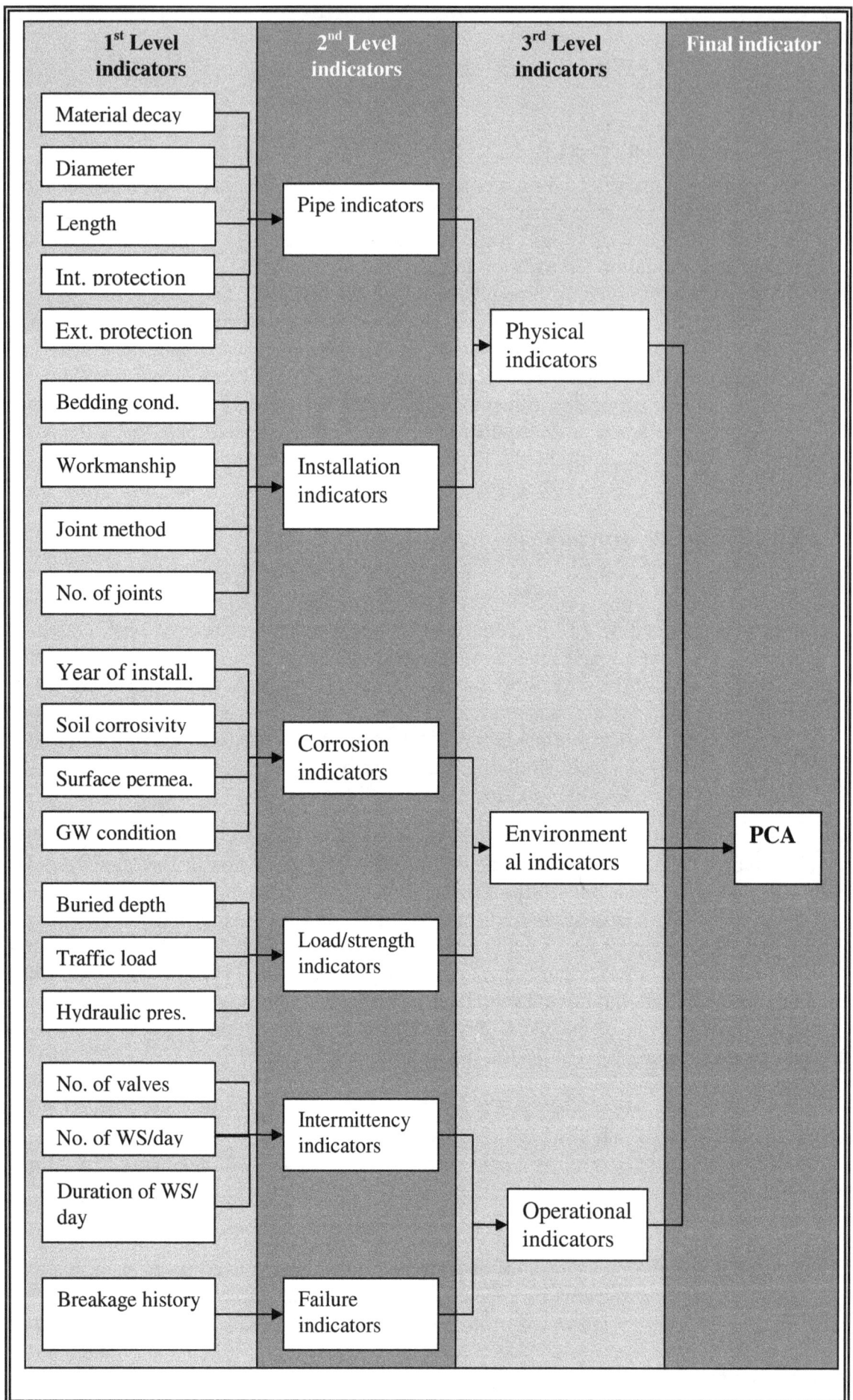

Figure 3.4. Composite structure of different pipe condition assessment indicators

INPUT

No. of levels (l=1.....L),

No. of groups at each level {(g=1....G_l), l=1.......L}

No. of indicators in each group at each level [{(i=1...I_{gl}), g=1....G_l}, l=1....L]

Weights for each indicator of each group at each level (w_{igl})

Balance factor for each group at each level (P_{gl})

f_{ig1}^{b} = max. possible/best value of ith crisp/fuzzy indicator of gth group at l^{th} level

f_{ig1}^{w} = min. possible/worst value of ith crisp/fuzzy indicator of gth group at l^{th}

PROCESS

Level l = 1

Group g = 1

l = 1?

Estimate $S_{ig1} = \begin{cases} \dfrac{f_{ig1} - f_{ig1}^{-}}{f_{ig1}^{+} - f_{ig1}^{-}} & f_{ig1}^{+} = f_{ig1}^{b} \\[2ex] \dfrac{f_{ig1}^{+} - f_{ig1}}{f_{ig1}^{+} - f_{ig1}^{-}} & f_{ig1}^{+} = f_{ig1}^{w} \end{cases}$

S_{ig1} = normalized value of ith crisp/fuzzy indicator of gth group at l^{th} level

Estimate $F_{g(l+1)} = \sum_{i=1}^{I_{gl}} w_{igl} S_{igl}^{P_{gl}}$

$F_{g(l+1)}$ = composite distance metric for g^{th} group at $(l+1)^{th}$ level

Yes — Next group ← More groups?

No

$F_{g(l+1)}$ are S_{ig1} for $(l+1)^{th}$ level.

Yes — Next level ← More levels?

No

OUTPUT: F_{1l}

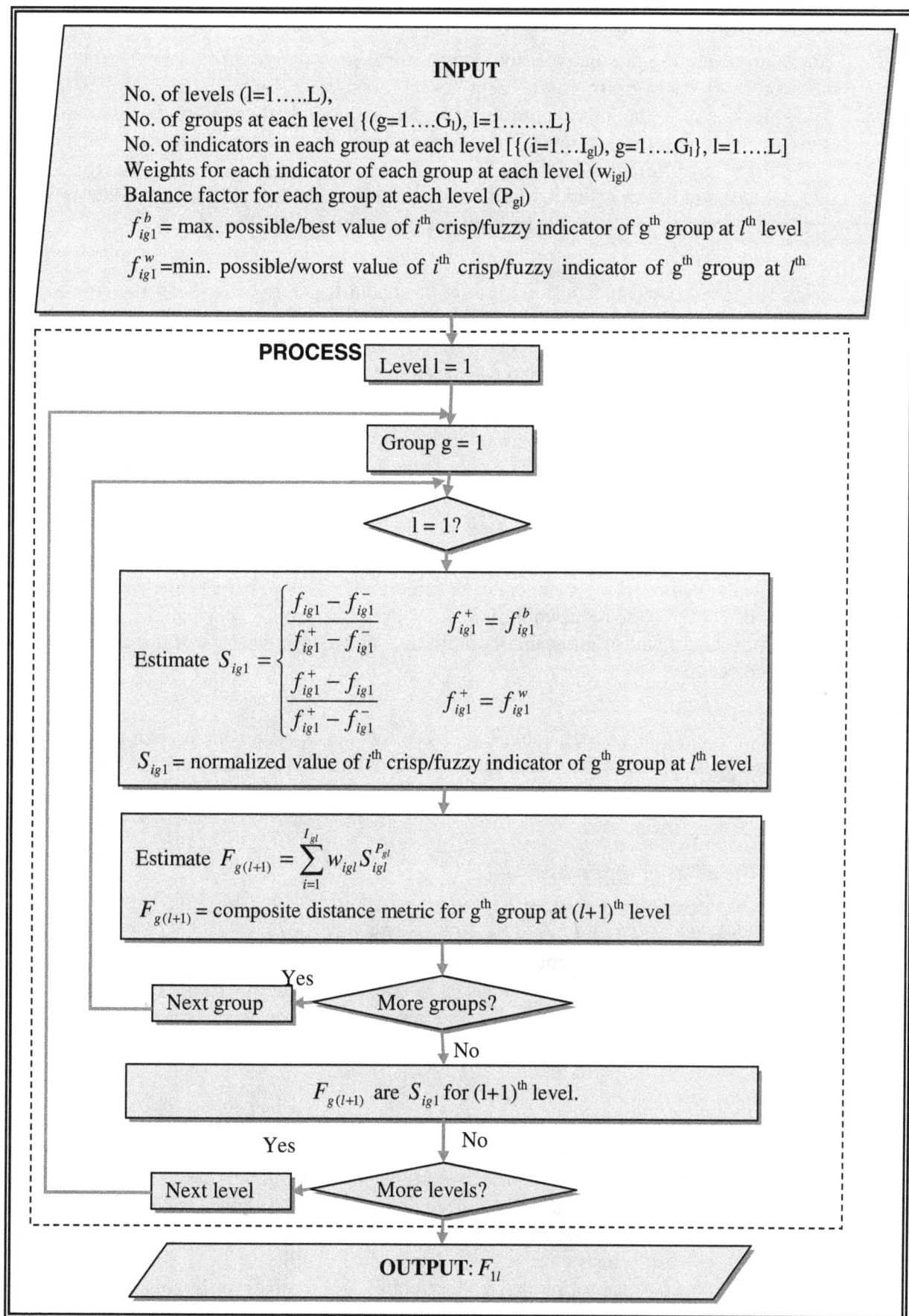

Figure 3.5. The flowchart for obtaining the final composite distance metric

3.5.4 Weights and balance factors

Prior to examining alternatives, the decision-maker is required to assign weights for indicators of each group at different levels. Assigning weights for different level indicators allows the incorporation of individual perceptions into the assessment system. This has the advantage of allowing users to recognize the importance of indicators in different analyses. There are several ways to assign weights for deterioration indicators (see Section 3.4.4). In this study the weights can be assigned by 'equal weight' and 'variable weights' or generated by AHP.

IRA-WDS provides an input dialog box to enable the user to perform the pair-wise comparison required for AHP (i.e. to indicate the preference of one indicator over another and the degree of preference). IRA-WDS then computes the weights for each indicator and these weights are stored in a file and displayed.

After assigning the weights using one of the methods described above, the user should be able to complete Table 3.8. The data from this table can then be directly inputted into IRA-WDS (see Chapter 4 of Book 4 to see input dialog window for IRA-WDS).

The decision-maker is required to determine balance factors in order to evaluate alternatives using fuzzy composite programming. Balance factors determine the degree of compromise between indicators of the same group. Low balance factors are used for a high level of allowable compromise between indicators of the same group and vice versa.

Balance factors are entered into IRA-WDS by means of an input dialog box (see Chapter 4 of Book 4 to see input dialog window for IRA-WDS). Using this information, the user is able to complete the Table 3.7.

3.5.5 The effect of pipe material

The above described indicators are interdependent: for example, the effect of pipe diameter on the pipe failure may be different for different pipe material; the effect of traffic load on pipe failure may be a function of pipe material and the buried depth. However, in this study the pipe material is considered the most important parameter and corrosion and load/strength indicators are considered to be influenced by the pipe material.

To represent the importance of pipe material, three surrogate measures are used, namely, corrosion resistance, maximum pressure and impact strength to indicate the influence of pipe material on pipe condition. The maximum pressure reflects the strength of pipe material and expressed in crisp form. The impact strength represents the ability of a material to withstand impact without damage and is expressed in crisp form. The corrosion resistance implies the intrinsic ability of pipe material to resist degradation by corrosion (internal and external) and is given in linguistic form with fuzzy description.

The weight based on the value of the appropriate measure is assigned to the indicator. The indicators that are influenced by pipe material and the corresponding measure are listed in Table 3.10.

Table 3.10. Indicators that are influenced by the pipe material and the corresponding measure

Indicator	Measure
Soil corrosivity	Pipe material corrosion resistance
Surface permeability	Pipe material corrosion resistance
GW condition	Pipe material corrosion resistance
Buried depth	Impact load
Traffic load	Impact load
Hydraulic pressure	Maximum pressure

The typical values of pipe material corrosion resistance, impact strength and maximum pressure are presented in Table 3.11.

Table 3.11. Typical values of pipe material corrosion resistance, impact strength and maximum pressure

Pipe material	Pipe material corrosion resistance		Impact strength m-kg/m	Maximum pressure kg/cm^2
	Internal	External		
DI	Highly corrodible	Corrodible	102.5	31.62-78.54
PVC	Non-corrodible	Non-corrodible	4.40	8.16-15.3
HDPE	Non-corrodible	Non-corrodible	20.5	10-20
AC	Mildly corrodible	corrodible	23.5	5.1-35.7
PE	Non corrodible	Corrodible	58.5	15-25
PC/RCC	Mildly corrodible	Corrodible	30	20.4-30
Steel/GI	Corrodible	Corrodible	150	14.28-97.92
CI	Highly corrodible	Extremely corrodible	150	14.28-97.92

3.5.6 Normalization

Pipe condition indicators are normalized using equation (3.2). The maximum and minimum values (or best and worst values) for normalization can be obtained from:

- *Criterion A:* Design values. For example, the crisp indicator, diameter, is normalized with the designed maximum and minimum values of the diameter for each pipe material. These designed maximum and minimum values can be obtained from the manufacturer for each pipe material.

- **Criterion B:** Global maximum and minimum. For example, the crisp indicator, soil corrosivity, is normalized with global maximum soil corrosivity (for clay soil) and global minimum soil corrosivity (for sandy soil).
- **Criterion C:** Normalized value. This criterion is used for the fuzzy variable in linguistic form. For example, for the fuzzy indicator, surface permeability, the global normalized membership function is used.
- **Criterion D:** Obtaining the maximum and minimum values by comparing the values of all alternatives (i.e. pipes in this case) for each indicator from the dataset. For example, the indicator, length, is normalized with the maximum and minimum lengths of the pipe from the data set.

The procedure is described in Figure 3.6. Table 3.12 narrates the different criteria used for the normalization of the indicators. Table 3.13 narrates the different criteria used for the normalization of the measures or attributes used for incorporating the effect of pipe material on different indicators.

Note: If two data sets (or water distribution systems) are to be compared, the maximum and minimum values in Criterion D should be obtained by comparing the values of all alternatives (i.e. pipes in this case) for each indicator from all the data sets.

3.5.7 Final composite fuzzy number using FCP

The final composite fuzzy number for each pipe is obtained by using fuzzy composite programming as described in Sections 3.4.1 and 3.4.2 and shown in Figure 3.6.

Table 3.12. Different criteria used for the normalization of the indicators	
Indicator	**Criterion**
Material decay	A
Diameter	A
Length	D
Int. protection	C
Ext. protection	C
Bedding condition	C
Workmanship	C
Joint method	C
No. of joints	D
Year of installation	A
Soil corrosivity	B
Surface permeability	C
GW condition	C
Buried depth	D
Traffic load	B
Maximum pressure	B
No. of valves	D
No. of water supply/day	D
Duration of water supply/day	D
Breakage history	D

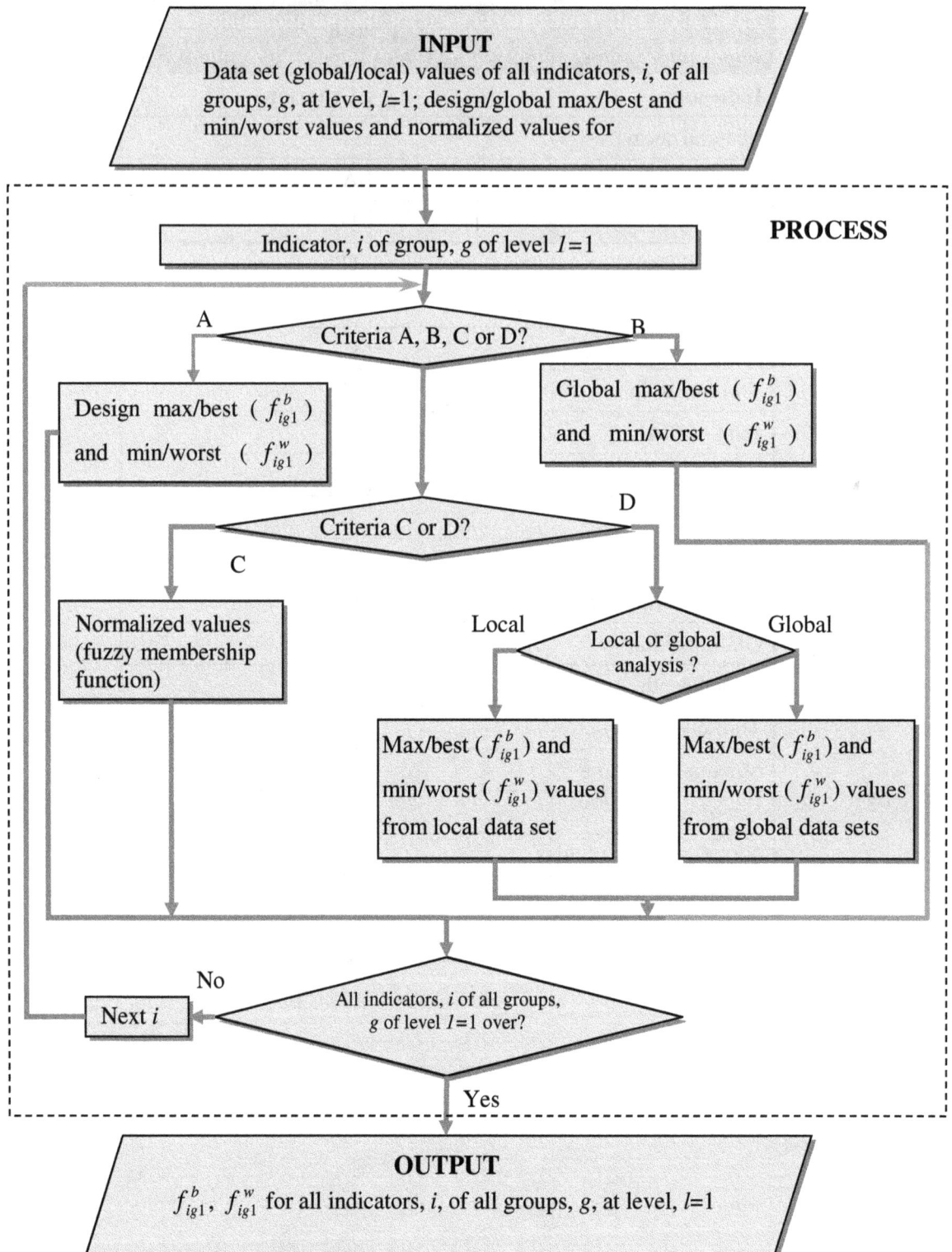

INPUT
Data set (global/local) values of all indicators, i, of all groups, g, at level, $l=1$; design/global max/best and min/worst values and normalized values for

PROCESS

Indicator, i of group, g of level $l=1$

Criteria A, B, C or D?

A

B

Design max/best (f_{ig1}^b) and min/worst (f_{ig1}^w)

Global max/best (f_{ig1}^b) and min/worst (f_{ig1}^w)

Criteria C or D?

D

C

Normalized values (fuzzy membership function)

Local or global analysis ?

Local

Global

Max/best (f_{ig1}^b) and min/worst (f_{ig1}^w) values from local data set

Max/best (f_{ig1}^b) and min/worst (f_{ig1}^w) values from global data sets

All indicators, i of all groups, g of level $l=1$ over?

No

Next i

Yes

OUTPUT
f_{ig1}^b, f_{ig1}^w for all indicators, i, of all groups, g, at level, $l=1$

Figure 3.6. Obtaining maximum/best and minimum/worst values for indicators of different groups at Level 1

80

Table 3.13. Different criteria used for the normalization of the pipe material attributes/measures	
Measure	**Criterion**
Pipe material corrosion resistance	C
Impact load	B
Maximum pressure	B

3.5.8 Ranking

By using the FCP hierarchical aggregation process, a final composite number was obtained to assess pipe condition for each pipe. The final composite number is fuzzy. Thus for a pipe network with n pipes, n fuzzy numbers $(L (j), j=1, 2... n)$ associated with the n pipes were obtained. These pipes need to be ranked according to the composite number. The following procedure is used to rank these fuzzy numbers.

The fuzzy number obtained from FCP process contains vague and imprecise information inherent from first-level indicators. Using fuzzy indicators instead of crisp ones is more realistic to reflect real systems, but it is not instinctive for people who are not familiar with fuzzy sets theory to understand the information included in the final fuzzy result. Thus some methods, such as defuzzification or fuzzy ranking method, should be applied to convert fuzzy results into crisp numbers or give a ranking order of fuzzy results respectively, which is more instinctive to practising engineers.

In the present research, we use the fuzzy ranking method to rank these n fuzzy numbers, which corresponds to the ranking of n pipes' condition. There are many fuzzy number ranking methods available from literature. Different fuzzy number ranking methods extract various features from fuzzy sets. These features may be a centre of gravity, and area under the membership function, or various intersection points between fuzzy sets. A particular ranking method extracts a specific feature, and then ranks fuzzy quantities according to the feature (Prodanovic and Simonovic 2002). In this study the fuzzy ranking method developed by Chen (1985), which determines the ranking of n fuzzy numbers by using the maximizing set and minimizing set, was used as it does not require subjective weightings for different parts of membership function to rank fuzzy quantities (Prodanovic and Simonovic 2002).

The maximizing set Max is a fuzzy subset with membership function $u_{Max}(x)$ given as:

$$u_{Max}(x) = \begin{cases} (x - x_{min})/(x_{max} - x_{min}), & x_{min} \leq x \leq x_{max} \\ 0 & , \quad \text{Otherwise} \end{cases} \tag{3.6}$$

where $x_{min} = \inf S$, $x_{max} = \sup S$, $S = \bigcup_{j=1}^{n} S_j$, $S_j = \{x \mid u_{L_j}(x) > 0\}$.

Then the right utility value, U_{Max}, for pipe j is defined as:

$$U_{Max}(j) = \sup\{\min[u_{Max}(x), u_{L_j}(x)]\} \tag{3.7}$$

The minimizing set *Min* is a fuzzy subset with membership function $u_{Min(x)}$ given as:

$$u_{Min}(x) = \begin{cases} (x - x_{max})/(x_{min} - x_{max}), & x_{min} \leq x \leq x_{max} \\ 0 & , \quad \text{Otherwise} \end{cases} \tag{3.8}$$

Then the left utility value, U_{Min}, for pipe j is defined as:

$$U_{Min}(j) = \sup\{\min[u_{Min}(x), u_{L_j}(x)]\} \tag{3.9}$$

The total utility or ranking value for pipe *j* is:

$$U_T = \frac{U_{Max}(x) - U_{Min}(x) + 1}{2} \tag{3.10}$$

$U_T(j)$, *j=1, 2…n* can be used to rank *n* fuzzy numbers associated with *n* pipes.

3.6 Implementation of the Pipe Condition Assessment Model in IRA-WDS

Using the information provided in this section, users should be able to complete Tables 3.1 to 3.6. These tables are required to use IRA-WDS for pipe condition assessment. The information required to complete Table 3.1 should be obtained from the records of organizations such as the Municipal Corporation or Water Authority, and from surveys and observations. The IRA-WDS has the default database for the properties of different pipe materials (Table 3.2). These properties are presented in tables in Appendix C. The user can add new pipe materials and their properties, and change the properties of the pipe materials in the default database with the help of an input dialog window provided in IRA-WDS (Chapter 4 of Book 4).

The IRA-WDS has the default membership for different linguistics and fuzzy indicators. However, users can construct the membership function for specified indicators by completing Table 3.3. The information provided in this section enables the user to construct the membership function for different indicators.

The IRA-WDS has the default database for the soil corrosivity for different soils (Table 3.4). These soil corrosivity values are presented in tables in Appendix C. However, users can modify these values. The information required to complete Tables 3.5 and 3.6 should be obtained from the Municipal Corporation or the appropriate Water Authority. These data are spatial; IRA-WDS needs the data in the form of shape files (Chapter 4 of Book 4).

3.7 Application

An example is presented to illustrate the applicability of the developed pipe condition assessment model. The example consists of five pipes and 10 pipe indicators at the first level. The example follows the procedures for pipe condition assessment described in Section 3.5 and obtains the final pipe condition distance metrics (a fuzzy number) for each pipe and their condition rankings.

3.7.1 Hierarchical composite structure

Two groups of water pipe deterioration indicators, i.e. physical and environmental indicators, have been selected in this example. Some of these indicators are expressed in crisp numbers whilst others are described in a linguistic way that could be interpreted with fuzzy numbers. The hierarchical composite structure of water pipe deterioration indicators is given in Figure 3.7.

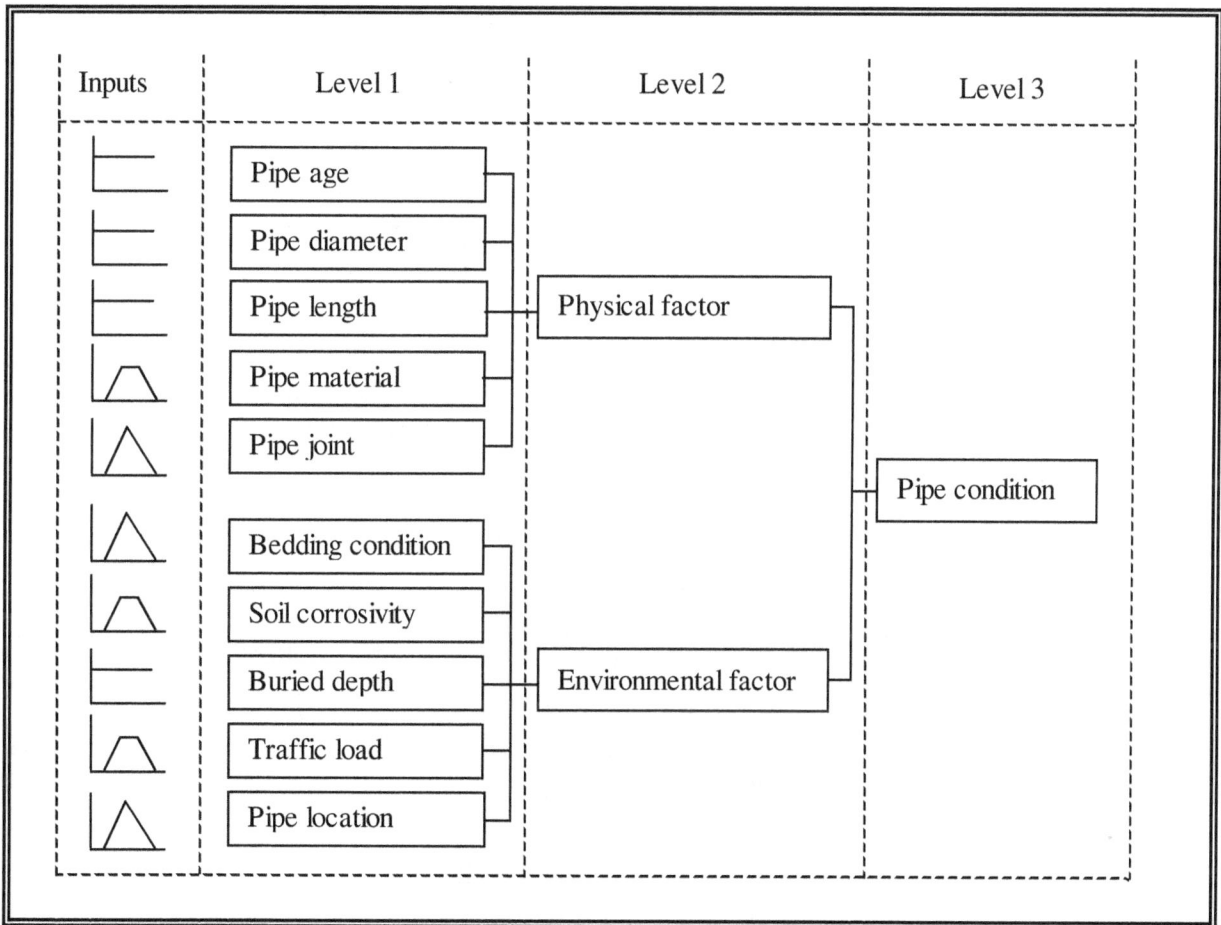

Figure 3.7. Pipe condition assessment composite structure

3.7.2 Values of basic indicators

The values of 10 indicators for all five pipes are shown in Table 3.14. Among these 10 first-level indicators, pipe material, pipe joint, pipe bedding, soil condition (corrosivity), traffic loads, and pipe location are expressed as fuzzy numbers. The fuzzy membership functions for these fuzzy indicators are shown in Figures 3.8 and 3.9.

Table 3.14. Values of first-level indicators for application example					
Pipe condition indicators	**Values of pipe condition indicator**				
	Pipe 1	**Pipe 2**	**Pipe 3**	**Pipe 4**	**Pipe 5**
Pipe age	1953	1964	1978	1988	1992
Pipe diameter (mm)	400	300	300	600	500
Pipe length (m)	600	400	800	400	300
Pipe material	CI	CI	DI	ST	PVC
Pipe joint	lead	leadite	rubber	rubber	rubber
Traffic loads	very quiet	very busy	busy	normal	very busy
Soil condition	high	low	high	low	medium
Location	poor	medium	excellent	excellent	good
Pipe bedding	clay	gravel	clay	sand	sand
Buried depth (m)	2.5	2.0	1.8	1.2	1.5

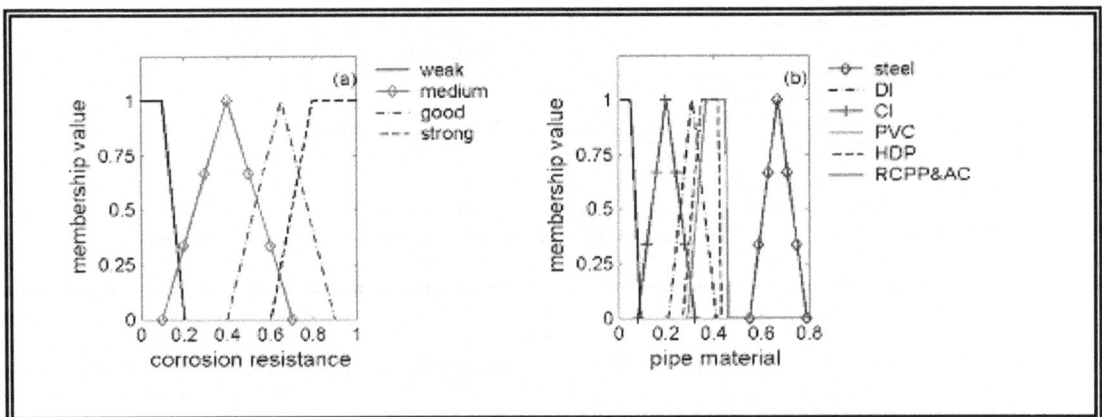

Figure 3.8. Fuzzy membership functions for corrosion resistance and pipe material

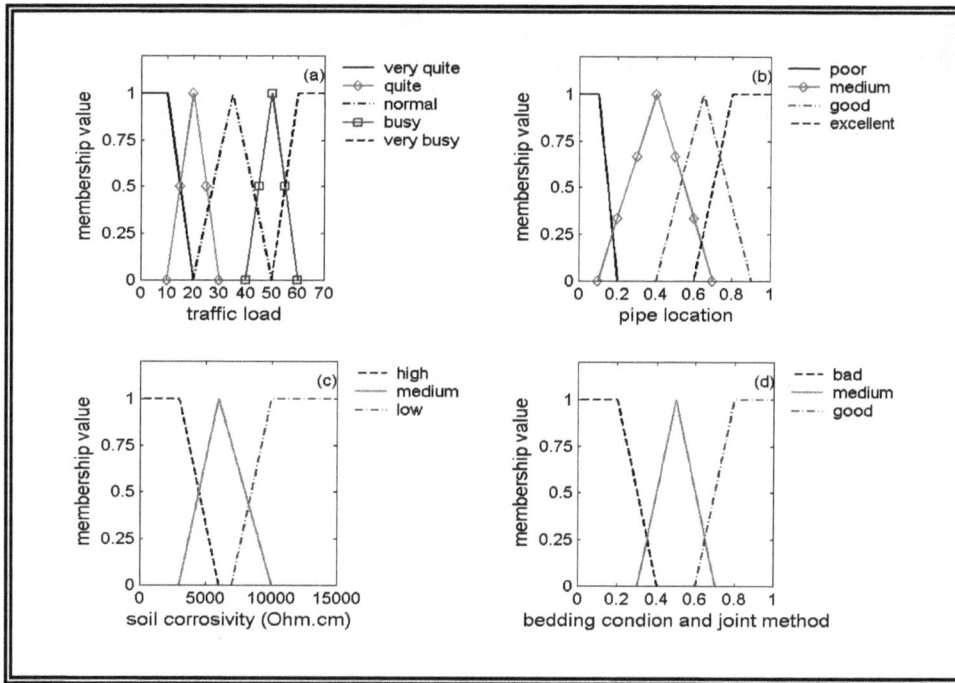

Figure 3.9. Fuzzy membership function of uncertain pipe indicators (traffic load, pipe location, soil corrosivity, and bedding condition and joint method)

3.7.3 Membership functions

To represent the importance of pipe material, two surrogate measures are used in this example, namely, maximum pressure and corrosion resistance. The comparisons of pipe material in terms of these two properties are given in Table 3.11. The maximum pressure reflecting the strength of the pipe material is expressed in crisp form, while the corrosion resistance that implies the capacity of pipe material to resist internal and external loads is given in linguistic form whose fuzzy description is as shown in Figure 3.8.

These two pipe material indicators are combined using appropriate weights (0.6 for maximum pressure of 0.6 and 0.4 for corrosion resistance are used in this example) to derive a single pipe material indicator, as given in Figure 3.5.

3.7.4 Weights and balance factors

Triangular fuzzy numbers were chosen to express the relative importance of different level indicators (column 4 of Table 3.15). The balance factor of 1 is used for first level indicators and a triangular fuzzy number is selected for the balance factor of second level indicators (column 5 of Table 3.15).

3.7.5 Normalization

Equation (3.2) is used to normalize the pipe condition indicators. The maximum and minimum values for normalization can be obtained from the design standard (criteria A) or can simply be obtained by comparing the values of all alternatives (pipes) for each indicator (criteria D) (see Section 3.5.6). Criteria D is used, based on the values given in Table 3.15.

Table 3.15. Best and worst indicators value, weights and balance factors				
Indicators	**Best value**	**Worst value**	**Weights**	**Balance factors**
(a) Level 1				
Pipe age	2000	1900	(0.2, 0.3, 0.4)	1
Pipe diameter (mm)	2000	50	(0.1,0.2, 0.3)	1
Pipe length (m)	50	2000	(0.1, 0.15, 0.4)	1
Pipe material	1	0	(0.2, 0.25, 0.3)	1
Pipe joint	1	0	(0.05,0.1, 0.2)	1
Traffic loads (vehicles/min)	0	100	(0.05, 0.15, 0.2)	1
Soil condition	50000	0	(0.1, 0.3, 0.4)	1
Location	1	0	(0.1, 0.2, 0.4)	1
Pipe bedding	1	0	(0.1, 0.25, 0.3)	1
Buried depth (m)	1	10	(0.05, 0.1, 0.2)	1
Maximum pressure (kPa)	20000	1000	0.6	1
Corrosion resistance	1	0	0.4	1
(b) Level 2				
Physical	*		(0.6, 0.7, 0.9)	(2.0, 2.5, 3.0)
Environmental	*		(0.2, 0.3, 0.4)	(2.0, 2.5, 3.0)

*Second level indicators are normalized, thus do not need best and worst values for normalization.

3.7.6 Results

The normalized indicator values are aggregated successively by using equation (3.4) until a final condition indicator is reached for each pipe as shown in Figure 3.5. The final indicator is used as criterion to rank the condition of pipes. The pipe condition indicators obtained from the FCP process are fuzzy numbers, which are shown in Figure 3.10. The fuzzy numbers were ranked using the method of Chen (1985) and the results are given in Table 3.16.

The results from Figure 3.10 show that the fuzzy number of pipe 1 is smaller than that of pipe 4. This indicates that pipe 1 has the worst condition whilst pipe 4 has the best condition, as shown in Table 3.16. It is noticed that the condition of pipe 4 is better than that of pipe 5, even though pipe 5 is new compared to pipe 4. This is probably due to the other contributing factors such as traffic. This illustrates that pipe condition assessment is a complex process resulting from many contributing factors and can hardly be decided from a single pipe condition indicator.

The pipe condition ranks given in Table 3.16 can be used when assigning priority for pipeline inspection and rehabilitation. It provides a quick and economical method of determining the relative quality of a large number of pipes.

Ascending order	Values of membership function				
	0.00	0.25	0.50	0.75	1.00
1 (very bad)	[0.047, 0.78]	[0.084, 0.66]	[0.014, 0.54]	[0.21, 0.41]	[0.028, 0.30]
2	[0.056, 0.82]	[0.096, 0.70]	[0.15, 0.57]	[0.22, 0.44]	[0.30, 0.31]
3	[0.077, 0.89]	[0.013, 0.78]	[0.20, 0.66]	[0.28, 0.53]	[0.37, 0.40]
5	[0.11, 0.96]	[0.17, 0.85]	[0.25, 0.73]	[0.34, 0.60]	[0.43, 0.46]
4 (very good)	[0.13, 1.00]	[0.20, 0.91]	[0.28, 0.78]	[0.38, 0.65]	[0.48, 0.50]

Table 3.16. Final pipe condition indicator values

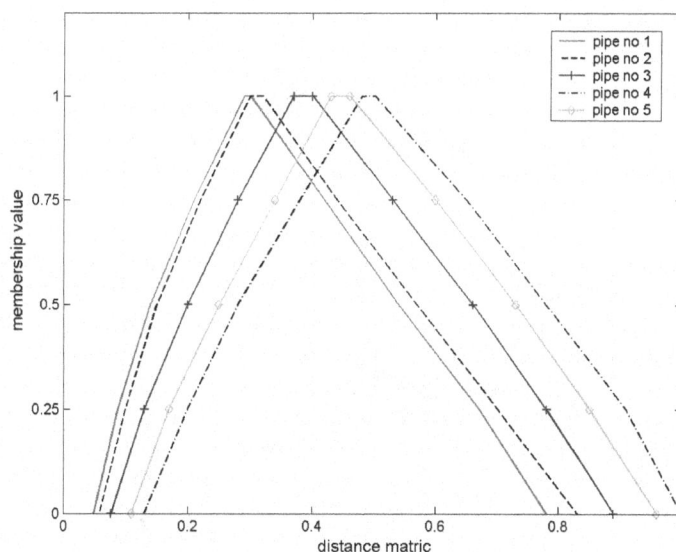

Figure 3.10. Fuzzy numbers representing water pipe condition

3.8 Conclusions

At this stage of the chapter readers should be able to complete Tables 3.1 to 3.9 for their particular area of study. These tables form the basis of the input data for the pipe condition assessment model part of IRA-WDS. The data contained in Tables 3.1 to

3.9 are entered into IRA-WDS by means of the several input dialog windows within the software. Figure 3.11 shows an example of these input dialog windows and more details of this can be found in Chapter 4 of Book 4 (IRA-WDS user manual).

An example of the output from a successful run of the pipe condition assessment model part of IRA-WDS are shown in Figure 3.12 and Table 3.17. These outputs are combined with the outputs from the contaminant ingress model part of IRA-WDS (discussed in Chapter 2), to give potential contaminant loads from pollution sources into the water distribution pipes.

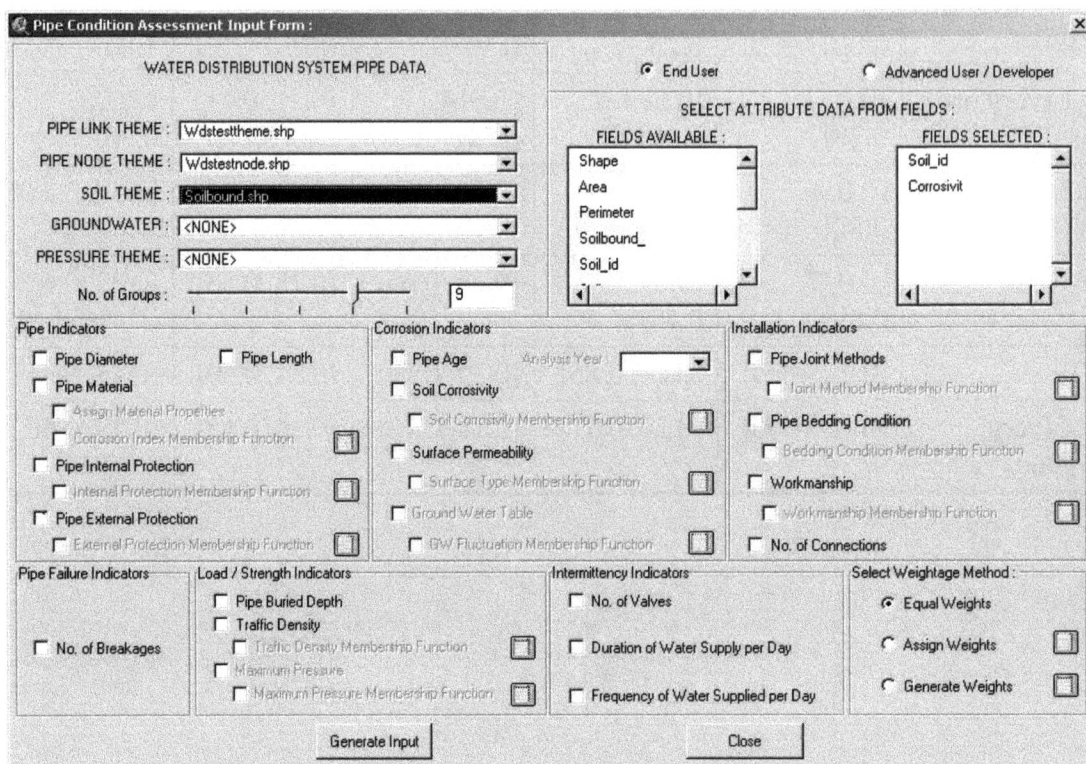

Figure 3.11. Example of input dialog window for PCA in IRA-WDS

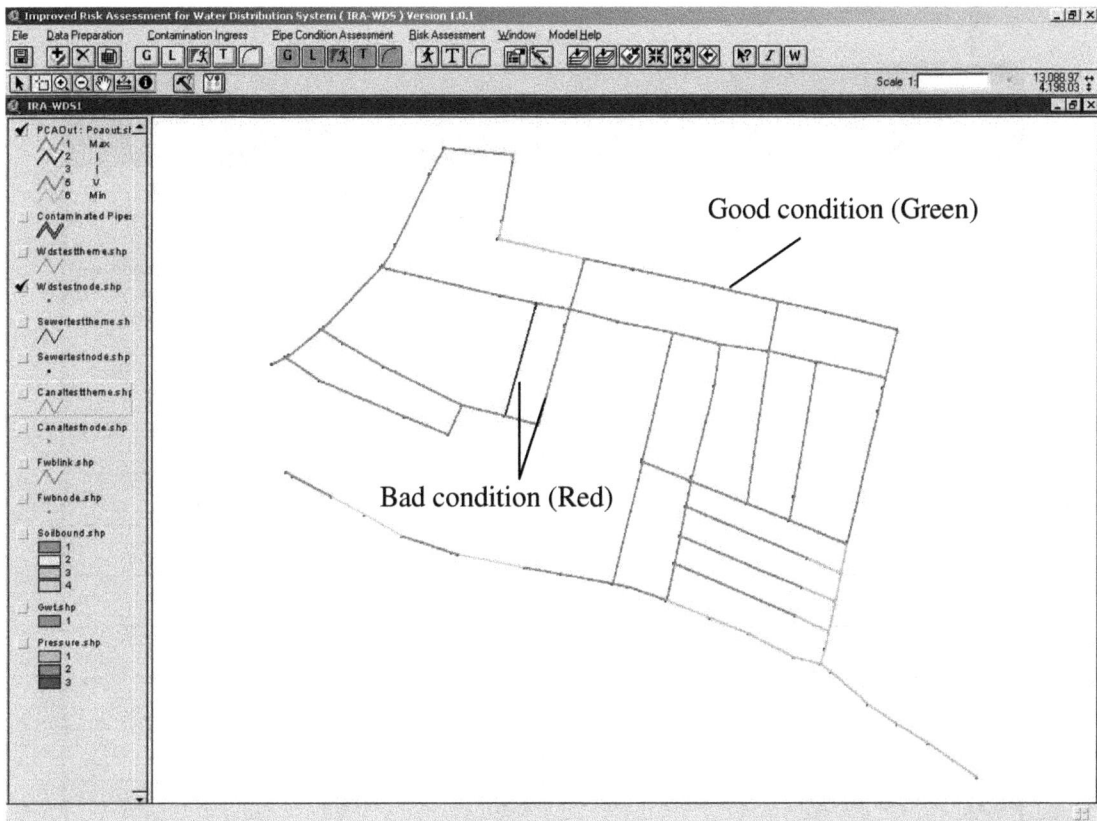

Figure 3.12. An example of the output from a successful run of the pipe condition assessment model part of IRA-WDS

Pipe ID	Defuzzy	Rank	Pipe ID	Defuzzy	Rank
950	0.000	1	883	0.805	8
944	0.283	3	994	0.805	8
1043	0.430	4	945	0.806	8
1074	0.448	4	956	0.806	8
1025	0.491	5	915	0.808	8
831	0.776	7	786	0.809	8
975	0.777	7	885	0.811	8
824	0.778	7	1017	0.814	8
880	0.781	7	949	0.814	8
852	0.793	7	855	0.815	8
866	0.797	7	976	0.817	8
837	0.797	7	856	0.817	8
951	0.797	7	993	0.817	8
936	0.799	7	1016	0.818	8
1083	0.799	7	995	0.818	8
957	0.800	8	1045	0.820	8
809	0.802	8	1012	0.821	8
989	0.804	8	800	0.823	8

Table 3.17. An example of the output from a successful run of the pipe condition assessment model part of IRA-WDS

CHAPTER FOUR

Risk Assessment Model

Risk Assessment of Contaminant Intrusion into Water Distribution Systems

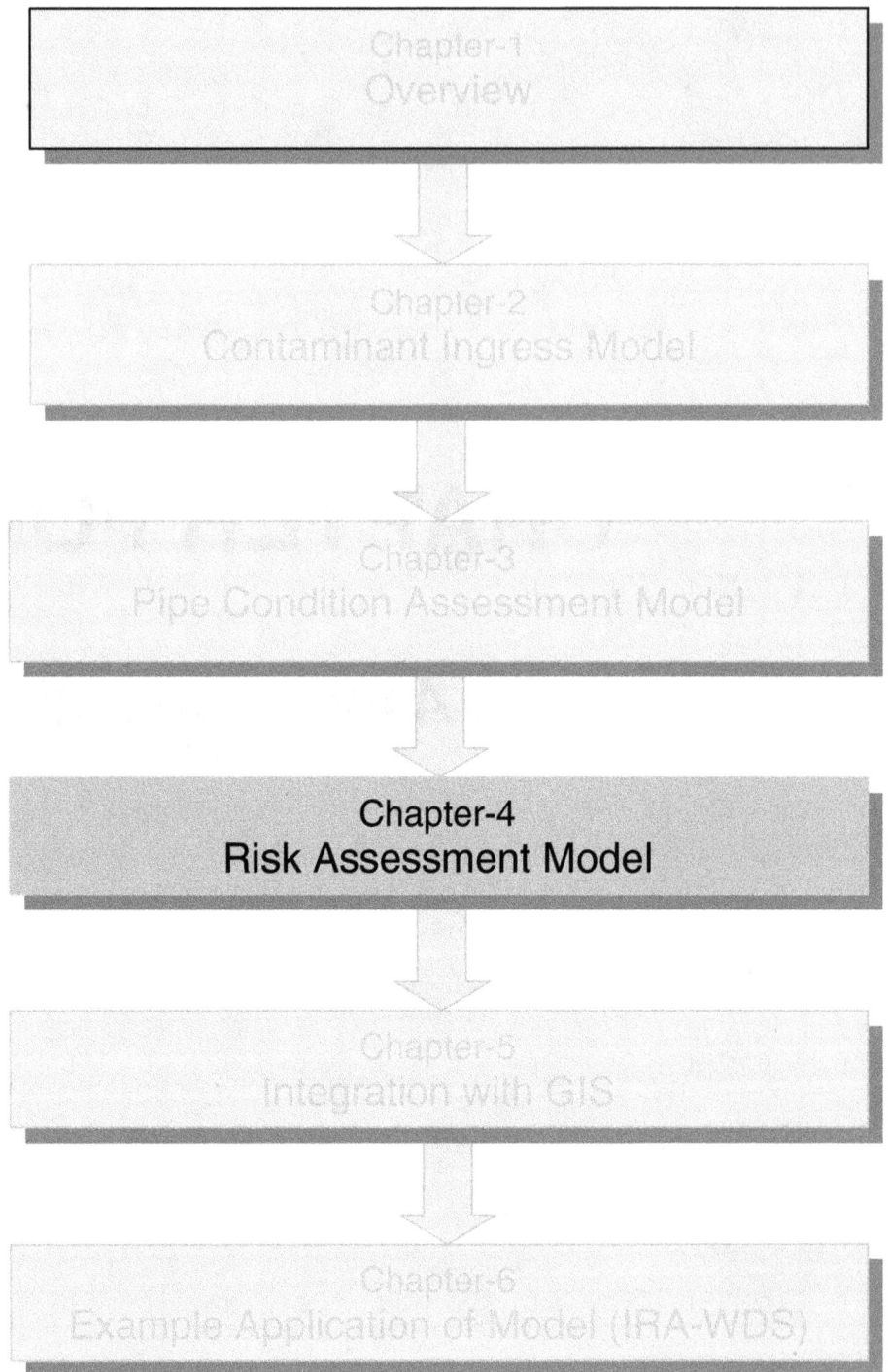

Chapter-1
Overview

Chapter-2
Contaminant Ingress Model

Chapter-3
Pipe Condition Assessment Model

Chapter-4
Risk Assessment Model

Chapter-5
Integration with GIS

Chapter-6
Example Application of Model (IRA-WDS)

Chapter 4: Risk Assessment Model

4.1 Introduction

This chapter presents the background to the risk assessment model part of IRA-WDS. The risk assessment model uses the outputs from the contaminant ingress model presented in Chapter 2 and pipe condition assessment model presented in Chapter 3. The model combines these outputs by using appropriate weights to generate a risk score for each pipe.

The outputs from the risk assessment model are risk maps showing the relative risk of contaminant intrusion into the entire water distribution system.

The purpose of this chapter is to provide an insight into the background and the techniques that underpin the risk assessment model, and to show how the outputs from the contaminant ingress and pipe condition model are combined to predict relative risk. This should enable the user of IRA-WDS to appreciate the significance of the data required and will aid in interpreting the results of the model. On completion of this chapter, the user should be able to complete Table 4.1, which holds the input data required to run the risk assessment model of IRA-WDS.

It should be noted, however, that to use IRA-WDS does not require a detailed understanding of the model presented in this chapter.

Table 4.1. Weights for different indicators	
Indicator	**Weight**
Hazard agent (contaminant load)	TO BE COMPLETED
Vulnerability of water pipe (pipe condition)	BY THE USERS

93

4.2 Background

There is growing concern about water quality variability within the distribution system. Treated water may undergo substantial changes in quality while being transported through the distribution system before reaching the end consumers. Recent evidence has demonstrated that external contaminant intrusion into water distribution network may be more frequent and of a greater importance than previously suspected (Besner et al. 2001; LeChevallier 1999). Both continuous and intermittent water distribution networks might suffer from the contaminant intrusion problem, although intermittent systems were found more vulnerable of contaminant intrusion.

The intrusion of contaminants into a water distribution system can have catastrophic consequences. Water-borne diseases have been reported historically. From 1971 to 1998, 619 water-borne disease outbreaks were reported in United States, of which 113 (18.3 per cent) outbreaks have been attributed to chemical and microbial contaminants intrusion into water distribution networks or water corrosive to plumbing systems within building or homes (Craun and Calderon 2001). More than half (53.1 per cent) of those 113 outbreaks are caused by cross-connection and back syphonage (Lindley and Buchberger 2002; USEPA 2002). It has been reported that approximately 40 per cent of outbreaks of water-borne disease have been caused by water distribution problems (Kramer et al. 1996; Lippy and Waltrip 1984). The consequence of outbreak posed on public health is enormous. Worldwide numerous cases of outbreak of different diseases were reported due to contamination of water distribution system (Craun and Calderon 2001; Danon-Schaffer 2001; Galbraith et al. 1992; Geldreich 1996; Kirmeyer et al. 2001; Wyatt et al. 1998).

Until now there has been no means of addressing the risk of contaminant intrusion into a water distribution system, even though it is widely recognized as a serious threat to public health. This is mainly due to the lack of methods for estimating the components of risk, i.e. hazards and vulnerability. In this chapter, the development of a risk assessment model for contaminant intrusion into the water distribution system is presented. This model makes use of the information on the section of water distribution pipes in a contaminant zone that has developed as a result of pollution sources (SPCZ), and the contaminant loading along the SPCZ, to estimate the hazard (Chapter 2); it uses the pipe condition assessment indicator to estimate the vulnerability of the pipe to contaminant intrusion (Chapter 3); and combines the two to estimate the risk of contaminant intrusion in the different pipes of the water distribution system. This enables engineers to undertake a rehabilitation programme to minimize the contamination of the water distribution system and thus the outbreaks of diseases; eventually it would provide safety to public health.

4.3 Methodology

To assess the risk of contaminant intrusion intoa water distribution system systematically, we need to look into the process of contaminant intrusion from the contaminant sources to the receptor system through the migration route (pathway). There are many pollution sources that exist around a water distribution system. These are the potential causes of drinking water contamination. The contaminants will migrate through their pathway to the receptor. Drinking water is contaminated if the water distribution pipe is vulnerable and passes through a contaminant migration route. Risk of contamination results from the interaction between a hazard agent and a vulnerable water distribution pipe. Risk assessment therefore requires information about water pipe vulnerability and any hazard agents resulting from the contamination sources. Hence the risk assessment model developed in this study consists of two components: hazard and vulnerability. These are obtained from the models developed in Chapters 2 and 3. The links between risk assessment model, pipe condition assessment model, contaminant ingress model are depicted in Figure 4.1.

4.3.1 Hazard assessment

The hazards are specific physical, chemical or biological agents that may cause an adverse health event. In the context of a water distribution system, hazards may be due to the polluted environment in which water distribution pipes are located such as those caused by surface or underground pollution sources. Hence, in this study, the hazard agent is considered to be any pollution sources around the water distribution pipeline that will potentially contaminate it. Three pollution sources, i.e. sewer pipes, open drains/canal and surface foul water bodies, are considered as the sources of hazards in this study. The contaminant load along the SPCZ is considered as the measure of hazard and is given by equation (4.1). The output of the contaminant ingress model in terms of SPCZ and the contaminant concentration at upstream and downstream ends of the SPCZ for each water distribution pipe are used to estimate the contaminant load along the SPCZ.

This is the input for hazard assessment (see Chapter 2).

$$HA_k = CL_k \qquad\qquad (4.1)$$

where
HA_k - hazard agent
CL_k - contaminant load given by equation (2.31) in Chapter 3

4.3.2 Vulnerability assessment

The vulnerability is the susceptibility of infrastructure to a hazard. In the context of a water distribution system, this may include the deterioration of water distribution pipe due to the physical, environmental and operational factors. The vulnerability of water distribution pipes is used to indicate the potential of contaminant ingress into the water distribution system in this study. The vulnerability assessment is performed using the pipe condition assessment (PCA) model presented in Chapter 3. For each pipe in the network, the PCA model assesses the vulnerability by assigning an index using fuzzy composite programming. This index combines the impacts of physical, environmental and operational indicators on water distribution pipe deterioration. The index is a fuzzy number represented by a membership function, and is defuzzified. The defuzzified value is used as a surrogate for pipe vulnerability, as given in equation (4.2).

$$VU_i = df(TF_i) \qquad i = 1, 2, ...NP \qquad\qquad (4.2)$$

where

VU_i - vulnerability of water distribution pipe i

df - method for defuzzification

TF_i - Trapezoidal fuzzy number for pipe I and NP - number of water distribution pipe

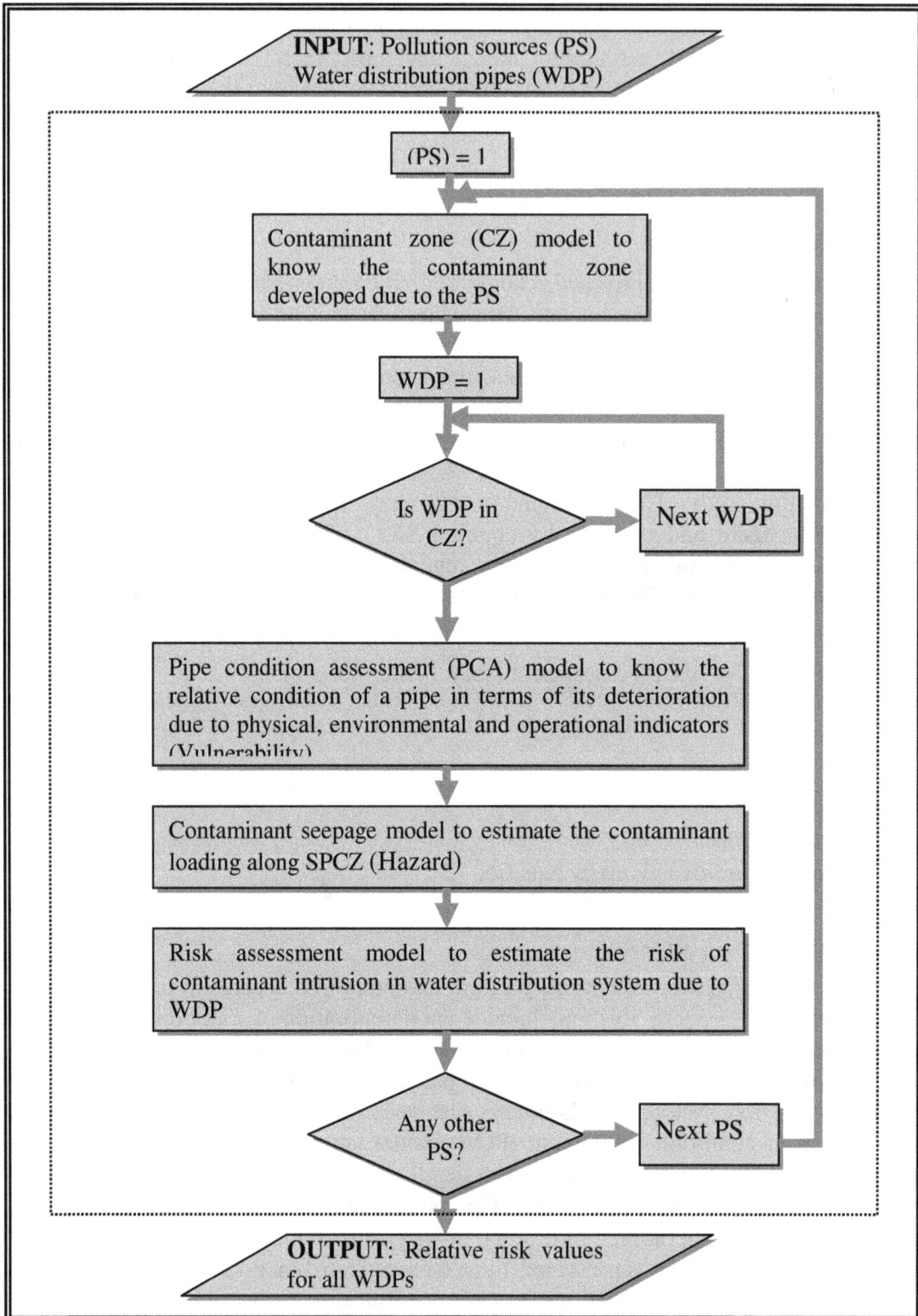

Figure 4.1. The linkage of contaminant ingress and pipe condition assessment models with the risk assessment model

4.3.3 Weight assignment

The relative risk of any particular combination of hazard and vulnerability will depend on the significance of each of these processes in relation to each other. This is expressed through weights that need to be established. Clearly, establishing the relative importance of the above processes is a difficult task. Details of procedures to obtain weights by different methods can be found in Section 3.4.2 of Chapter 3. In this study, the analytical hierarchy process (AHP) is recommended for generating the weights for multiple risk factors. Interviews with experts are required to perform pair-wise comparisons of risk factors to generate the weights (Appendix B). These weights will be used to perform risk assessment by the method proposed in Section 4.3.4.

By using one of the proposed procedures for generation of weights for risk factors (hazard and vulnerability), the user will be able to complete Table 4.1. On completion of this table, the data can be entered into IRA-WDS by means of an input dialogue window.

4.3.4 Multi-criteria evaluation method for risk assessment

The risk of contaminant intrusion into water distribution system results from the interaction between a hazard agent and a vulnerable water distribution pipe. These two risk components are combined using multi-criteria decision-making (MCDM) methods. MCDM (see Figure 4.2) allows us to tackle multiple factors simultaneously, provide insight into various value judgements and help decision-makers and experts penetrate complex and implicit decision-making tasks (Thill 1999). Two types of multi-criteria evaluation (MCE) methods are possible: conventional methods (e.g. weighted linear combination (WLC)) and artificial intelligence based methods (e.g. artificial neural networks (ANN)), fuzzy logic approximate reasoning, optimization methods such as genetic algorithms (GA) and simulated annealing). In this study a weighted linear combination (WLC) method is chosen to assemble weights, and synthesize and analyse different risk criteria.

In WLC methods, the risk factors are integrated to produce the risk index of contaminant intrusion into water distribution. The risk index (RI) for contaminant intrusion into water distribution systems is a function of the hazard agent and vulnerability of water pipe and is obtained by equation (4.3).

$$RI_k = (w_h \times HA_k) + (w_v \times VU_k) \qquad k = 1, 2, ...NC \qquad (4.3)$$

where
RI - risk index
w_h - weight for hazard agent
w_v - weight for vulnerability of water pipe

Note that the model uses output from the contaminant ingress and pipe condition assessment models to perform the hazard and vulnerability assessment. Hence the user is only required to input data related to the weights.

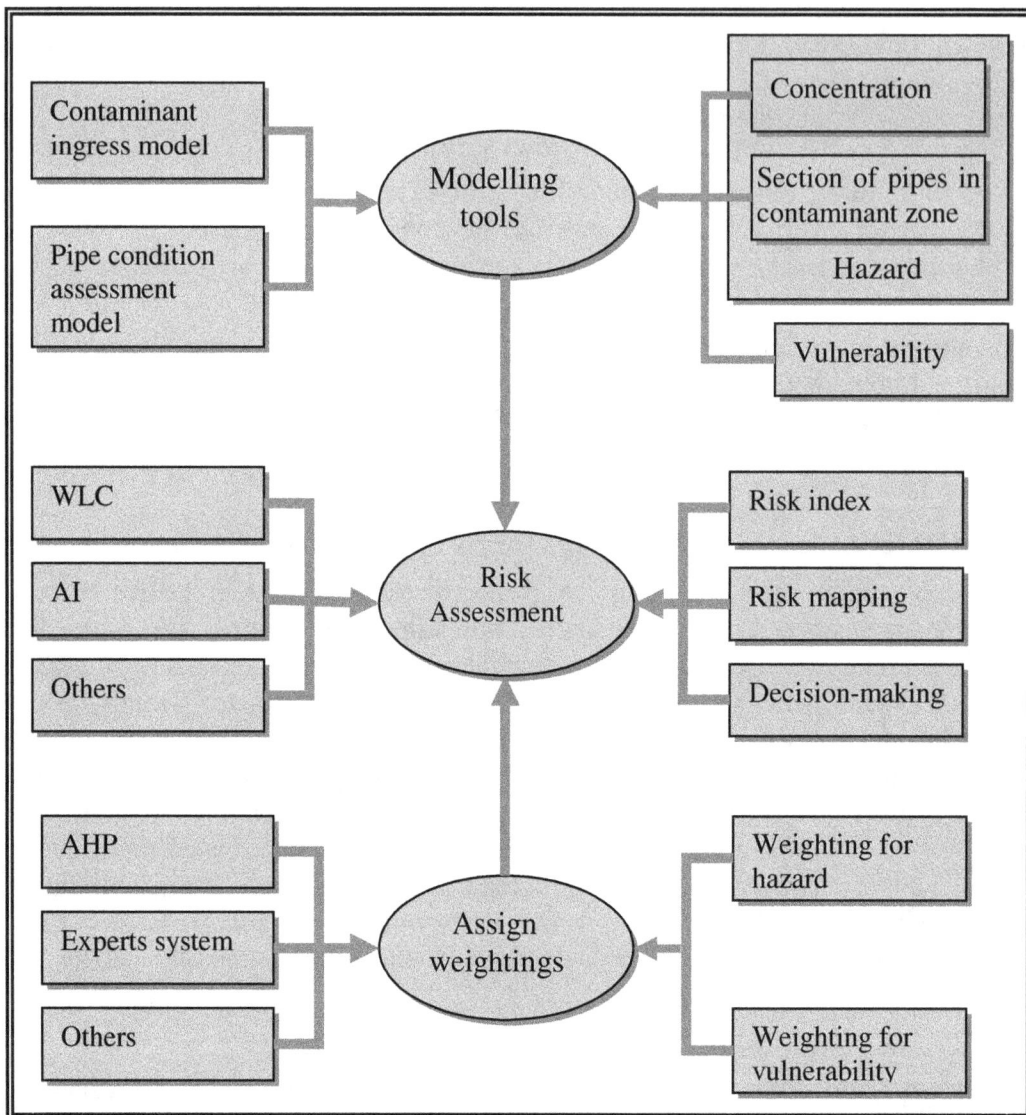

Figure 4.2. Flowchart for risk assessment of contaminant intrusion into WDS

4.4 Conclusions

Based on the risk map, engineers can take decisions for the rehabilitation programme.

At this stage of the chapter the reader should be able to complete Table 4.1 for their particular area of study. This table forms the basis of the input data for the risk assessment model part of IRA-WDS. The data contained in Table 4.1 is entered into IRA-WDS by means of the input dialog window within the software.

Figure 4.3 shows an example of the input dialog window and more details of this can be found in Chapter 5 of Book 4.

An example of the output from a successful run of the risk assessment model part of IRA-WDS is shown in Figure 4.4. Using these outputs the decision-maker can identify sections of the distribution system that are of particular concern (high risk areas), and take appropriate remedial action.

It should be noted that the outputs from the risk assessment model can then be coupled with a water network quality model (e.g. EPANET (Rossman 1994)) to show the movement of contamination within the distribution system. Note that this extension is beyond the scope of this study.

The use of a water quality model will enable the decision-makers to identify areas and consumers most at risk to contaminated water. Water quality models are able to track the fate of discrete parcels of water as they move along pipes and mix together at junctions between fixed-length time steps. To develop a water quality model of the distribution system, a fully calibrated hydraulic network model will be required. This will require additional investment in terms of time and effort for data collection.

If a fully calibrated network model is developed then water quality simulation can be performed by first adding dummy input pollutant nodes to areas where the risk assessment model shows a high risk of contamination. Then, by adding pollutant loads at these nodes it is possible to simulate their propagation. It is recommended that, when performing water quality analysis, source tracing is performed. Source tracing tracks over time the percentage of water reaching any node in the network that had its origin at a particular node (in this case the dummy pollutant node). In the analysis the pollutant will be treated as a non-reacting constituent. Source tracing can show to what degree water from a given source blends with that from other sources, and how the spatial pattern of this blending changes over time.

Note that although the use of water quality models is beyond the scope of this study, an example application to the case study area (described in Chapter 6) is shown in Appendix F.

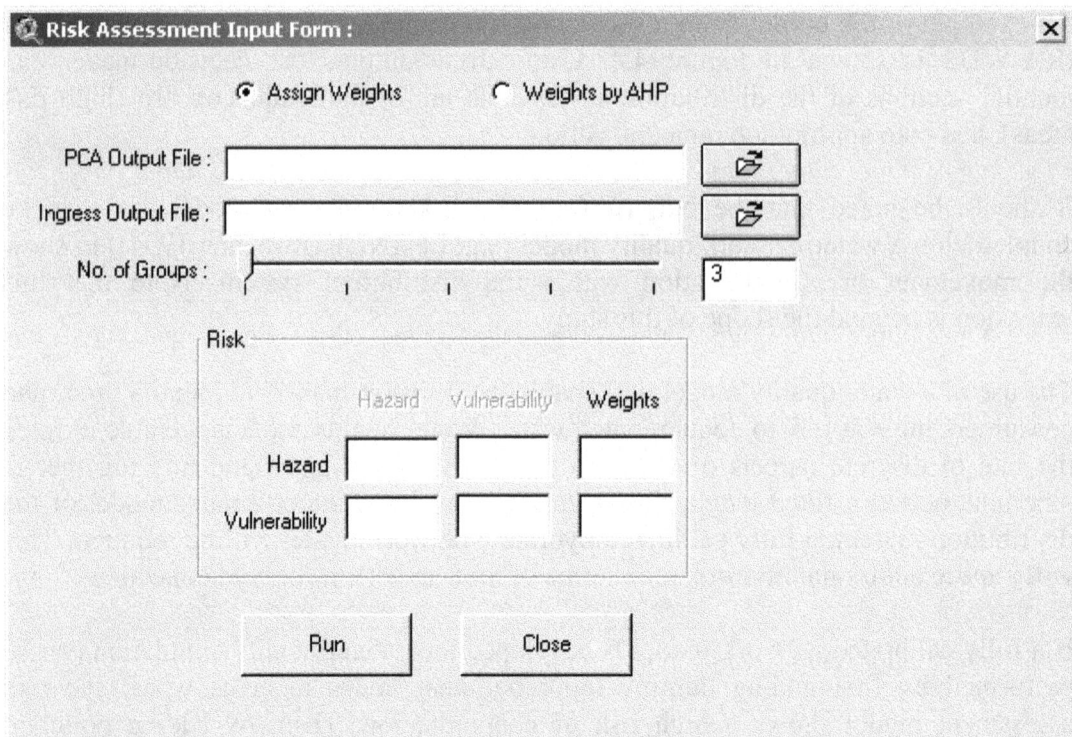

Figure 4.3. An example of the input dialog window of the risk assessment model part of IRA-WDS

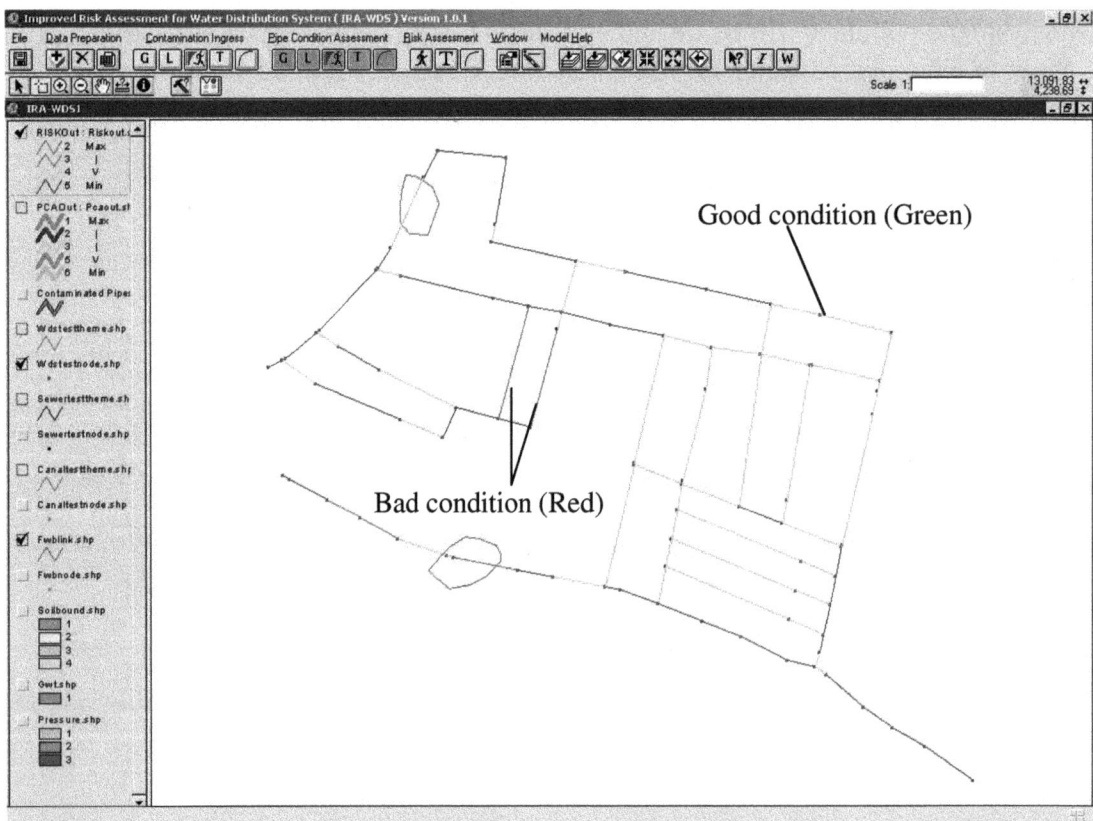

Figure 4.4. An example of the output from a successful run of the risk assessment model part of IRA-WDS

CHAPTER FIVE

Integration with GIS

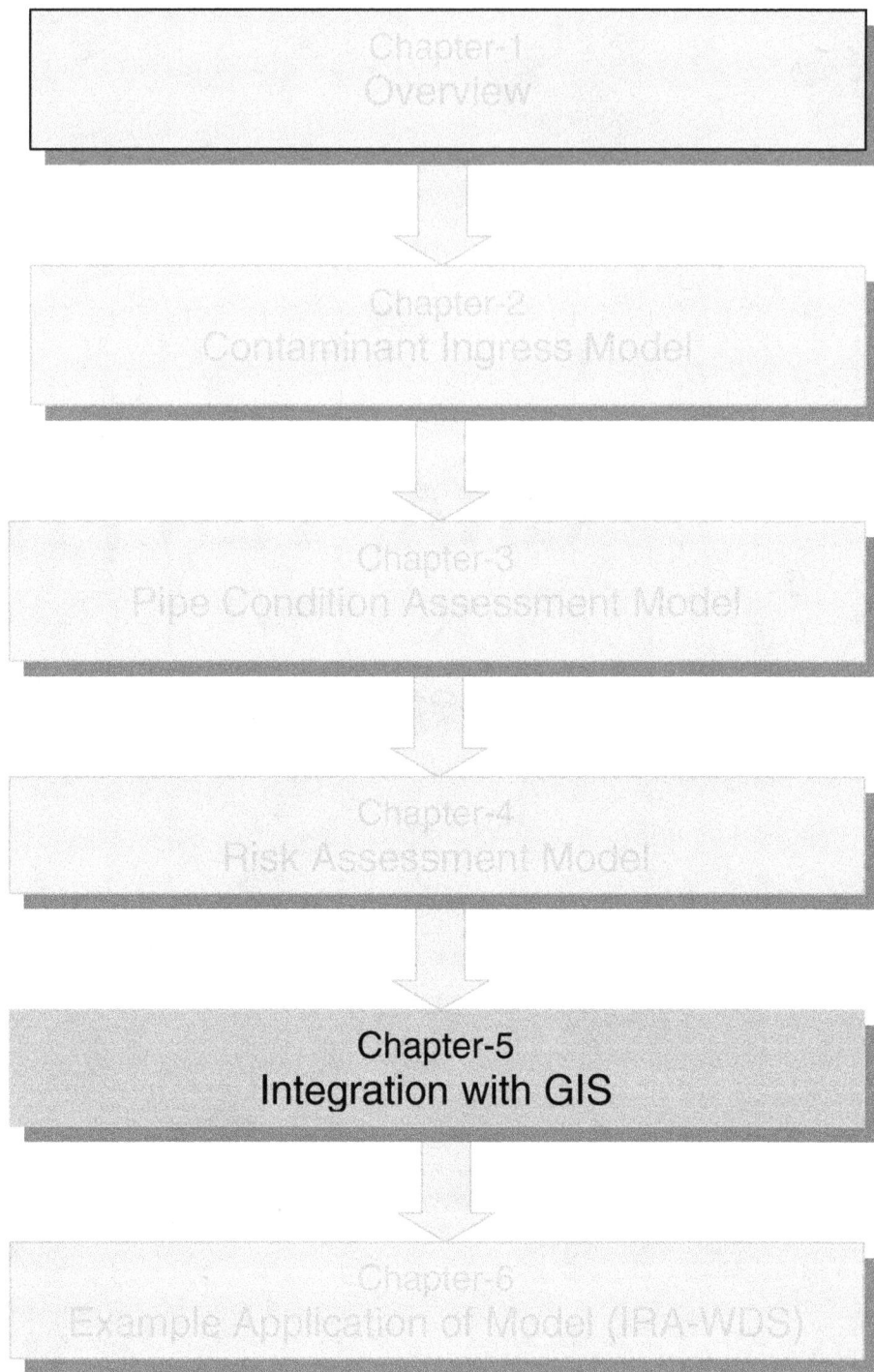

Chapter 5: Integration of the Model with GIS

5.1 Introduction

This chapter provides information about how a geographic information system (GIS) can be developed for the area of study. IRA-WDS is GIS-based software and hence, in order to use it, one needs to build a GIS for the area of study. This chapter begins by introducing GIS and its applications in the area of risk assessment. It then outlines the process of data collection and preparation of maps, and provides an introduction to IRA-WDS.

5.2 Why GIS?

Risk is an inherently spatial phenomenon. It is clearly not sufficient to report risk non-spatially. A risk map should be considered as the ultimate product of any risk investigation, and should be the first resource sought for any risk decision or evaluation. As the process of risk assessment requires the assimilation of data that are spatially variable in nature, geographic information systems are an ideal tool for such assessments. GIS techniques can be central to these important and critical processes of risk identification, quantification, and evaluation. It has proved to be a useful tool for risk assessment and management. Coupling of GIS with the contamination, pipe condition assessment and risk assessment models enhances the value of the models and makes the models more user-friendly. In the present study, an attempt has been made to assess and manage risk by integrating the contamination ingress, pipe condition assessment and risk assessment models with GIS. The database required for the models is prepared using GIS, the model is processed through GIS, and the output maps can be used for printing, display and investigation purpose.

5.3 Geographic Information Systems and Risk Assessment

A geographic information system (GIS) is an integrated system of computer hardware and software designed to capture, store, analyse, manipulate and display spatial data. It acts as an integration platform and offers the possibility of a consistent, interactive user-friendly environment. The advantage of GIS lies in its ability to relate data sets through a common denominator, which is a spatial location. GIS also provides the tools for managing the modelling process, organizing model input parameters, analysing the model results and displaying both model input and output in an user-defined scale.

In order to assess potential pollution risks, the stored data has to be manipulated beyond simple digital mapping of the existing features. A number of tools within a GIS make it possible to analyse, combine, update, interpolate and query the records to create new or redefined information, thus adding value to the original data. Complex geographical analysis, such as map algebra or overlay, essentially combining the attributes of two or more data layers depending on their geographic location, can be used to identify hazard source areas. Selections based on a map layer's attribute information can be used to provide input data for calculations of risk frequency. Logical overlay (using *and, or, not* terms) can be used to combine data where map attributes are represented on a nominal (e.g. soil type, land cover type) or ordinal (e.g. data ranked from poor to excellent) scale. Arithmetic overlay (addition, subtraction) can be used when the map attributes need to be represented by an interval level of measurement such as rainfall values.

In general, the intrinsic capacity of a GIS to store, analyse, query and display large volumes of data makes it an ideal tool for performing risk assessment.

5.4 Tool Used for Integration

The GIS software tool used for the process of integration in the present study is ArcView GIS 3.2 developed by ESRI. It is one of the most widely used commercial Windows GIS packages. It is primarily designed for the manipulation of spatial vector data, extended with optional modules for the analysis of network data (Network Analyst extension), raster data (Spatial Analyst extension), and other types of data. The object oriented Avenue script language supported by ArcView allows external programs or computer packages to be integrated into the ArcView environment to offer enhanced functionality for spatial analysis, and the customizing facility of ArcView GUI (Menus, Buttons, Tools) provides a user-friendly approach to using the integrated tools. ArcView also has integration capabilities that allow users to access system resources (i.e. clipboard and system variables), issue operating system commands inside ArcView, and support Dynamic Data Exchange (DDE) in the Microsoft Windows environment and Remote Procedure Call (RPC) in UNIX.

In the present study, contaminant ingress, pipe condition assessment and risk assessment models have been integrated with ArcView GIS in such a manner that the model can be used effortlessly.

5.5 Strength of GIS in Risk Assessment

Within the past five years, many conferences/workshops have been organized which primarily discussed research in environmental modelling and engineering practices using GIS. The area of risk assessment/management modelling and integration of GIS with user models have also been studied. The purpose of this section is to explain the strengths of GIS in environmental modelling.

5.5.1 State of the art

Previous research studies on use of GIS were mainly focused on the type of connection established between different water quality related models and GIS software. In addition, the type of GIS software used was a concern. Tim and Jolly (1994) presented a good overview of three types of model interfaces possible with GIS. They described three levels of integration as (1) ad hoc integration, (2) partial integration, and (3) complete integration. In the first level, the GIS data structure and environmental model are developed independently. The data is extracted from GIS, the model is run separately, and the outputs are analysed at the user's discretion. In the second level, i.e. partial integration, GIS supplies the data and then accepts the modelling results for processing and presentation. In this case GIS plays more of an integrated role in modelling. The third level, i.e. complete integration, consists of complete model development within the GIS software. The user has a single operating environment, where the data stored in the GIS is structured to meet the demands of the model and vice versa. It should also be noted that there are numerous types of GIS software with which a model link can be accomplished. The earlier works were reviewed and some important reported works are explained herein to show the utility of GIS for the current study.

5.5.2 Integration of environmental modelling and GIS

For over a decade, the integration of GIS with environmental modelling has been an important research topic. The use of GIS for modelling provides ease and accuracy in the management and spatial representation of data. Recent projects which have conducted environmental modelling directly in the GIS have included studies in simulating hydrologic processes, river basin planning and management, predicting chemical concentrations in rivers, and assessing non-point source loading over a watershed (Maidment 1992).

Akcakaya (1994) developed an integrated model linking GIS and models of ecological risk assessment. In this work, a model that links GIS for viability analysis and risk assessment which was applied to endangered species was explained in detail. The model integrates landscape data on habitat requirements with demographic data to analyse risks of extinction, evaluate management options, and assess human impact on wildlife populations. Other applications of the model involve design of nature reserves, wildlife management, and population viability analysis. The model analyses habitat data exported from a GIS, and identifies the patches of habitat that can support a population. The structure of these patches, including their locations, sizes and distances from each other, define the spatial structure of the meta-population. The spatial structure is combined with demographic data and other information on the ecology of the species to complete a meta-population model, which incorporates age or stage structure and density dependence for each population, spatial correlation and dispersal among populations, environmental and demographic stochasticity and catastrophes. The model performs a risk analysis, and runs multiple simulations, automatically changing parameters to analyse the sensitivity of risks to input data.

Kumar et al. (1997) demonstrated an approach to integrate GIS software and models using their design of the Solar Analyst and TopoView, tools for calculation of incoming solar radiation (insolation) over landscape scales. The calculation engine of these models was implemented in DLL format using C++. The DLLs were then loaded into ArcView to create the Solar Analyst extension. The ArcView GRIDIO library was used to read a DEM as input and write insolation GRIDs as output. They used techniques such as ArcView GRIDIO usage, procedure communication (system call/DDE/DLL/ActiveX), design of DLLs, and on-line help systems for use with ArcView. Extending these models to large areas in a GIS environment can be accomplished by obtaining data layers of parameters for the areas. System integration can be accomplished by using common files, system calls, DDE/RPC, DLLs, or Active X controls, according to specific user needs. There is growing interest in extending point-specific processes to broader spatial scales, using spatially explicit raster models. ArcView GRIDIO provides an easy way for non-ESRI products to directly access ESRI grid data and this paper explained ways to export C++ functions and workarounds to call C++ member functions when developing DLLs for use with ArcView. As GIS is used in more and more ways to solve more complex problems, the topic of integrating GIS with user models becomes increasingly important.

Yates and Bishop (1997) developed a simple and comprehensive approach for the integration of separately developed software systems. According to them, any information system can be integrated using the methodology without the complexities introduced by providing an interpretation of a universal language. The design of the integration methodology consists of four separate components: the protocol for communication, a message queuing system, wrapping software, and an integration manager. Relevant conceptual models and implementation techniques are discussed in this paper. Some examples of the software that have been successfully integrated were also presented with an example script for managing a simple integration activity.

Fedra (1998) described an overview of integrated risk assessment and management. He explained the role of GIS in risk assessment and management, and concluded that the risk assessment and management strategy is not only a spatially distributed problem, but also a dynamic problem. While geographic information systems provide powerful tools for spatial analysis, their capabilities for complex and dynamic analysis are limited. Traditional simulation models, on the other hand, are powerful tools for complex and dynamic situations, but often lack the intuitive visualization and spatial analysis functions that the GIS offers. Obviously, the integration of GIS and simulation models, together with the necessary databases and expert systems, within a common and interactive graphical user interface should make it more powerful and easy to use. He has demonstrated the integration process with the development of a risk information system for the Netherlands. In this integrated model, GIS is considered as the central tool, and the user-interface, database on hazardous installations and hazardous chemicals are linked in a hypertext structure. They include tools for spatial risk assessment based on externally generated risk contours, and links to models describing accidental and continuous atmospheric releases, spills into surface water systems, and transportation risk analysis.

Hornung et al. (1994) developed models that are fully geo-referenced and integrated with the underlying GIS layers, and include an embedded rule-based expert system to help with model input specifications, and the interpretation of model results. Model results take the form of interactive graphics and animated topographical maps for an intuitive understanding, and a more efficient interactive analysis.

Steele et al. (1999) explained the development of a GIS-based risk assessment methodology that incorporates contaminant source, groundwater vulnerability and abstraction, and catchment elements in order to prioritize areas and boreholes potentially at risk from chlorinated solvent pollution on a regional scale. Factors incorporated in the vulnerability assessment such as the nature of soils, presence or absence of superficial or glacial deposits, fault density and depth to water table were employed with a simple ranking system from which the derived vulnerability assessment index was combined with current chlorinated solvent user-industry data and source protection zone components. Results indicated that the presence of high-risk areas in urban locations where locally dense distributions of chlorinated solvent user industries combine with high vulnerability aquifers within the catchment of supply boreholes. Ranking of catchment-specific risk reveals the abstraction points under greatest stress. The proposed methodology has applications as a regional-scale initial screening tool to guide site selection for regulatory inspections and assist in prioritizing monitoring strategies for existing boreholes. The study was concluded by indicating that future developments will provide guidance for locating new urban boreholes in areas of lowest risk.

How (1998) explained a model that linked the naUTilus model, to GIS technology in order to facilitate prediction of volatile organic compound (VOC) emissions from large industrial sewer networks. The connection of naUTilus with a GIS software package, ArcView®, was achieved through a series of Avenue scripts. The integrated naUTilus/GIS model was used to predict VOC emissions from actual industrial sewer systems under varying environmental, flow, and sewer conditions. Stripping efficiency was predicted to (1) increase with increasing wind speed, (2) increase with increasing temperature (liquid and ambient), (3) decrease with increasing liquid flow rates, and (4) decrease with an increasing number of sealed drains. The integrated model was also used to analyse emission estimates on a spatial level. Ventilation patterns assumed in the naUTilus model were found to have a significant effect on predicted emissions.

Geter et al. (1995) discussed a GIS interface to four Agricultural Research Service (ARS) pollutant loading models: Agricultural Non-Point Source (AGNPS), A Basin Scale Simulation Model for Soil and Water Resources Management (SWRRBWQ), Erosion Productivity Impact Calculator (EPIC), Groundwater Loading Effects of Agricultural Management Systems (GLEAMS). The goal of this research was to develop an interface which resulted in standardized and consistent input data to all the water quality models, while providing a platform for interpreting the model results through tables, graphs, and maps. The user first enters the necessary model data in the form of attributed coverages within the GIS software, Geographic Resource Analysis System (GRASS). The total connection requires five raster-based maps linked to sixteen attribute tables. This base information is then interpreted by the GRASS interface and consistent model input is determined. The link established actually writes the derived input into the formatted file necessary for the models' input, and the connection provided a means for the user to view the model output through charts, tables, and raster maps.

Tim and Jolly (1994) demonstrated the concept of integrating an agricultural non-point source water quality model, AGNPS, with an Arc/Info interface. GIS provided the means to generate and spatially organize the data needed for the non-point source modelling effort, while AGNPS was used to predict water quality related parameters such as soil erosion and sedimentation. A partial integration link was established, by developing computer programs which provided 'access points' between the GIS database, the AGNPS model, and the user. The link read the model input from raster coverages imported into Arc/Info's subprogram, Grid. Once the grid-based data were converted to a readable format by AGNPS and the model executed, the output was re-imported into Grid and displayed through ArcPlot.

Besides hydrologic processes, GIS has been used to assess pollutant loadings entering a water body and to explain the transport of chemicals in surface water. Various studies have investigated the concept of non-point source (NPS) loadings from watershed areas. Two projects in particular used GIS to develop projected aerial loadings of different chemical constituents (Saunders and Maidment 1996). Mitchell and McDonald (1995) developed a grid-based model which assessed NPS loadings of nitrogen, phosphorus, cadmium, and faecal coli-forms into a small coastal bay in South Texas. The method used a grid of land-use-based estimated mean concentrations (EMCs) multiplied by spatially distributed runoff volumes to obtain an annual aerial loading over the watershed. A similar study also used the concept of EMCs and runoff volumes to develop an assessment of NPS loads into Galveston Bay, Texas (Newell et al. 1992). They used GIS to spatially distribute runoff volumes, land use characteristics, EMCs, and final loading values. A slightly different pollutant study is applying GIS to project chemical concentrations in the Upper Mississippi River Basin (Mizgalewicz 1996). Using data collected in the United States Geological Survey (USGS) toxic chemical program throughout the Midwest, this GIS model is meant to explain the relationship between chemical concentrations in a stream and parameters such as chemical application, runoff, precipitation, season, and watershed characteristics. In addition, this research aims to describe chemical losses due to transport downstream using GIS as the ultimate modelling interface for these processes.

In summary, various concepts have been developed within the GIS framework to assist in traditional environmental modelling by development of an interface between the water quality/quantity models with GIS. Of more concern for this research, though, is the establishment of a connection between developed models relating to contamination ingress, pipe condition assessment and risk assessment and the GIS software. Many earlier research workers have investigated the feasibility of linking various models to GIS to assist in data management, manipulation, and output processing. Of particular interest for this project were those previous studies which concentrated on water quality and quantity model links. These projects have ranged from incorporating an entire model into the GIS software, to concentrating on a subprogram of the model to connect to the interface.

5.6 Methodology in Developing IRA-WDS

The various steps involved in developing IRA-WDS are as follows:
- Data collection
- Preparation of maps
- Development of IRA-WDS

- Integration of models
- Generation of output.

5.6.1 Data collection

First there is collection of field data on the existing water distribution system and sewerage collection system including canals/open drains, surface foul water bodies.

The major steps in the data collection process are as follows.

1. Identify the needed data/information
    The data required includes: thematic maps (base maps, contour maps etc.); network data (water distribution system, sewers etc.).
2. Determine data availability

    Check sources and availability of the data identified in Step 1. Determine which data are currently not available and which are out of date.
3. Physically collect data

    Once the data requirements are identified and the availability ascertained, decide on how to collect the required data (e.g. a relevant department might be a good place to start). A work-plan needs to be prepared, clearly identifying the required data, the methodology to be employed for its collection, and the time period (and money) available to collect it (schedule the data collection process).
4. Verifying the accuracy of the data

    An important aspect of the data collection process is to verify the accuracy of the data. Errors may be clerical, subjective or methodological. It is important to appraise your data to eliminate known and suspected errors.

Sources for obtaining maps

Maps can be collected/requested from sources such as:

- Local government sources
- Water authorities
- Other state departments such as irrigation, electricity, highway etc.
- GIS / Topographical Department (remote sensing)
- Town Planning Department
- The Ministry of Defence
- Private companies / consultants.

If the maps obtained from the above sources are not up to date, then a survey of the area may be required to reveal elements missing from the map. It is of a great importance that the base map should be very accurate and that it includes areas of settlement (this could be identified by roads and properties) in the study area, as all these play an important role in the design of a water distribution system.

Sources of data for network identification

Sources of network data include water authorities, municipalities and other local agencies. It is the experience of the authors that the data availability with the local agencies is generally poor and collection may be required. It is useful to contact local contractors and the operators (lineman), as they often have a better knowledge of the system than the managing authorities. Below, details of how data can be collected are given.

1. Existing data can be obtained from:

    • Water authorities

    • Consultants/organizations

    • Past reports/projects

    • Interviews: engineers from the water authorities, consultants/contractors, linesmen, valve operators.

2. Data can be physically collected in the field by:

    • Identifying the pipes that can be seen on/under culverts/bridges

    • Identifying valves

    • Actual excavations if necessary.

5.6.2 Preparation of maps

The data preparation part includes the preparation of various data/layers required for IRA-WDS, viz.:

    • Thematic layers

    • Network database

    • Derived maps.

Figures 5.1 and 5.2 illustrate the process of converting maps into a GIS format. More details of this process can be found in Chapter 2 of Book 4.

Thematic layers

The first step in data preparation is thematic layers preparation. The following thematic layers of the study area need to be prepared by using the collected field data and data from other sources such as remote sensing.

    • Base map: infrastructure and contour maps

    • Environmental maps: soil, groundwater, and pressure maps.

The various maps are prepared by digitizing, editing and projecting the coordinates to a polyconic projection system using ArcView GIS. The output from this process will be a collection of shape-files containing each theme. See Chapter 2 of Book 4 for details of the data associated with the thematic maps.

Base map

Infrastructure This map should be prepared from Survey Toposheets of the available scale (for example 1:50,000 from Survey of India (SOI), Government of India). The entire area needs to be divided into different major classes, viz. settlement, surface foul water bodies, vegetation and roads. The final map consists of details such as roads, water bodies, railways etc.

Contour map The contour map needs to be prepared from reduced level data obtained by a levelling survey.

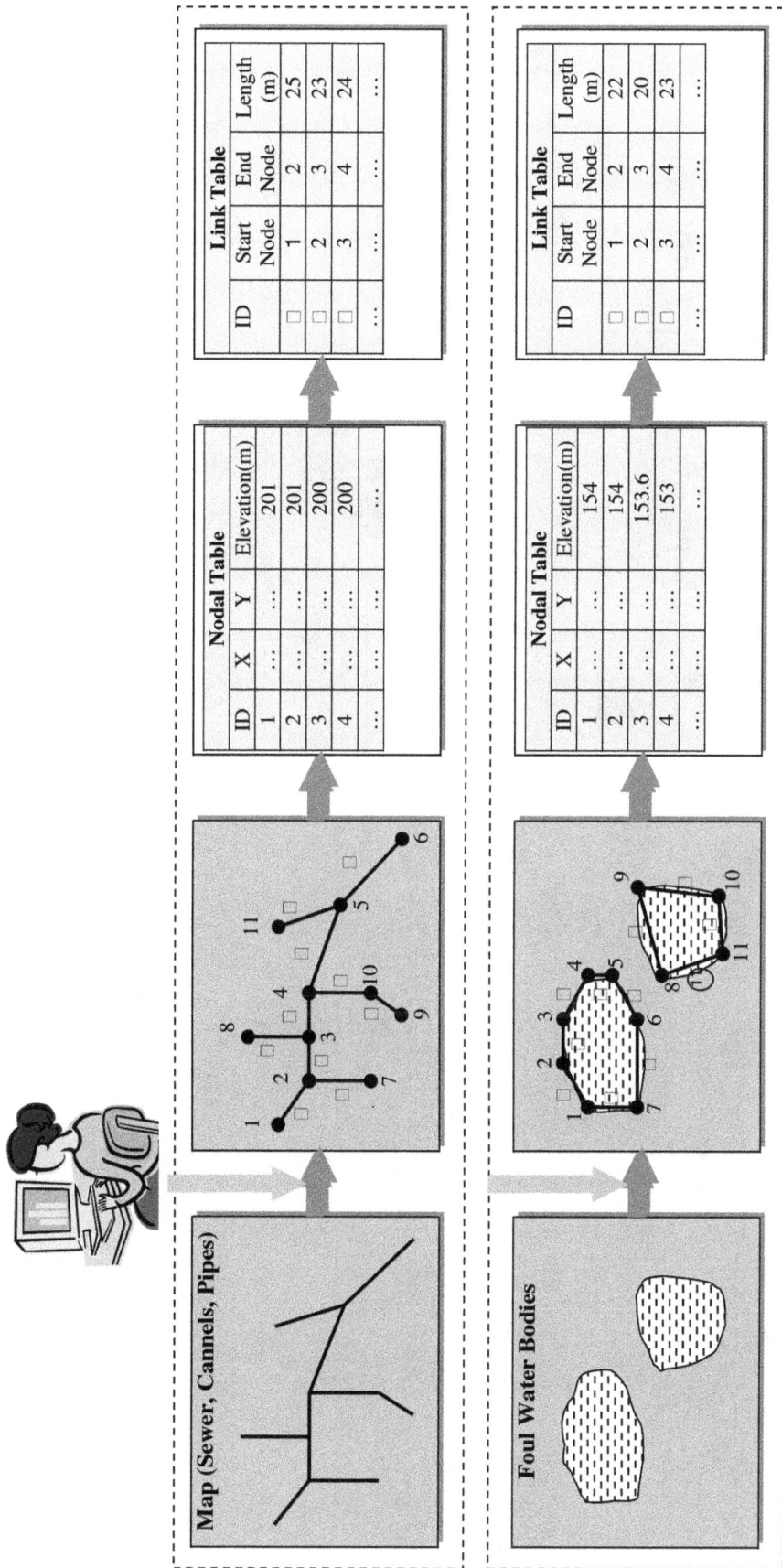

Figure 5.1. Digitization of real-world network

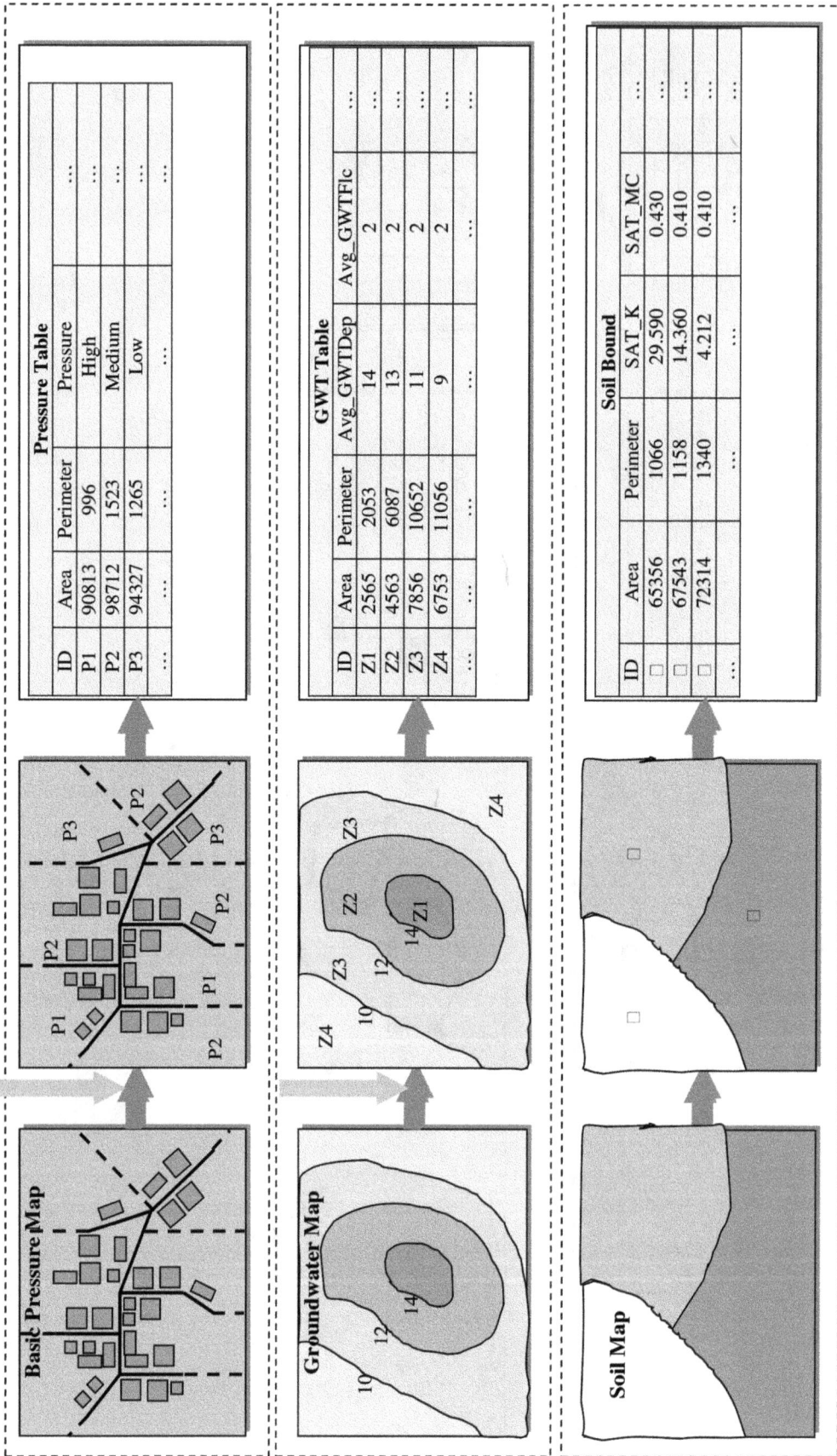

Figure 5.2. Digitization of thematic maps

Pressure Table

ID	Area	Perimeter	Pressure	...
P1	90813	996	High	...
P2	98712	1523	Medium	...
P3	94327	1265	Low	...
...			...	...

GWT Table

ID	Area	Perimeter	Avg_GWTDep	Avg_GWTFlc	...
Z1	2565	2053	14	2	...
Z2	4563	6087	13	2	...
Z3	7856	10652	11	2	...
Z4	6753	11056	9	2	...
...	...	...	...	...	...

Soil Bound

ID	Area	Perimeter	SAT_K	SAT_MC	...
☐	65356	1066	29.590	0.430	...
☐	67543	1158	14.360	0.410	...
☐	72314	1340	4.212	0.410	...
...			...	...	...

Basic Pressure Map

Groundwater Map

Soil Map

112

Environmental maps

Soil map The soil map can be prepared by conducting a detailed soil survey or by collecting the information from soil survey and soil testing laboratories. The soil maps should contain data pertaining to various soil properties (see Chapter 2 of Book 4).

Groundwater map The groundwater table map can be prepared using the data pertaining to groundwater depth and average fluctuation data.

Pressure zone map The pressure zone map can be prepared by recording actual pressure or from the hydraulic analysis of the network. It should provide information on operating pressure zones.

Network database

Data preparation includes the construction of network data required for the contamination ingress and pipe condition assessment models.

Network model A network model is a simple representation of complex reality. A network comprises of number of interconnected links/elements and nodes.

- Nodes represent points at which there is an input, output or a junction of two or more links (or pipes). They also include points where there is a change in characteristics or connections to system features.
- Link (or pipe) refers to connection between two nodes.

GIS network maps are required to be developed on the following themes, by incorporating nodes and links data:

1. Water distribution system network
2. Sewer system
3. Canals/open drainage network
4. Surface foul water bodies.

Each of the network maps will need to be digitized and unique identification (ID) assigned to all elements/links/pipes and nodes. The network maps will then be stored as shape-files and all other attribute data added (e.g. diameter, age and material of links etc.).

Water distribution network theme: The water supply system consists of tanks, reservoirs, junctions which are represented as nodes, and pipelines that are represented as links (see Figure 5.3 for example). The water supply link comprises data attributes such as pipe length, diameter, age, material, leakage frequency etc. The node consists of attributes like x, y, z coordinates and bury depth.

Sewer distribution network theme: Sewer pipes are represented as elements and junctions, manholes are represented as nodes (see Figure 5.4 for example). Details of sewer pipes such as pipe diameter, pipe length, pipe material, direction of flow, joint type, location of manholes, depth of manholes, age of pipe, bury depth etc. need to be included in the sewer network theme.

Canal network theme: Open drainage canals are represented as elements/links. Junctions and points where there is a change in direction are represented as nodes (see Figure 5.5 for example). The open drainage network theme database includes data on the type of drainage, geometry of the canal, slope. Canal node consist of attributes like x, y, z coordinates.

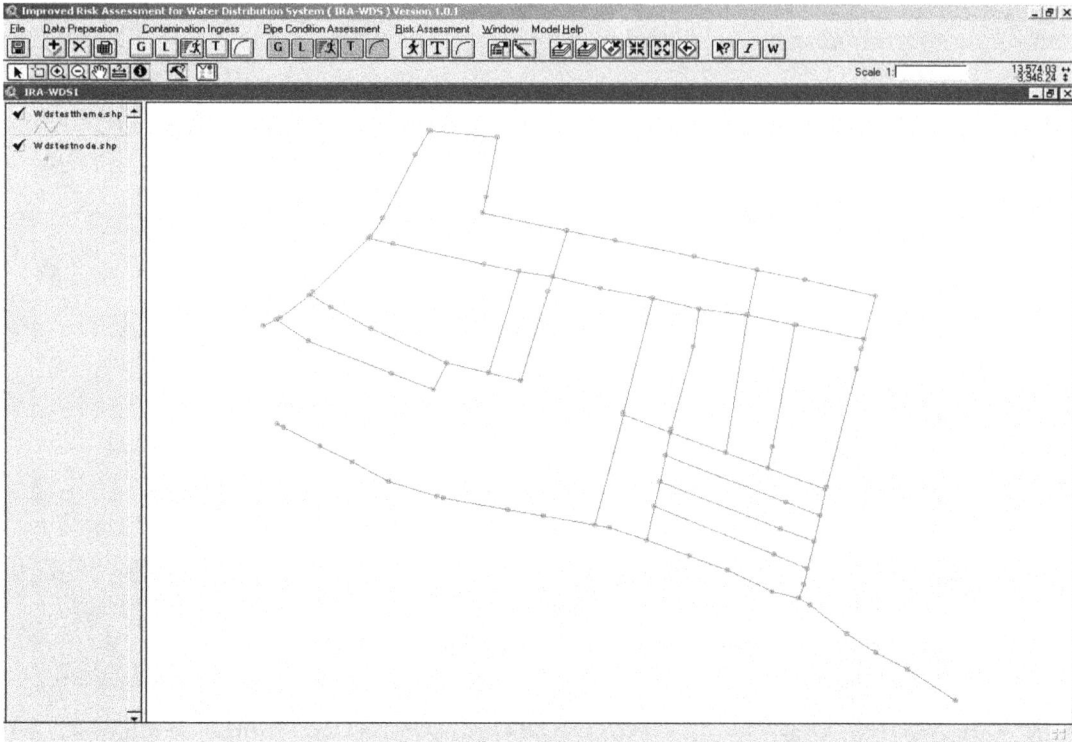

Figure 5.3. Water distribution network

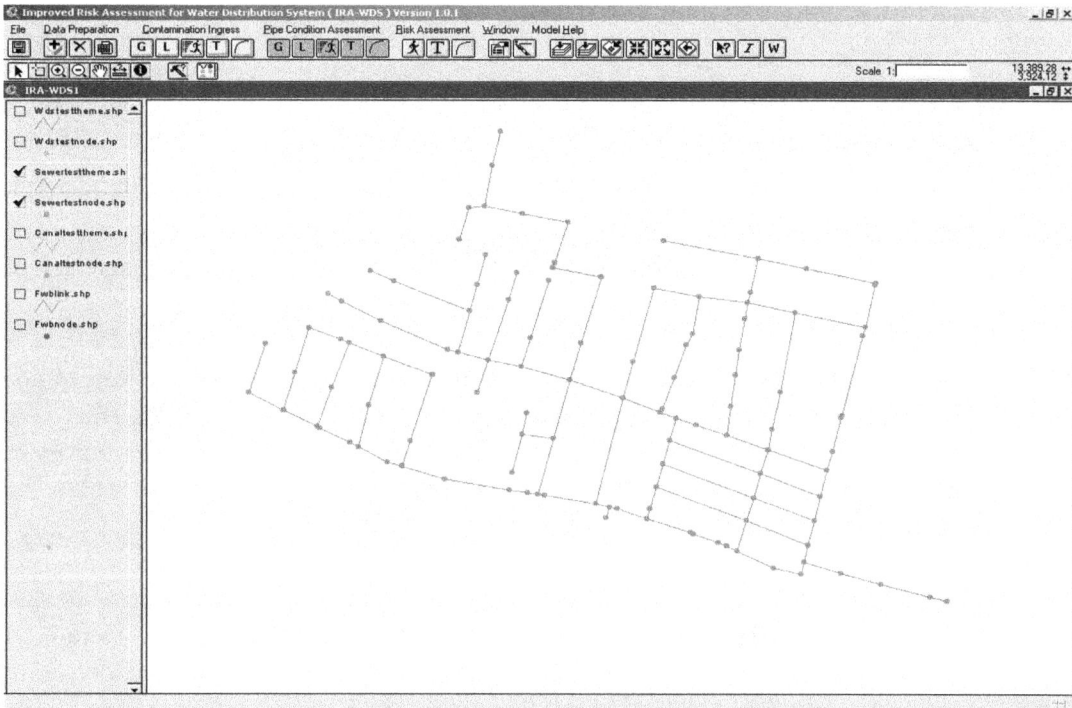

Figure 5.4. Sewer distribution network

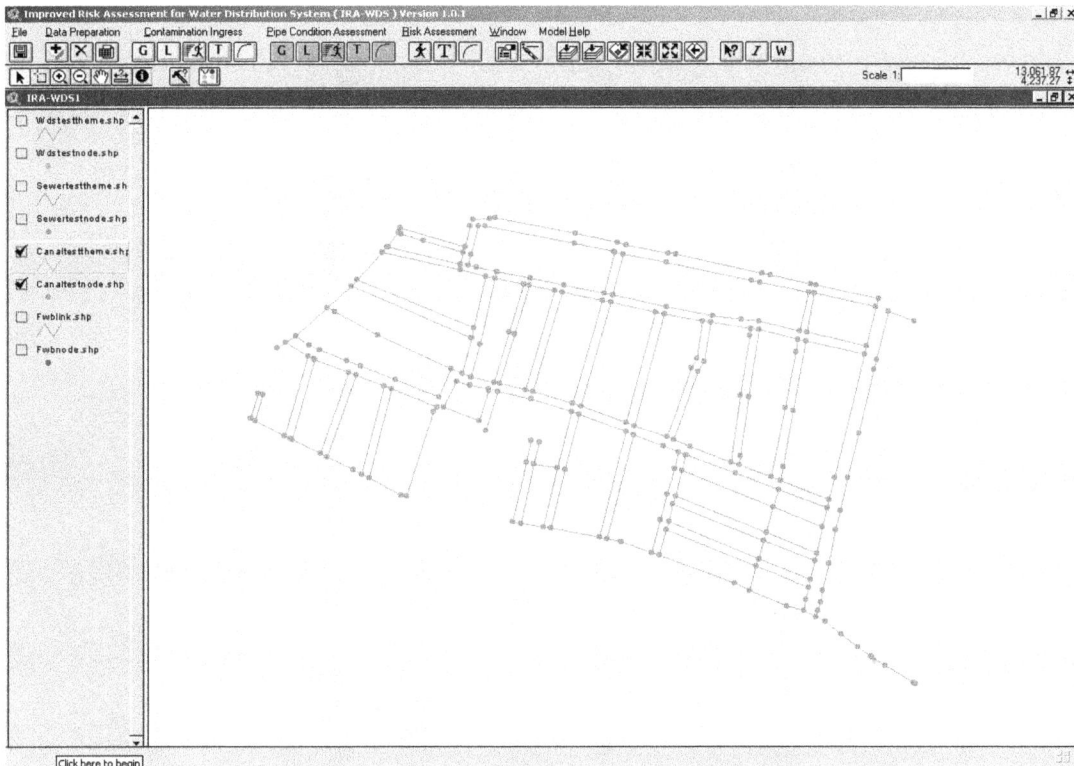

Figure 5.5. Canal distribution network

Surface foul water bodies: The foul water bodies are represented as polygon features in the network. The boundary of the polygon is represented as the link and points where the direction of the boundary changes are represented as nodes (see Figure 5.6 for example). The database includes the link, start and end node of link, coordinates of node of polygon, average depth of surface foul water body.

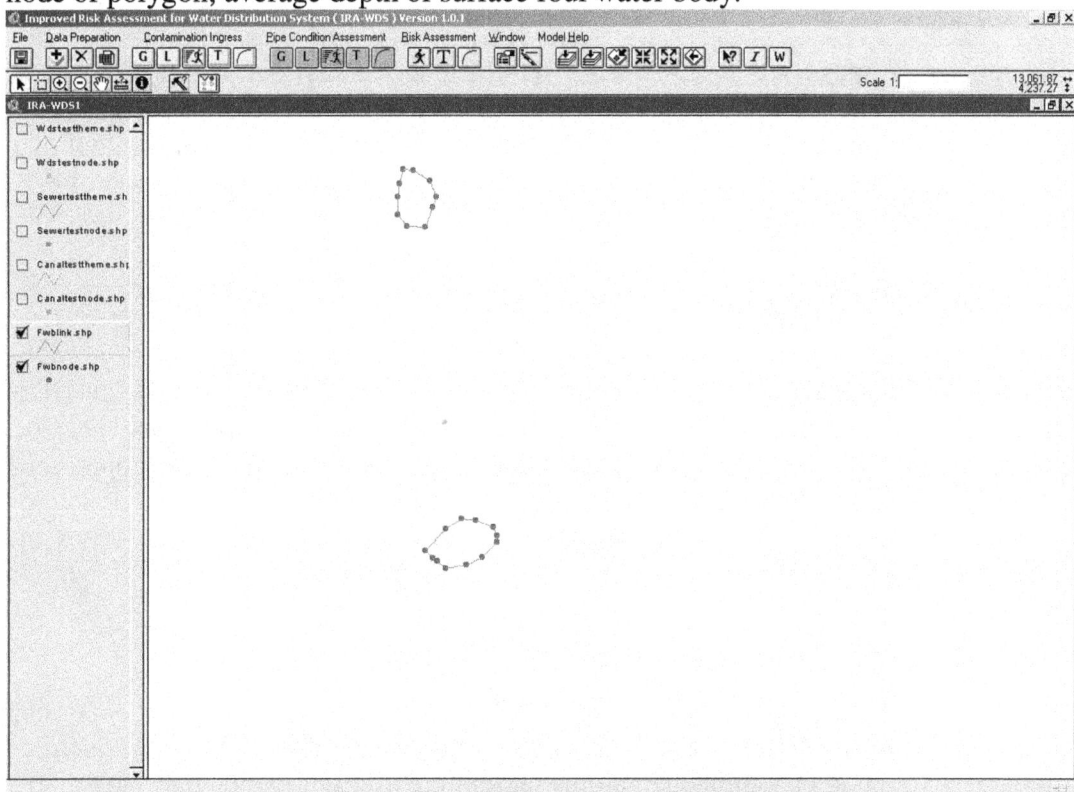

Figure 5.6. Surface foul water body theme

115

Overlay of above themes: Figure 5.7 shows all the above network themes overlaid into a single derived map.

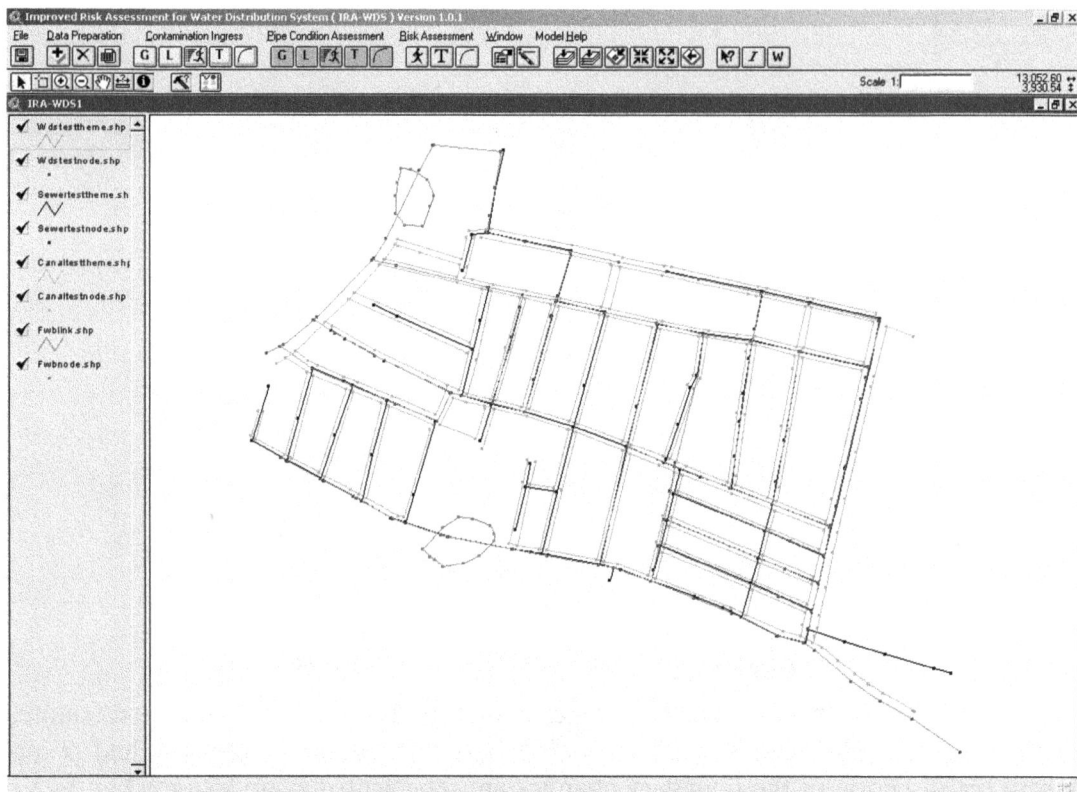

Figure 5.7. Representation of the scenario (by overlaying themes)

Derived maps

The secondary maps are derived from the thematic maps and the attribute data collected from the Municipal Corporation. A Triangular Irregular Network (TIN) and/or Digital Elevation Model (DEM) can be derived from the elevation contour map. The TIN represents the surface of the area and DEM represents the elevation of each grid cell in the study area.

5.6.3 Development of model

The three models presented in Chapters 2, 3 and 4 are developed in the C++ programming language and then converted to a dynamic link library (DLL). These DLLs are then installed in the ArcView GIS installation BIN directory. The DLL procedure is called using the Avenue script while running the model. The appropriate input parameters for the DLL procedure are provided by the avenue script (pertaining to input and output files). The DLL then executes the programme and writes the respective output file. The model is integrated within GIS using the partial integration approach.

5.6.4 Integration with GIS and generation of output

One of the most important concerns in GIS design is simplifying the user's learning curve. Many current GIS implementations present the user with a bewildering number of functions, which confuses both the novice and expert. The challenge is to propose

116

an interface which adequately conveys the data model, without posing a complex learning task on the developed model. Data input and retrieval data to and from the model must be performed in a user-friendly manner. Keeping the above criteria in mind, an interface has been developed in order to input and retrieve the data to and from the contamination models. The network data, viz. Pipe link data, Pipe node data, Pipe soil data, Sewer link data, Sewer node data, Sewer soil data, Canal (open drain) link, Canal node data, Canal soil data, and Surface foul water body link data, Surface foul water body node data and Surface foul water body soil data are the input data required for the model.

The different developed models were integrated with GIS to form the 'IRA-WDS' software (see Figure 5.9). The next section deals with different components of the interface and describes various controls and tools used for the interface development (Figure 5.8).

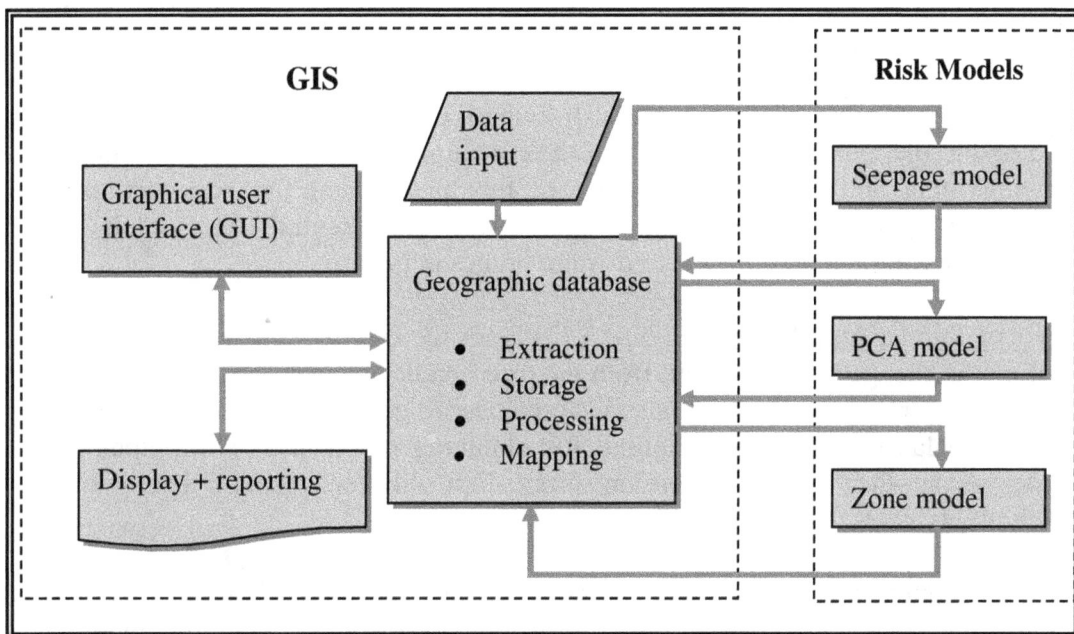

Figure 5.8. Integration of different developed models with GIS

5.7 IRA-WDS User Interface

A document graphical user interface (DocGUI) based IRA-WDS (Figure 5.9) has been created by using the ArcView GIS tool in the form of ArcView Project. IRA-WDS includes the collection of controls such as menus, buttons and tools that are used to interact with documents like IRA-WDS view, table and chart.

The IRA-WDS view is an interactive document graphical user interface that lets the user display, explore, query and analyse geographic data in ArcView. Similar to 'View' document, any number of IRA-WDS documents can be opened and same data can be saved in more than one IRA-WDS documents viz. IRA-WDS 1, IRA-WDS 2, IRA-WDS 3, etc.

5.7.1 Components of interface

The major components of the GIS-based IRA-WDS interface (Figure 5.9) are:

1. File
2. Data preparation
3. Contamination ingress
4. Pipe condition assessment
5. Risk assessment
6. Window
7. Model help

<u>File</u> helps with all file operations such as opening, closing, saving etc.

<u>Data preparation</u> aids the user in converting a file from one mode to another, adding shape files, creating and importing tables etc.

<u>Contamination ingress</u> (see Figure 5.10) helps the user in generating an input file, loading the file, generating output from the contaminant ingress model (running) and viewing input and output. The output of the model identifies the contaminated segments of water supply distribution pipes due to the potential effects of the sewer system, canal system and surface foul water bodies in the area.

<u>Pipe condition assessment</u> (see Figure 5.11) helps the user in generating an input file, loading the file, generating output from the pipe condition assessment model (running) and viewing input and output. It also aids the user to generate membership functions, weights, balance factors etc. required for obtaining the output. The output of the model ranks the water distribution pipes into different groups based on the vulnerability of the pipes (Figure 5.11).

<u>Risk assessment</u> (see Figure 5.12) helps in loading the outputs of the contaminant ingress and pipe condition assessment models as input, running the model and viewing the input and output. It also aids the user to generate the weights required for obtaining the output. The output of the model enables the user to delineate critical zones of water supply network combining the contaminant ingress potential and the pipe vulnerability (Figure 5.12).

<u>Window</u> performs standard ArcView windows menu operations such as arranging and showing documents.

<u>Model help</u> aids the user in assessing the help file created for the various components of the IRA-WDS Interface.

The interface is designed in such a manner that data input and retrieval data to/from the model can be performed in a user-friendly way.

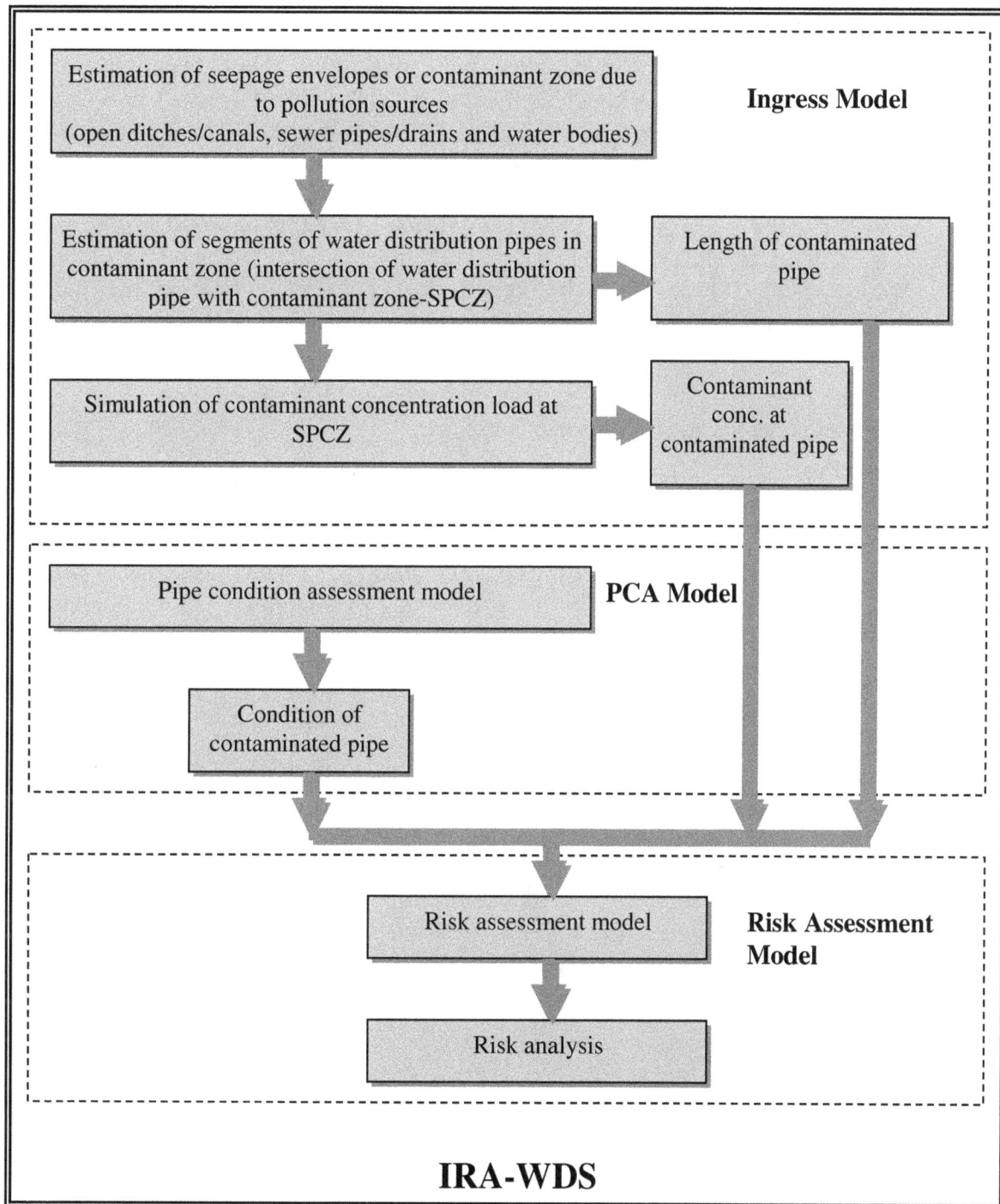

Figure 5.9. Overview of IRA-WDS

5.8 IRA-WDS Extension

An extension is a kind of object database that can be used to provide new functionality to ArcView without altering existing projects and to permit multiple individuals to contribute without conflict to a single ArcView-based development effort. IRA-WDS has been developed as an extension. Once the extension is loaded, all the controls, viz. menus, tools, buttons, dialog, are automatically loaded into the ArcView's project document. The user can also choose to make the extension default, i.e. whenever the user opens any ArcView project, IRA-WDS interface will be loaded.

The IRA-WDS extension can be loaded automatically by running the shortcut installed by the IRA-WDS setup or through the Program menu. If the user has already opened ArcView and wants to run IRA-WDS he/she should carry out the following steps:

- Activate the ArcView Project window.
- From the File menu, choose Extensions. This will bring up the Extensions dialog.
- Check the box adjacent to IRA-WDS in the Extensions dialog. If user wishes the IRA-WDS extension to load automatically every time user starts ArcView, press the Make Default button after ticking the IRA-WDS. The next time user starts ArcView, the IRA-WDS will automatically be loaded.
- Press OK in the Extensions dialog box.
- The IRA-WDS welcome screen will be opened and the user can opt to cancel/ quit ArcView or continue with IRA-WDS loading.

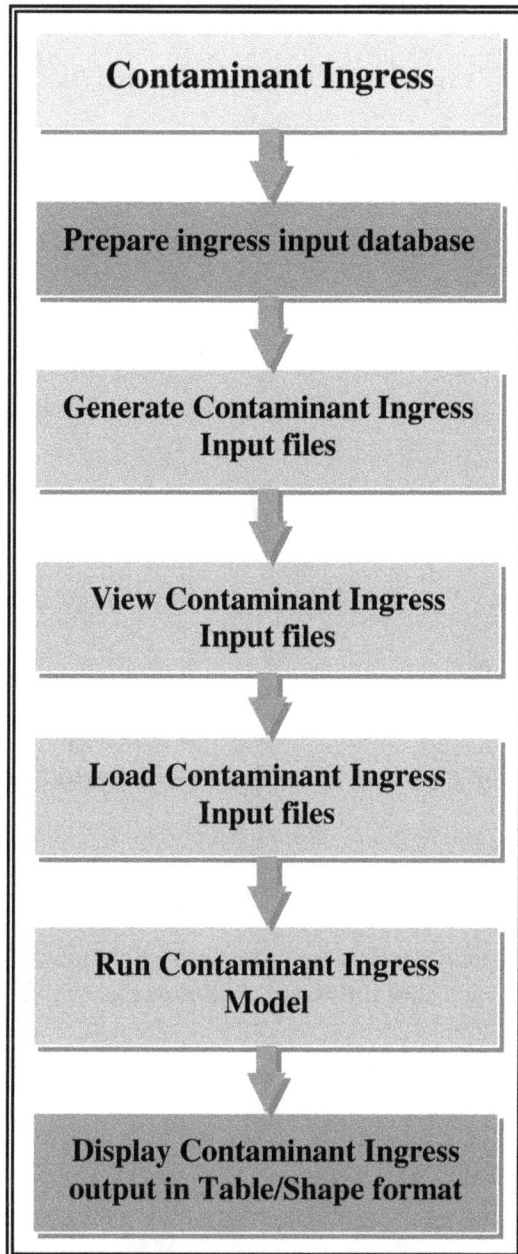

Figure 5.10. Overview of Contaminant Ingress Model of IRA-WDS

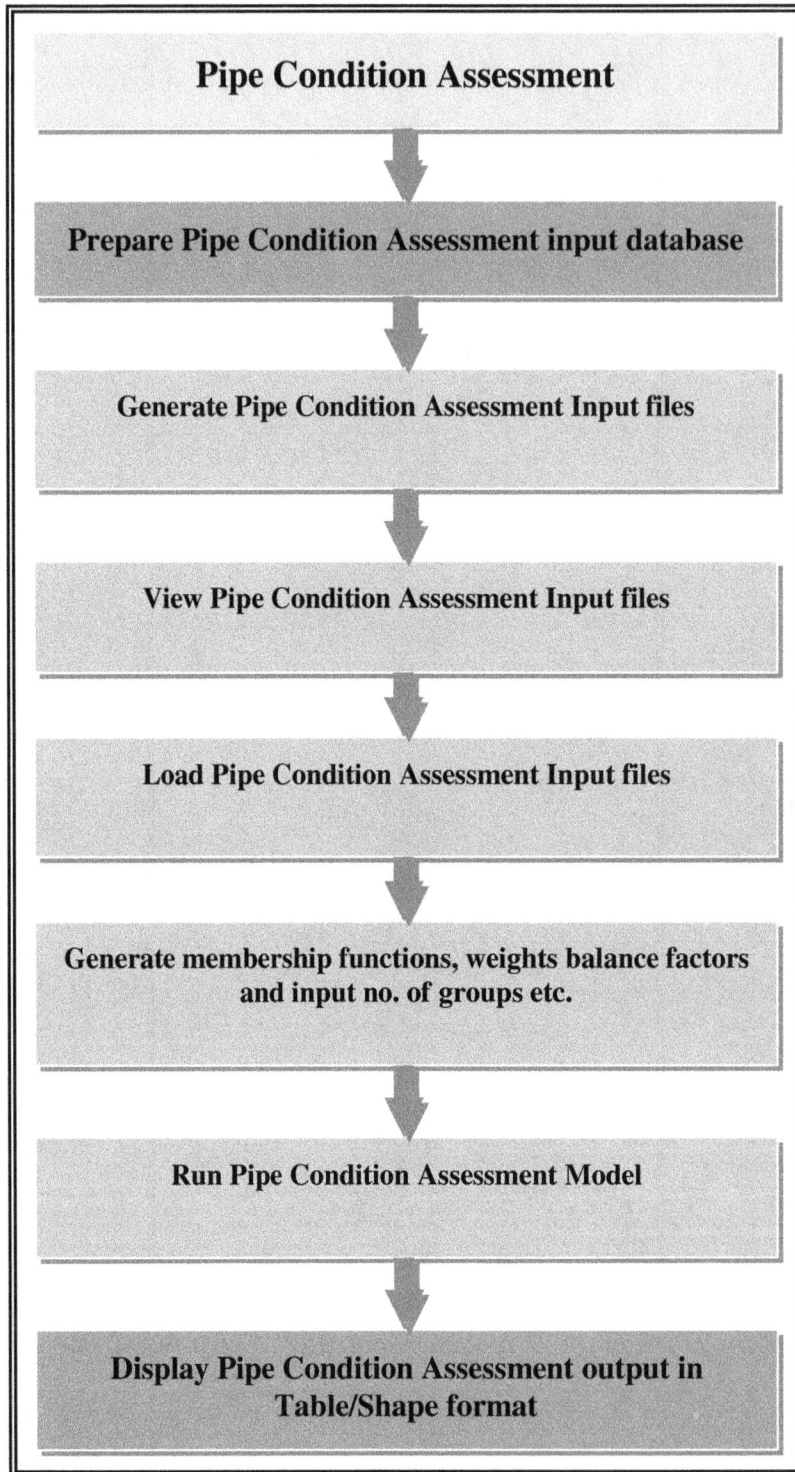

Figure 5.11. Overview of Pipe Condition Assessment Model of IRA-WDS

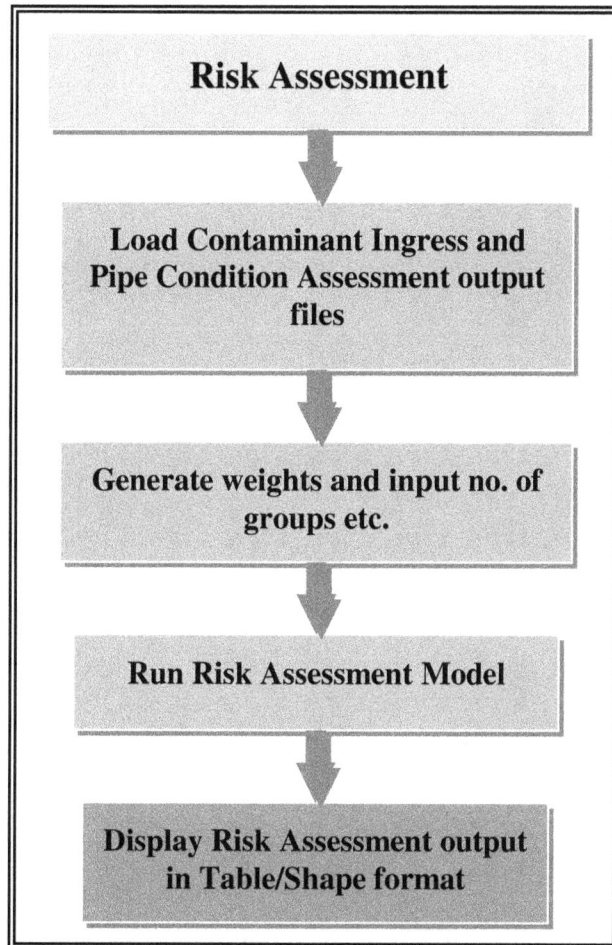

Figure 5.12. Overview of Risk Assessment Model of IRA-WDS

CHAPTER SIX

Example Application of Model (IRA-WDS)

Risk Assessment of Contaminant Intrusion into Water Distribution Systems

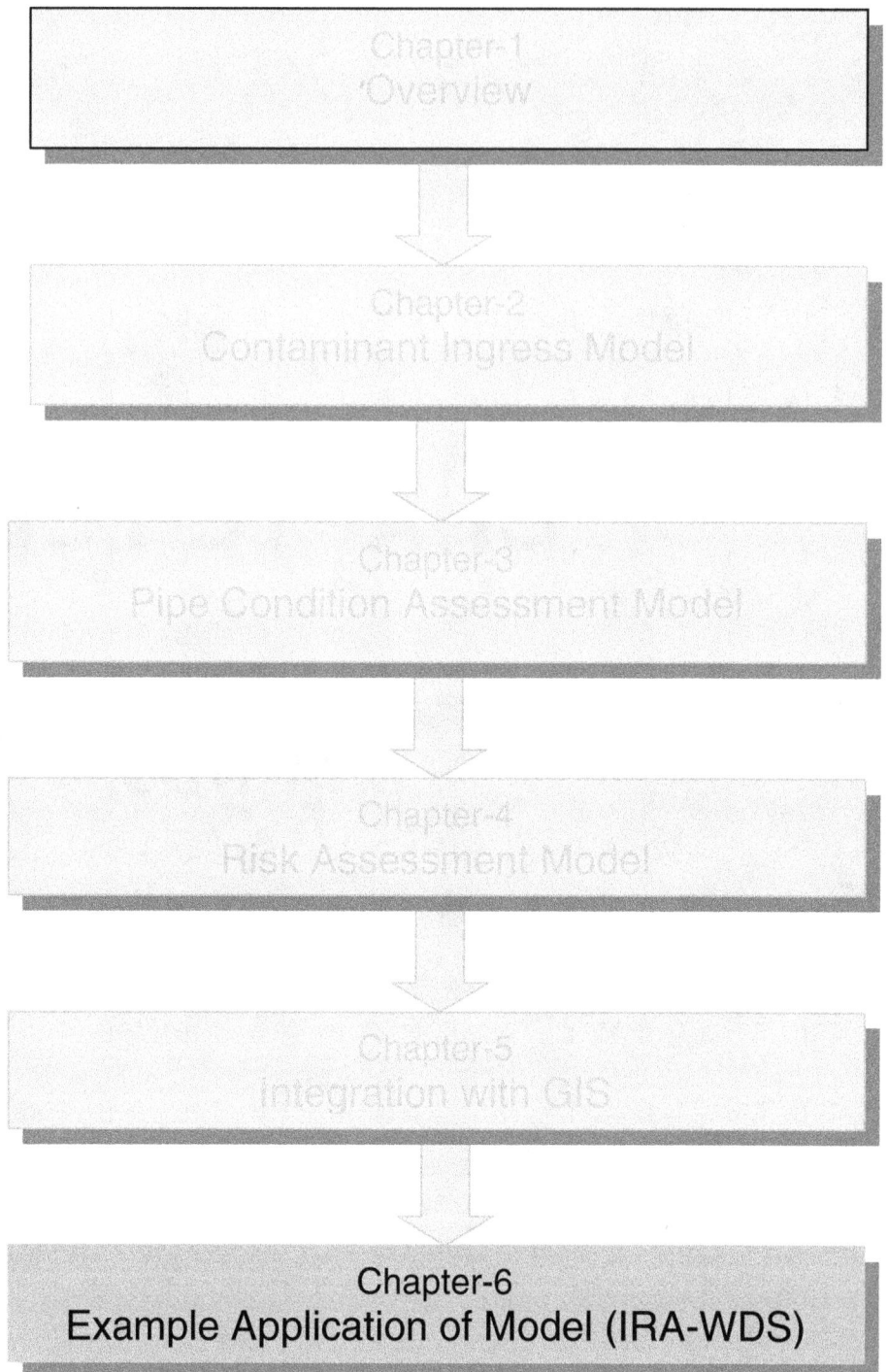

Chapter-1
Overview

Chapter-2
Contaminant Ingress Model

Chapter-3
Pipe Condition Assessment Model

Chapter-4
Risk Assessment Model

Chapter-5
Integration with GIS

Chapter-6
Example Application of Model (IRA-WDS)

Chapter 6: Example Application of Model (IRA-WDS)

6.1 Introduction

Previous chapters of this book have provided an introduction into the technical background of the mathematical models provided, how the outputs of the model are combined to estimate risk, and how the models are integrated into a GIS framework.

In this chapter an application to a real case study area is presented. The chapter provides details of data collection, model construction, its integration with GIS, and finally interpretation of the results.

As far as possible this chapter is structured in a way that mirrors the steps presented in the previous chapters. It is anticipated that by reading this chapter, the user will get a good insight into all the processes involved in using these models and IRA-WDS.

This chapter is structured in the following way.

- Background to the study area and details of the data collection

- Details of GIS development and model construction

- Application of IRA-WDS and interpretation of the results.

6.2 Case Study – Guntur

Guntur is one of the five largest cities in Andhra Pradesh, India (see Figure 6.1) and is bounded by latitudes 150 50'N and 160 50'N and longitudes 790 10'E and 790 55'E.

The present population of the city is around 580,000 and the city attracts on average approximately 120,000 population every day. The mean annual temperature in Guntur is 28°C with an average annual rainfall of about 800-1000 mm (Sources: NATMO; Indian Meteorological Department, Hyderabad). The climate in the area is very warm and in summer temperatures of as high as 49°C are recorded. The groundwater is available at about 10-20 m depth in this area (Sources: Central Ground Water Board, Irrigation Division, Guntur).

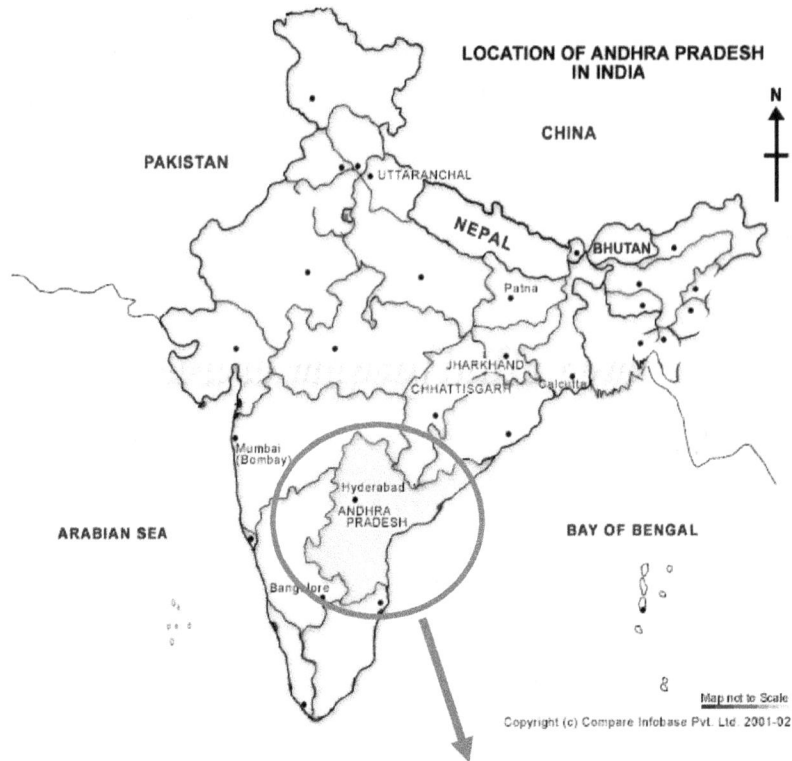

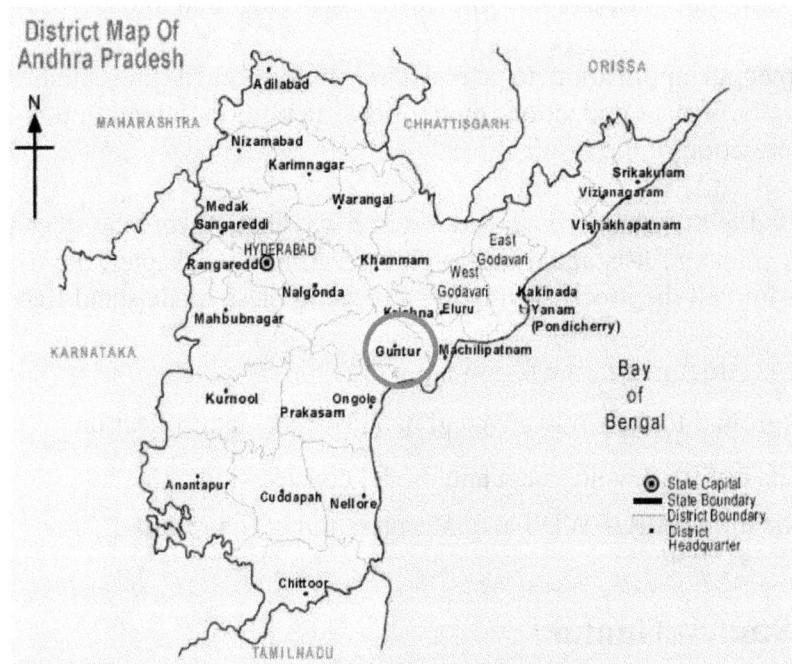

Figure 6.1. Location of Guntur in Andhra Pradesh, India

6.3 The Study Area

Guntur is divided into 10 zones for administrative purpose and the area chosen for the this study is the B R Stadium (zone VIII). Water is supplied for approximately one hour a day and during non-supply hours most of the population depends on groundwater.

The data available for zone VIII include maps of the road network, water distribution networks, sewer networks, surface foul water bodies, stand pipe locations and house connections details.

6.3.1 Water supply distribution system

Guntur Municipal Corporation is responsible for providing the city with its drinking water supply through a piped network. As in most parts of India, Guntur's water supply is intermittent and available for one hour a day. In addition to being intermittent the water supply is also reported to experience frequent ingress of contaminants (particularly in zone VIII). Zone VIII covers an area of approximately 4 km^2 and has a population of about 60,000. The vast majority of the population depends on the public water supply through house connections and standpipes.

The source of water for the study area is the Krishna River. Through canals the water flows to Takkellapadu reservoir. At Takkellapadu reservoir the water is treated and the treated water is collected in clear water sumps. From these sumps the water is pumped and distributed to zone VIII water tanks through cement concrete pipes of 1200 mm diameter. There are two overhead water tanks supplying this zone.

The main supply lines from the tanks are 600 mm diameter RCC pipes. The distribution lines are mainly AC pipes with a few CI and GI pipes ranging in diameter from 60 mm to 600 mm. The total length of the network is 62 km, which includes 829 pipes of various sizes.

There are various points along the network where pipes pass through open drains, and where sewage flows over the pipes. Since, majority of the population depends on public water supply any contamination in the network affects large number of people.

A peculiar feature of this zone is that, once the water supply has stopped, at many locations the public uses handpumps (or even electric pumps) to suck water out of the distribution system. Clearly this will encourage foul water from leaking sewers and open drains to enter the main drinking water network (through leaks at joints, pipe segments or valves etc.).

6.3.2 Underground sewer system

Only a part of the study area is served by underground sewers. There are two types of sewer pipes, viz. RCC and stoneware, the total length of which is approximately 26 km (most of this is RCC). The age of the sewers varies from 1 to 28 years and the buried depth of the sewers varies from 0.9 to 4.5 m. The minimum and maximum diameters of the sewers are 150 mm and 1200 mm respectively. The main sewer of diameter 1200 mm conveys the sewage to the wastewater treatment work located at Suddapalli Donka.

6.3.3 Open drainage system

All but 1 per cent of the study area is covered with the open drains. There are two types of drains, lined (Pucca drain) and unlined (Kutcha drain). The majority of the lined drains are made of brick and lined with cement. Unlined drains exist in only a few locations. The standard width and depth of the drains is approximately 0.3 m (however, there are a few larger drains that connect with several smaller drains). It has been reported that there is considerable seepage from the open drains. As the open drains are at ground level, there is a potential of seepage reaching water supply pipes.

6.3.4 Surface foul water bodies

Stagnant water is found in depressions around the city (especially during the rainy season). There are several such water bodies in the study area, of which four are polluted. In several places, the open drains release water into these water bodies, making them foul. The depth of water in these foul water bodies ranges from 9 to 14 m and the area varies from 1055 to 13266 m^2. Note that water distribution pipelines pass near and in some cases below these water bodies and it is quite common for there to be reports of water supply contamination immediately after rain.

6.3.5 General observations in the study area

Several field visits were undertaken to the study area. To give an indication of the conditions that exist in the area, a brief selection of observations are given below.

Culvert on an open drain in Nandhi Velugu Road with two main water supply lines along the drain was visited in which one of the two pipelines (300 mm) was fully submerged and the other was just above the existing water level in the drain.

- In the main water supply pipeline near the Railway Junction, leakages were found in the 1200 mm main pipeline (18 years old), which conveys water from the water treatment plant to the rest of the pipe network.

- Leakages were also found in the valves and pipelines near the water tank. Treatment of water is being done by adding lumps of bleaching powder at the open source and flocculation (using Alum) in the tank. There are garbage disposal areas at different locations along the opposite side of the road. This poses the threat of contamination in the pipelines as the main pipelines from the treatment plant lie close to this area.

- The facilities at the wastewater treatment plant include screening, two settling tanks, one pumping station and sedimentation canals. At the time of the study, the plant was not functioning and the untreated wastewater was released to the nearby farmlands.

- The local drains empty into the surface foul water body at Balaji Nagar (zone VIII).

- Many open drains were found in the IPD Colony with water supply lines in close proximity.

- Two overhead tanks are located near BR Stadium, each with a capacity of 1500 kilolitres. At present only one tank is in use. The supply pattern is one hour per day in all the areas. At this rate the per capita water supplied is approximately 40 litres per day.

- Drainage channels and water supply pipes run along both sides of the narrow street and at many locations the pipelines are submerged in the sewage water. At some locations the water distribution pipes are corroded to a great extent.

6.4 Data Collection and Database Preparation

Several field visits were undertaken to the study area and a local NGO, KAKATOS, was engaged to collect data.

- Data collected included characteristics of the water supply distribution system, sewer and open drain system and surface foul water bodies.
- Data preparation included the production of thematic layers:
  - base map theme - land use, elevation contour, ward map, etc.
  - network map themes - pipe network, sewer network, canal network, foul water bodies etc.
  - derived themes - population density, proximity of pipeline to sewers etc.

6.4.1 Data collection

The following are the various types of data collected in the study area:

- Base map data (elevation, land use etc.).
- Network data
  - Water distribution data
  - Sewer data
  - Open drains/canals data
  - Surface foul water body data
- Demand data (not required to run models).

With a reference map made available by the Guntur Municipal Corporation, the boundary of the area was marked through physical survey and all the important features were identified and marked on the map.

6.4.2 Compass survey

Data was collected in relation to road type, length of the road and width of the road (using a road meter and tapes), and then plotted using AutoCAD. The total length of the roads is 90 km.

6.4.3 Levelling survey

The levelling survey was performed using the auto level instrument. The Takkellapadu reservoir was taken as the benchmark and levels at all junction points of the roads were measured.

6.4.4 Network surveys

The network maps (water distribution, sewers and open drains) were collected from the Public Health Engineering Department of Guntur. A survey was carried out to verify and add details to the network maps. This was done with the help of municipal engineers, tap inspectors and other workers from the Guntur Municipal Corporation.

6.4.4.1 Water distribution system

The water distribution system is shown in Figure 6.2. Water is distributed twice a day to different areas – area 1, morning 6:00 am to 7:00 am; and area 2, evening 6:00 pm to 7:00 pm. Additional data collected included: pipe characteristics (pipe, material, age, buried depth, diameter, length, road loading, break frequency and reduced levels). Locations and details of pipe joints (bends, tees cross etc.), were also obtained, as they could be potential entry points of pollutants.

Figure 6.2. Water distribution network of Guntur (Zone VIII)

6.4.4.2 Sewer network

The sewer network is shown in Figure 6.3. It can be seen that only a small part the study area is served by underground sewers. Manholes are placed at regular intervals; however, many are now covered over with soil or roads. When there are problems with sewage flow, therefore, it is difficult to locate the manhole for repair.

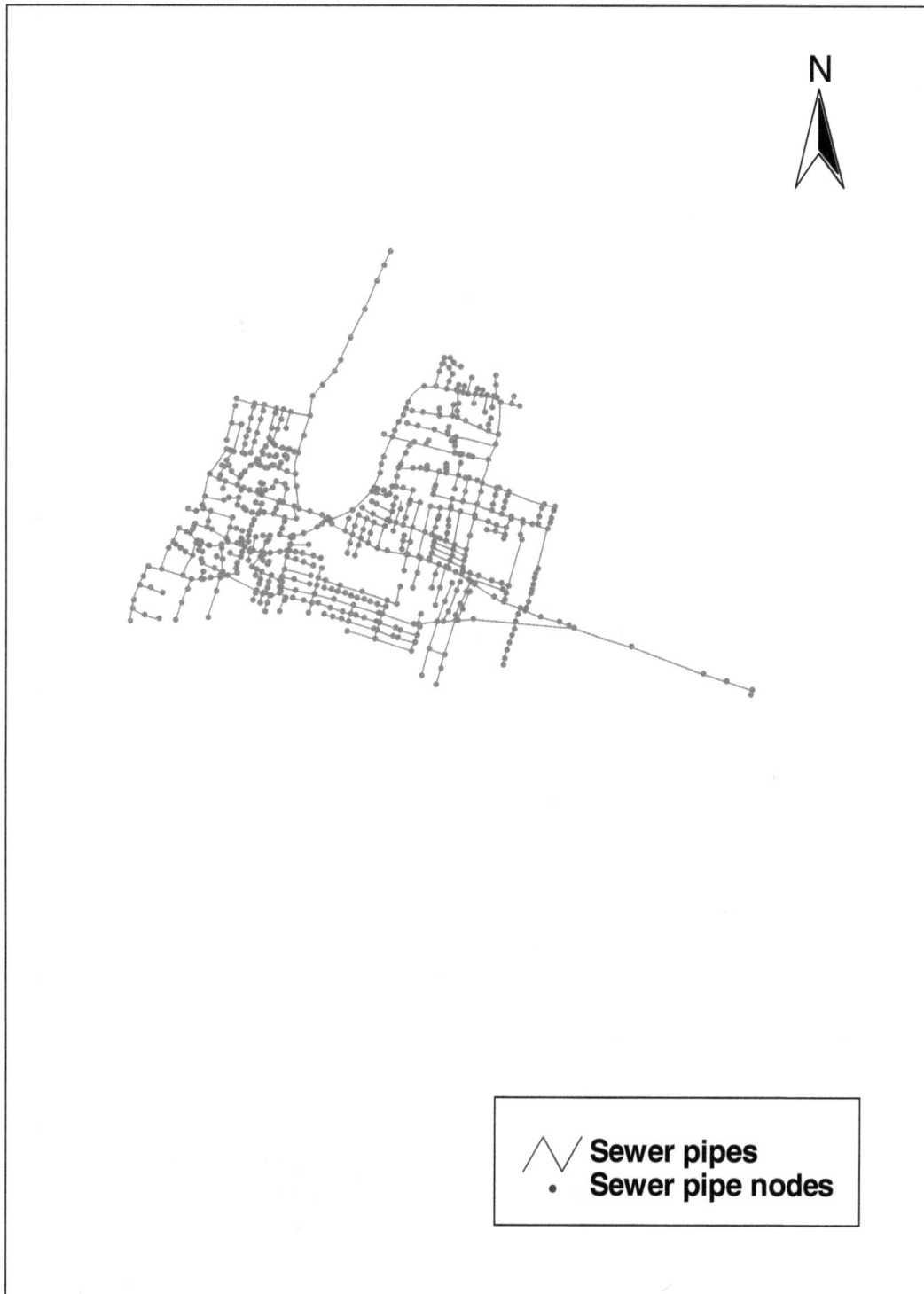

Figure 6.3. Sewer network of Guntur (Zone VIII)

6.4.4.3 Canal/Drain network

The canal/open drain network is shown in Figure 6.4. Most of the data related to the open drains was collected by visual inspection. Data collected included: type of drain (lined or unlined); age; length; width; and depth. It was observed that most of the drains were in bad condition and that the drain water was not flowing freely at many places. In some areas, the open drain is feeding nearby water bodies, making them foul water bodies. There are also several locations where drinking water pipes pass through the open drain.

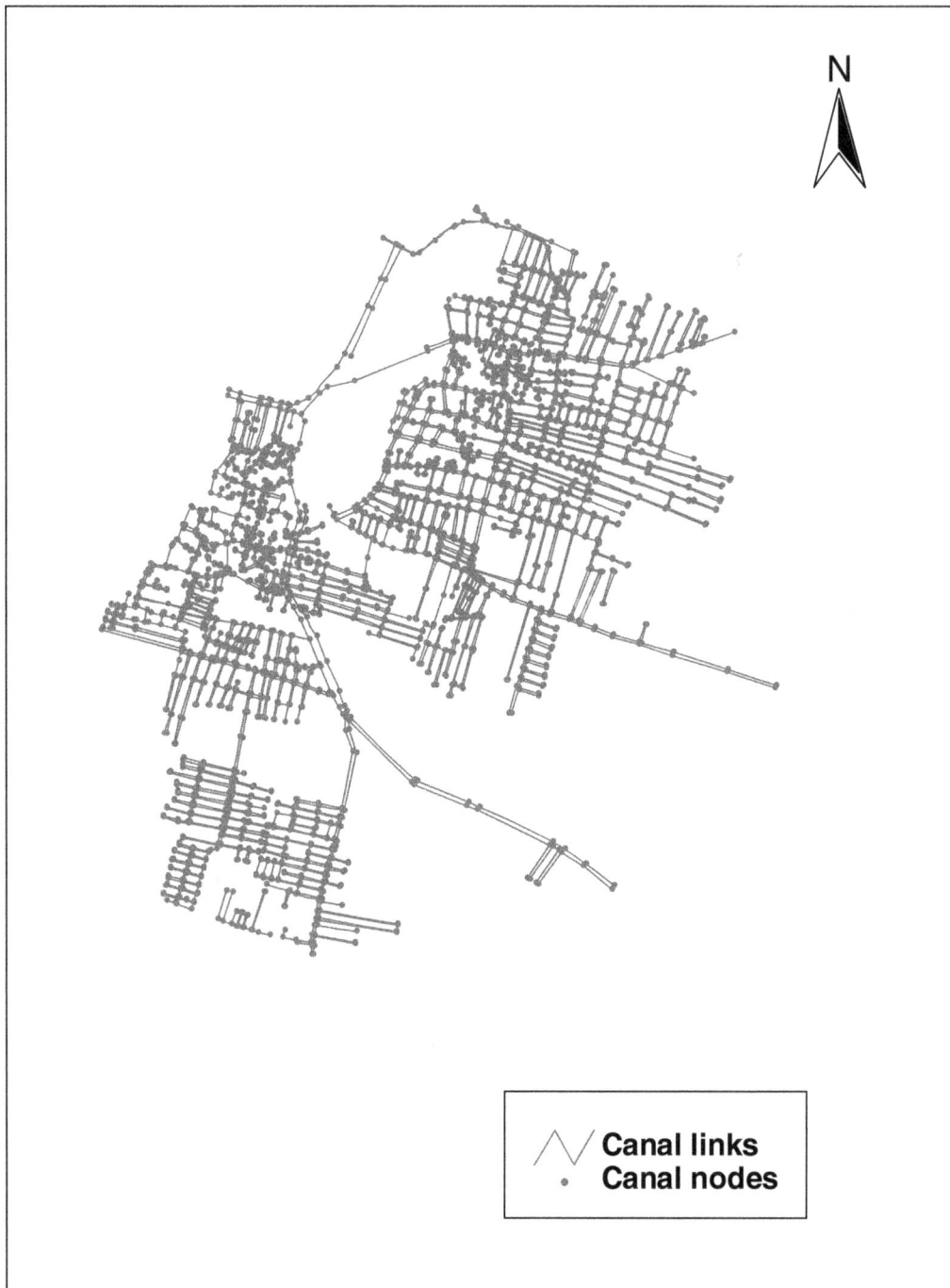

Figure 6.4. Canal/open drain network of Guntur (Zone VIII)

6.4.4.4 Surface foul water bodies

The foul water body polygon network is shown in Figure 6.5. There are several depressions around the city, of which four are polluted. Data collected for the foul water bodies included: their location; size (perimeter); and depth. The depth of water in the foul water bodies ranges from 9 to 14 m and the area varies from 1055 to 13266 m^2. Water supply pipelines pass near and in some cases below these water bodies.

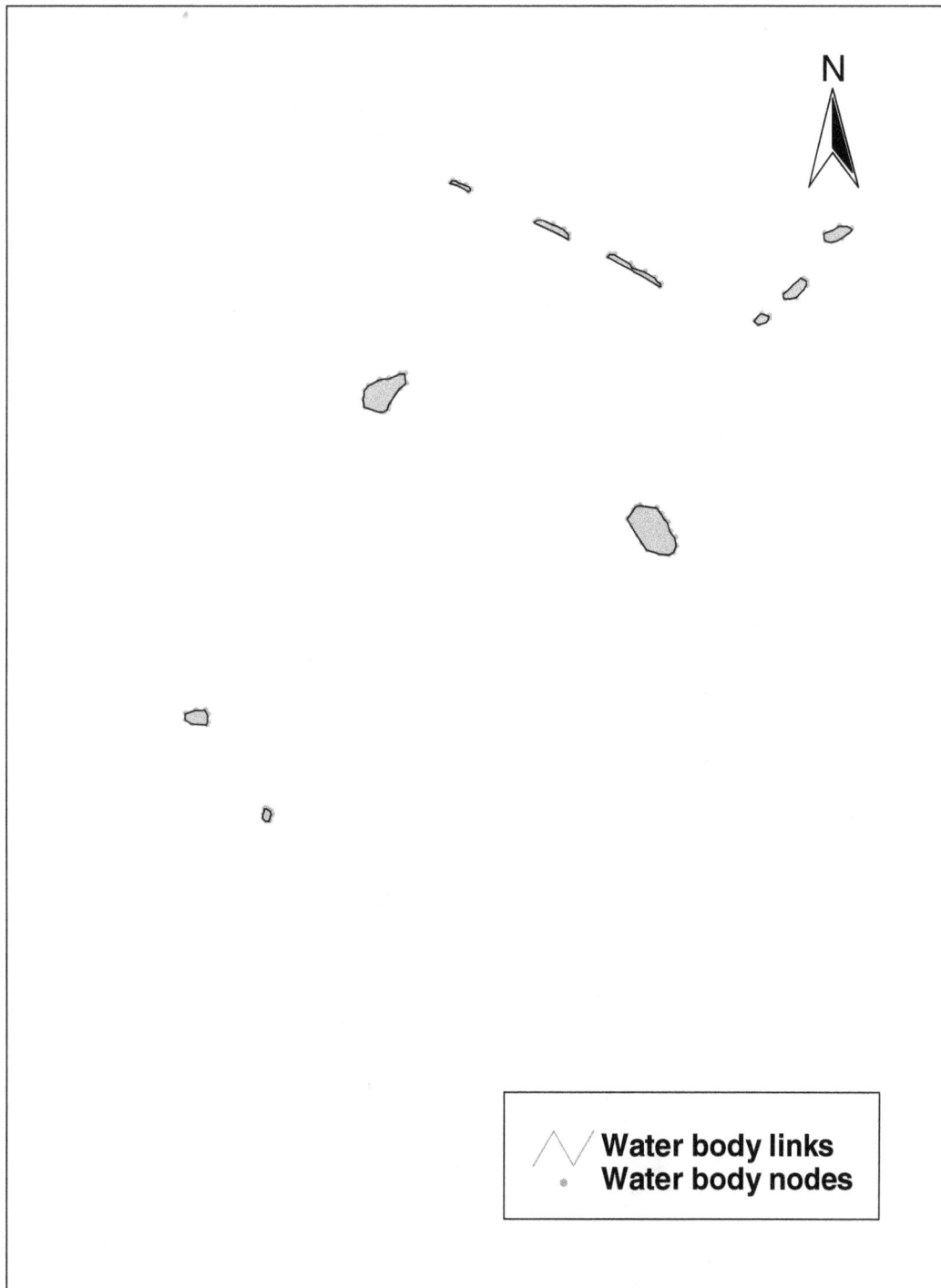

Figure 6.5. Foul water body polygon network of Guntur (Zone VIII)

6.4.5 Data preparation

As described in Section 5.5 of Chapter 5, the data preparation stage includes the preparation of various data/layers:

- Thematic layers
- Network database
- Derived layers.

6.4.5.1 Thematic layers

The first step in data preparation is thematic layers preparation. The following thematic layers of Guntur study area were prepared using the field data collected.

- Base map: infrastructure and contour maps
- Environmental maps: soil, groundwater, and pressure maps.

<u>Base map</u>

This map was prepared from a Survey of India (SOI) toposheet with a scale of 1:50,000. The SOI toposheet was obtained from the Guntur Municipal Corporation. ArcView GIS tools were used and the map was prepared by digitizing, editing and projecting the coordinates to a polyconic projection system. The entire area was divided into major classes, e.g. settlement, vegetation, roads etc. The following themes were added to generate the base map.

- Elevation contour map - The contour map (Figure 6.6) was prepared from reduced level data obtained by levelling survey. The elevation level in the study area varies from 18.5 m to 25 m.
- Land use/land cover map - The land use/land cover map (Figure 6.7) was prepared using IRS ID/LISS III & PAN merged data, scale 1:25,000. The major land-use classes that are found in the study area are shown in Table 6.1.
- Ward map - The ward map (Figure 6.8) of zone VIII was prepared from the data obtained from the Guntur Municipality. The study area consists of 10 wards.

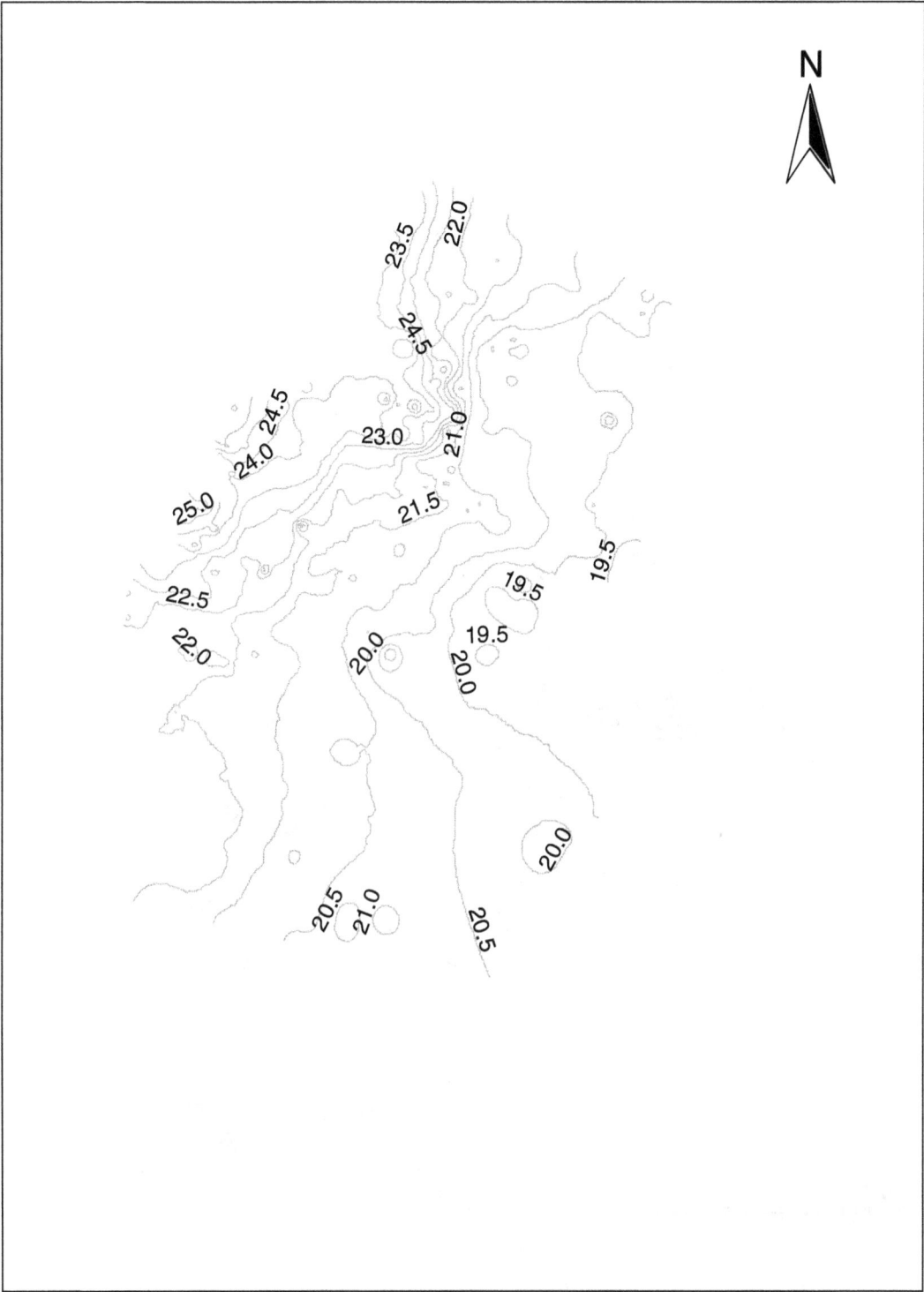

Figure 6.6. Contour map of Guntur (Zone VIII)

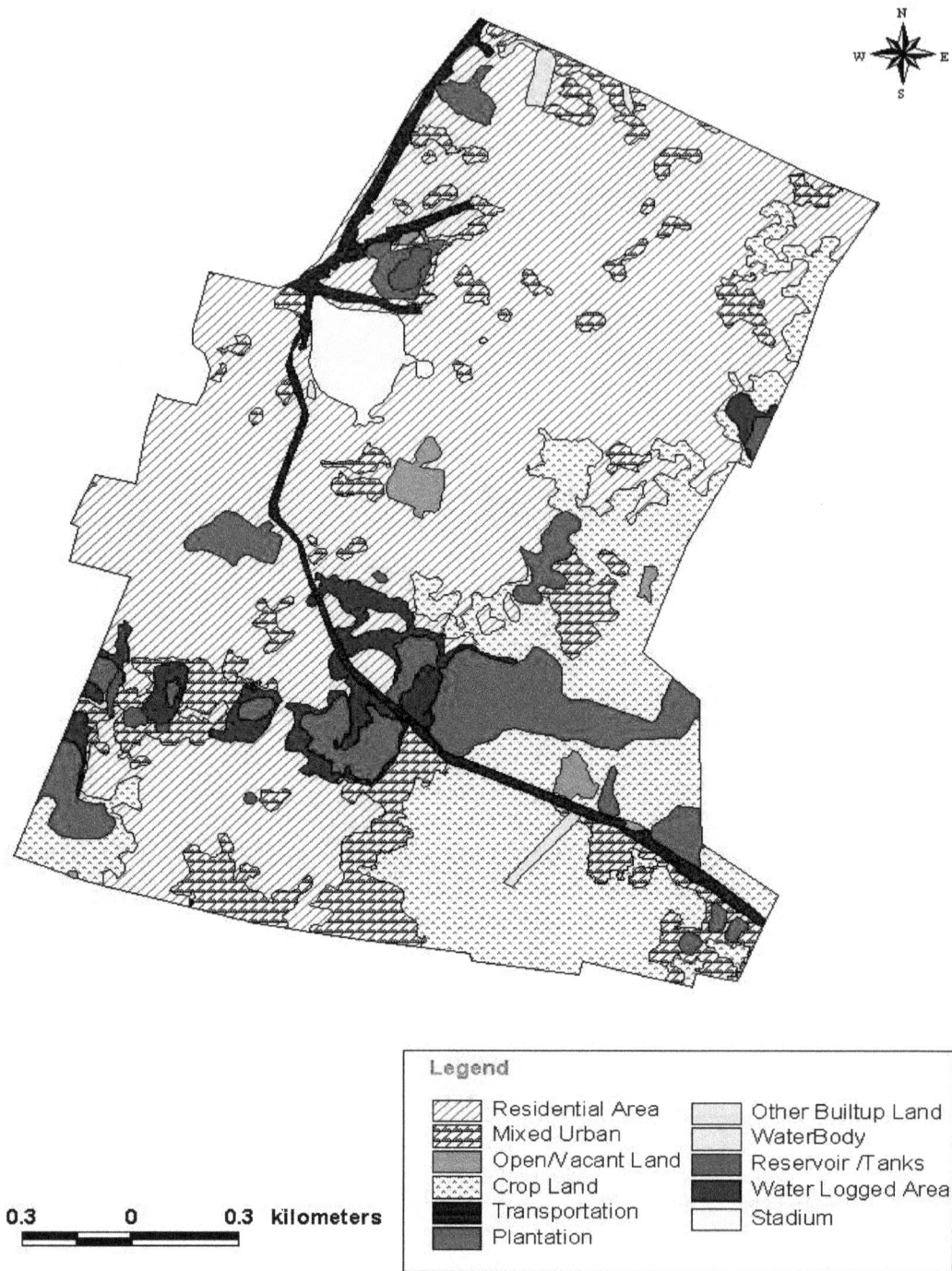

Legend

	Residential Area		Other Builtup Land
	Mixed Urban		WaterBody
	Open/Vacant Land		Reservoir /Tanks
	Crop Land		Water Logged Area
	Transportation		Stadium
	Plantation		

0.3   0   0.3 kilometers

Figure 6.7. Land use/land cover map of Guntur (Zone VIII)

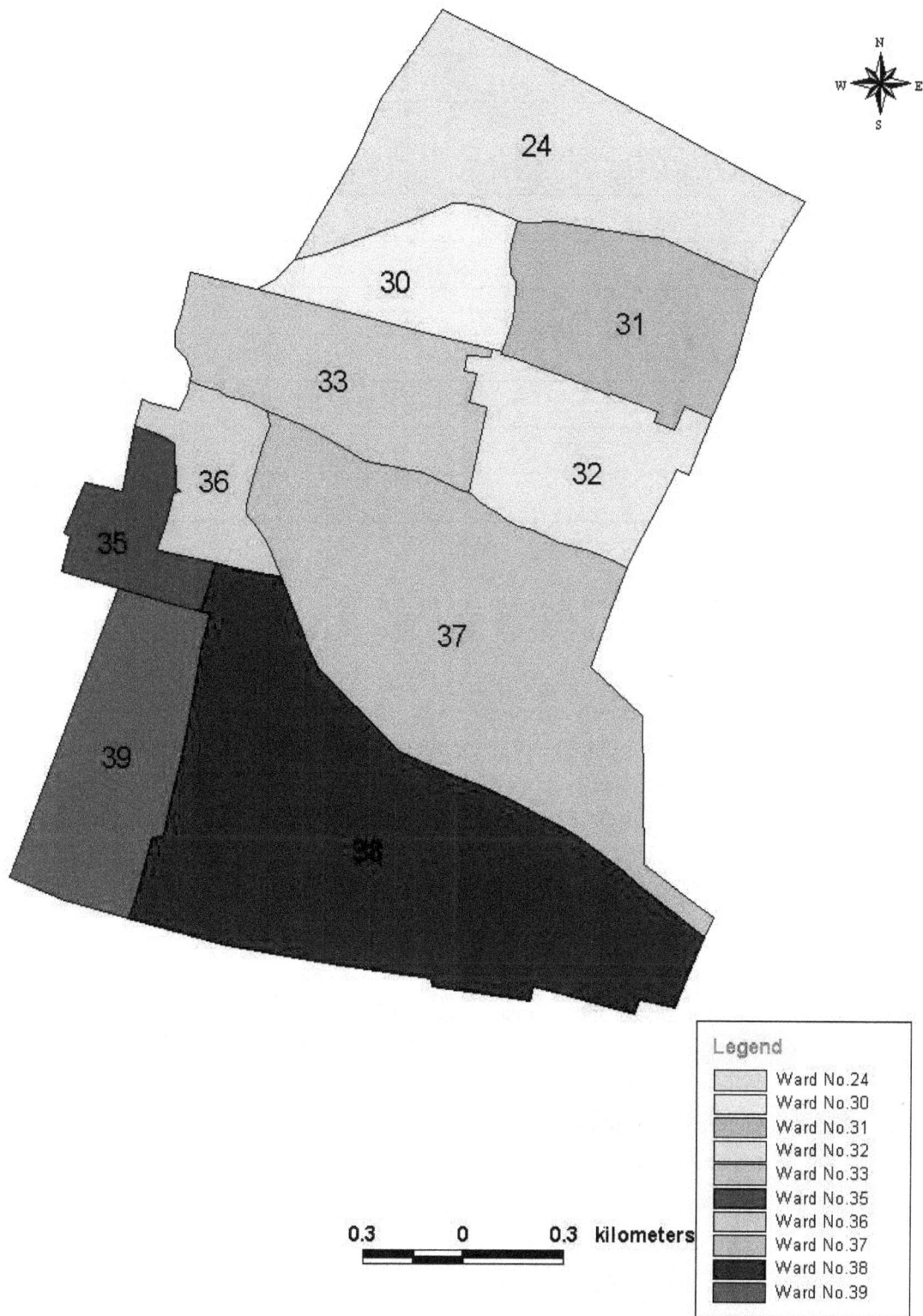

Figure 6.8. The ward map of Guntur (Zone VIII)

Legend
Ward No.24
Ward No.30
Ward No.31
Ward No.32
Ward No.33
Ward No.35
Ward No.36
Ward No.37
Ward No.38
Ward No.39

0.3　　0　　0.3　kilometers

Table 6.1. Major land use classes found in Guntur (Zone VIII)	
Land use category	Area (km^2)
Residential area	2.11
Mixed urban	0.45
Open/vacant land	0.04
Crop land	0.77
Transportation	0.11
Plantation	0.33
Other built-up land	0.01
Stadium	0.07
Waterlogged area	0.14
Water bodies	0.03

Environmental maps

As discussed in Section 5.5.2 of Chapter 5, environmental maps are created from soil maps, groundwater maps and pressure zone maps. For the case study the following observations were made:

- The groundwater depth in Guntur is low (much lower than the water distribution pipes), and hence a groundwater zone map was not required.

- In the Guntur study area the soil is homogenous and is fully covered by black cotton soil. Hence there is no need for a soil zone map.

- Field study indicated that the pressures in the water distribution in Guntur study are low. Hence a pressure zone map is not required.

6.4.5.2 Construction of network database

Data preparation includes the construction of network data required for the contaminant ingress and pipe condition assessment models. Note the details of all the attributes required to run these models are given in Chapters 2 and 3.

The following GIS network maps were prepared for the study area:

1. Water distribution system network
2. Sewer system
3. Canals/open drainage network
4. Surface foul water body.

The steps involved in preparation of the network maps for IRA-WDS are as follows (see also Section 5.5.2 of Book 4):

1. Creation of appropriate shape-files: These are GIS files that contain the spatial information of all objects considered by IRA-WDS

140

2. Input of additional model data: These files contain specific characteristics of the objects generated in the shape-files.

In order to implement the above steps for the study area network maps, the following was performed (refer to Chapter 2 of Book 4 for more information):

- Maps converted from AUTOCAD to GIS format

- Nodes created for each of the networks (junctions and locations where there is a change in the characteristics of a link).

- Unique identification (IDs) assigned to all elements/links and nodes

- Shape-files generated containing key attribute data (IDs, elevation, length, diameter, material, etc.)

- Additional attribute data added to shape-files using the spreadsheets ('Data requirement Ingress Model.xls' for Contaminant Ingress Model and 'Data requirement PCA Model.xls' for Pipe Condition Assessment Model) enclosed with IRA-WDS.

Water distribution network

Figure 6.9 shows the water distribution network model for zone VIII (study area). Tables 6.2 and 6.3 show the attributes included in the link and nodal shape-files for the water distribution system from the data collected for the contamination ingress model. Table 6.4 and 6.5 show the attributes included in the link and nodal shape-files for the pipe condition assessment model.

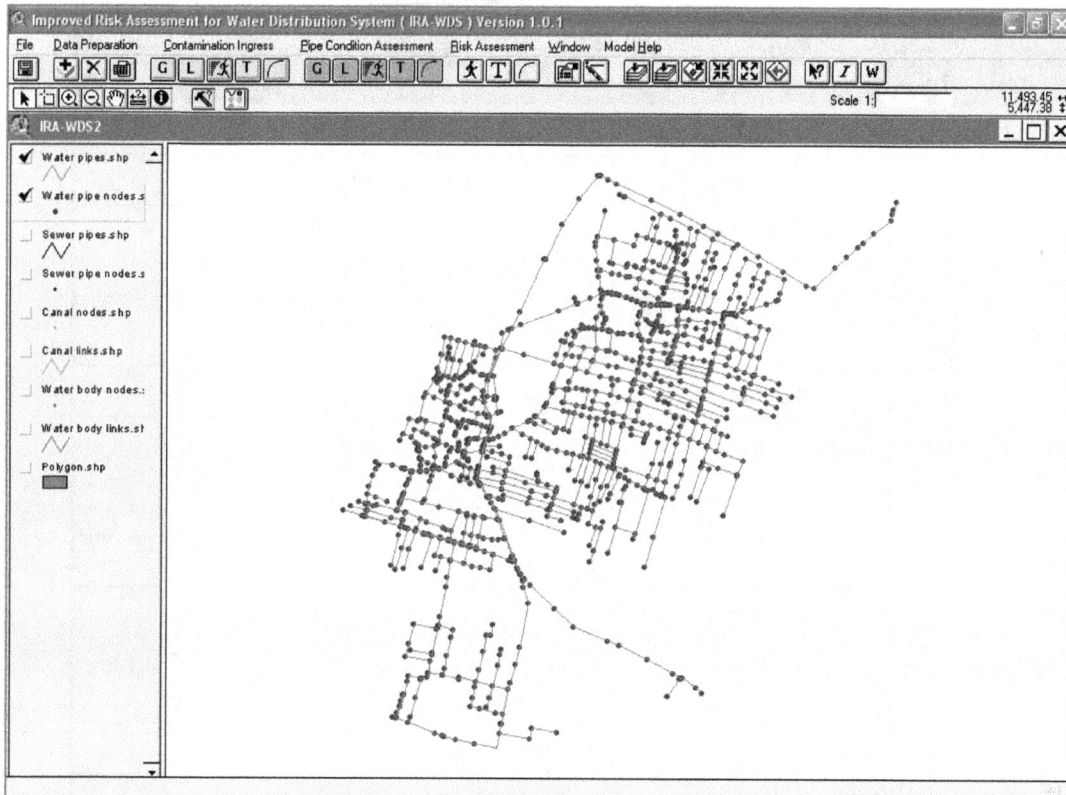

Figure 6.9. Water distribution network model for zone VIII of Guntur

Table 6.2. Attributes included in the link shape-files for water distribution system for contaminant ingress model

Data Name	Data Type	Descriptions
Pipe ID	Integer	Unique ID for each pipe
Start node ID	Integer	Node ID at pipe's starting point
End node ID	Integer	Node ID at pipe's ending point

Table 6.3 Attributes included in the node shape-files for water distribution system for contaminant ingress model

Attribute	Data Type	Description
Node ID	Integer	Unique ID
Node coordinate (x)	Float	Unit in metres
Node coordinate (y)	Float	Unit in m
Node coordinate (z)	Float	Unit in m
Bury depth	Float	Unit in m
Elevation	Float	Unit in m

Table 6.4. Attributes included in the link shape-files for water distribution system for pipe condition assessment model

Data Name	Data Type	Descriptions
Pipe ID	Integer	Unique ID for each pipe
Start node ID	Integer	Node ID at pipe's starting point
End node ID	Integer	Node ID at pipe's ending point
Pipe diameter	Float	In mm
Pipe material	Char	CI=cast iron; PVC=polyvinyl chloride; RCC=reinforced concrete; ASB or AC=asbestos cement
Pipe length	Float	In metres
Year of installation	Integer	Unit in year
Traffic loading	Integer	0=very busy; 1=busy; 2=normal; 3=quiet; 4=very quiet
Complaint frequency	Float	In times/year
Break frequency	Float	In times/year
Pipe location	Integer	0=very hard; 1=hard; 2=grassed; 3=open land; 4=water body

Table 6.5. Attributes included in the node shape-files for water distribution system for pipe condition assessment model

Attribute	Data Type	Description
Node ID	Integer	Unique ID
Node coordinate (x)	Float	In metres
Node coordinate (y)	Float	In metres
Node coordinate (z)	Float	In metres
Bury depth	Float	In metres
Elevation	Float	In metres
Joint type	Char	CID, Clamped, Collar, FW, lead
Number of connected pipes	Integer	Number of pipes at a joint

Sewer network

Figure 6.10 shows the sewer network model for zone VIII (study area). Tables 6.6 and 6.7 show link and nodal shape-files for the sewer network from the data collected, for the contaminant ingress model

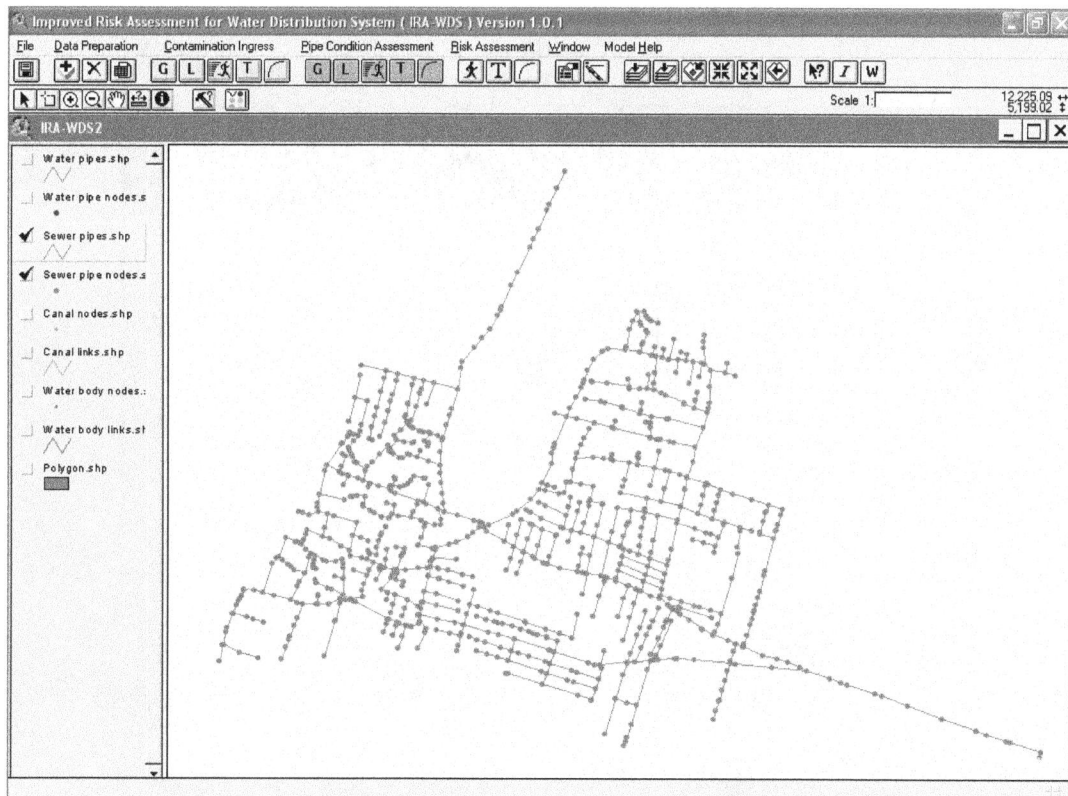

Figure 6.10. Sewer network model for zone VIII of Guntur

Table 6.6. Attributes included in the link shape-files for sewer system		
Attribute	**Data Type**	**Description**
Pipe ID	Integer	Unique ID for each pipe
Start node ID	Integer	Node ID at pipe's starting point
End node ID	Integer	Node ID at pipe's end point
Pipe diameter	Float	In mm
Pipe material	Char	Such as SWP, RCC.
Pipe length	Float	In metres
Pipe age (year installed)	Integer	Unit in year
Road loading above pipe	Integer	0=very quiet; 1=quiet; 2=normal; 3=quiet busy; 4=busy; 5=very busy. (prefer to give some numerical value for each category)
Pipe location	Integer	0=main road-urban; 1=main road-suburban/rural; 2=light road; 3=footpath; 4=others (prefer to indicate the type of area)
Sewer use/purpose	Integer	0=combined; 1=foul; 2=surface water;
Slope	Float	
Soil condition	Integer	0=non-aggressive; 1= slightly aggressive; 2=moderately aggressive; 3=highly aggressive; 4=very highly aggressive

Table 6.7. Attributes included in the node shape-files for sewer system		
Data Name	**Data Type**	**Descriptions**
Node ID	Integer	Unique ID for each node
Node coordinate (x)	Float	In metres
Node coordinate (y)	Float	In metres
Node coordinate (z)	Float	In metres
Bury depth	Float	In metres
Elevation	Float	In metres

Canal/open drain network

Figure 6.11 shows the canal/open drain network model for zone VIII (study area). Tables 6.8 and 6.9 show the link and nodal shape-files for the canal/open drain network from the data collected, for contaminant ingress model.

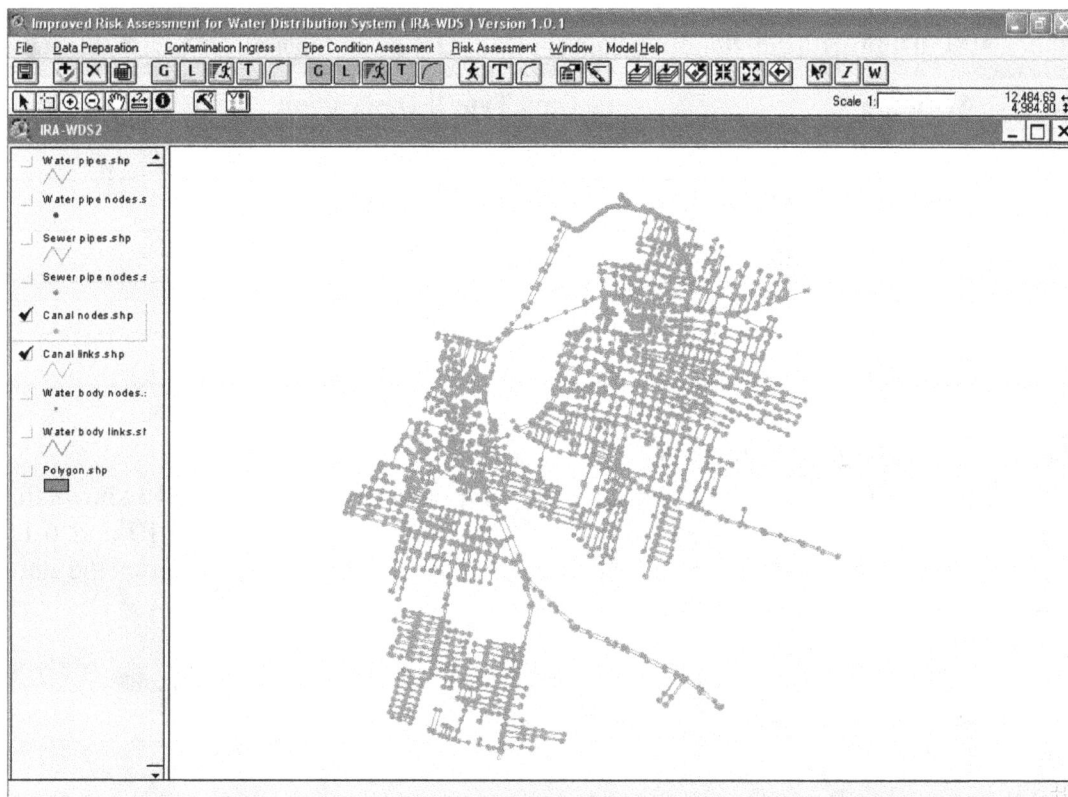

Figure 6.11. Canal/open drain network model for zone VIII of Guntur

No.	Attribute	Data Type	Description
Table 6.8. Attributes included in the link shape files for canal/open drain system			
1	Drainage canal ID	Integer	Unique ID for each link
2	Start point ID	Integer	Node ID at starting point of link
3	Endpoint ID	Integer	Node ID at ending point of link
4	Type of cross-section	Char	Circular, rectangular, triangular, trapezoidal, etc.
5	Cross-section	Float	Width, depth, angle, etc.
6	Length of canals	Float	In metres
7	Slope	Float	
8	Bed protection	Boolean	1=bed lining; 0=unlining
9	Soil condition	Integer	0=non-aggressive; 1= slightly aggressive; 2=moderately aggressive; 3=highly aggressive; 4=very highly aggressive

No.	Attribute	Data Type	Description
Table 6.9. Attributes included in the node shape files for canal/open drain system			
1	Canal node ID	Integer	Unique ID for each node
2	Canal node coordinate (x)	Float	In metres
3	Canal node coordinate (y)	Float	In metres
4	Canal node coordinate (z)	Float	In metres
5	Water depth	Float	In metres

Surface foul water bodies network

Surface foul water bodies are represented as polygon networks. Figure 6.12 shows the foul water bodies network model for zone VIII (study area). Tables 6.10 and 6.11 show the link and nodal shape-files for the foul water body networks from the data collected, for use in the contaminant ingress model.

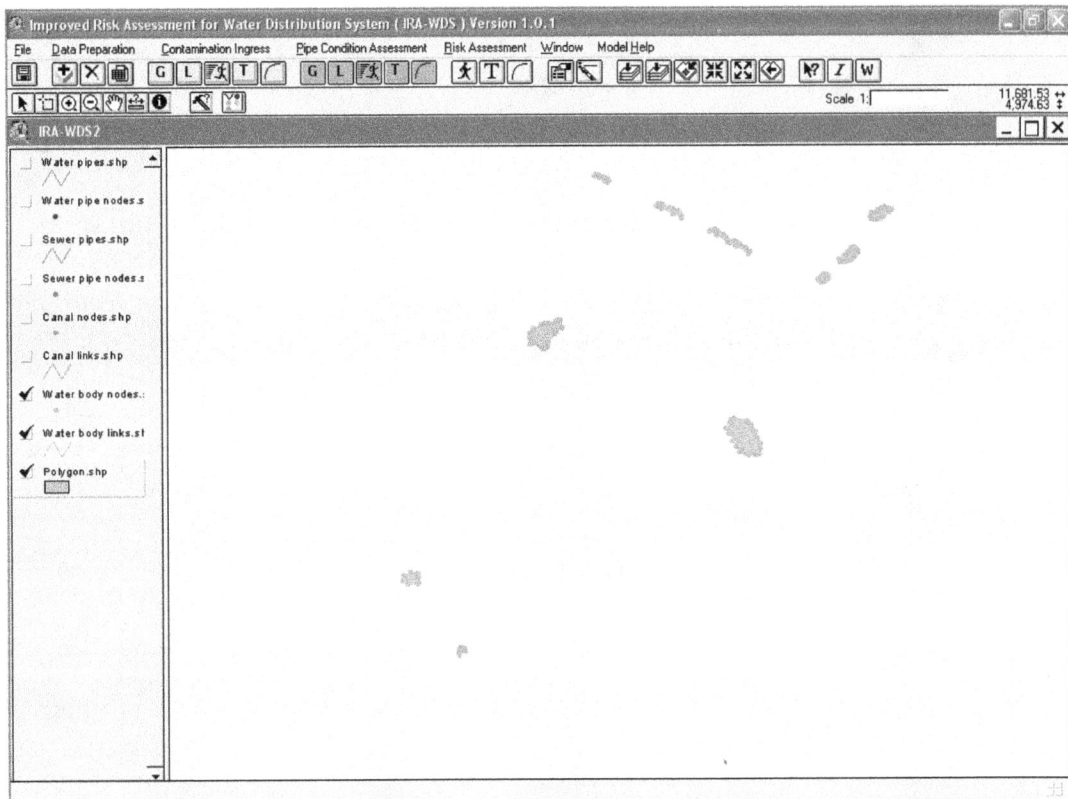

Figure 6.12. Surface foul water bodies network model for zone VIII of Guntur

Table 6.10. Attributes included in the link shape-files for surface foul water bodies			
No.	Attribute	Data Type	Description
1	link ID	Integer	Unique ID for each link
2	Start node ID	Integer	Node ID at starting point of link
3	End node ID	Integer	Node ID at ending point of link
4	Water depth	Float	In metres
5	Slope of water body bed	Float	Distance/elevation

Table 6.11. Attributes included in the node shape files for foul water bodies.			
No.	Attribute	Data Type	Description
1	Node ID	Integer	Unique ID for each node
2	Node coordinate (x)	Float	In metres
3	Node coordinate (y)	Float	In metres
4	Node coordinate (z)	Float	In metres

6.5 Model Application

Using the data collected, the maps, database and shape-files generated, the contaminant ingress, pipe condition assessment and risk assessment models were run using IRA-WDS. Details on how to execute these models through IRA-WDS are given in Chapters 4, 5 and 6 of Book 4. Below is a brief summary of the outputs obtained.

6.5.1 Contaminant ingress model

Figures 6.13 and 6.14 and Table 6.12 show the results obtained from the contaminant ingress model for the study area. The SPCZ shown in Figure 6.13 indicates that some water distribution pipes are within the contaminant zone of the pollution sources (sewers, canal/open drains and foul water bodies). A hazard map that is derived from SPCZ and contaminant concentration at upstream and downstream of SPCZ is given in Figure 6.14. Thus these outputs give an indication of the sections of water pipes that are in danger of being contaminated and highlights the risk areas within water distribution system due to pollution sources.

Figure 6.13. SPCZ map for Guntur (Zone VIII)

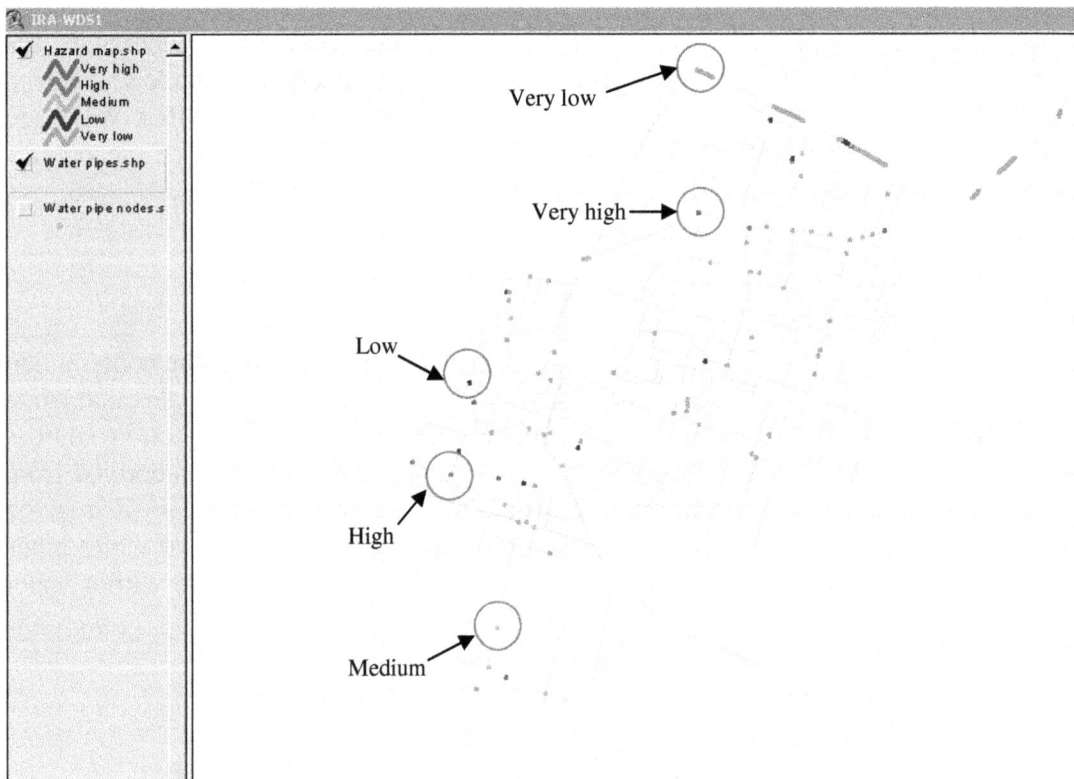

Figure 6.14. Hazard map for Guntur (Zone VIII)

Table 6.12. Results obtained from the contaminant ingress model for Guntur (Zone VIII)

Pipe ID	Start pollution point			End pollution point			Start C/C_o	End C/C_o	Pollution sources
	X	Y	Z	X	Y	Z			
305	12717.77	4545.922	24.50268	12717.58	4545.966	24.50225	0.028168	0.002896	Sewer 228
305	12743.89	4540.023	24.56024	12738.08	4541.334	24.54745	0.028168	0.128344	Sewer 809
303	12743.95	4506.873	24.47796	12745.82	4513.557	24.49958	0.009858	1	Sewer 811
313	12949.24	4146.949	21.21824	12951.1	4147.349	21.2079	1.14E-06	1.3E-07	Canal 1
823	12936.75	4117.176	21.42281	12937.86	4117.172	21.44787	3.4E-07	1	Canal 4
395	12932.87	4093.07	21.11469	12931.81	4093.229	21.10199	0.00014	8.75E-05	Canal 6
397	12908.37	4001.869	21.14883	12909.64	4001.574	21.14137	1.25E-05	9E-08	Canal 10
403	12901.88	3967.267	20.97322	12902.84	3967.049	20.96998	0.000172	1.31E-06	Canal 11
412	12957.66	3874.648	20.43584	12958.37	3874.517	20.43235	3.36E-05	0.000127	Canal 15
288	12815.99	4401.565	23.00558	12815.83	4401.658	23.0077	0	1.1E-07	Canal 33
285	12742.89	4351.888	22.5018	12742.95	4352.129	22.50285	3E-08	4E-08	Canal 36
300	12755.67	4440.881	24.194	12755.81	4441.425	24.194	5.82E-05	0.000104	Canal 37
202	12846.43	4221.799	21.85554	12846.31	4221.378	21.86952	2E-08	0.000126	Canal 44
229	12833.27	4091.534	21.15412	12833.05	4090.918	21.15261	2E-07	7E-08	Canal 53
263	12684.32	4110.998	22.03195	12684.3	4111.65	22.03903	0	1.1E-07	Canal 56
271	12607.54	4119.167	23.6308	12607.71	4119.558	23.64173	0.000129	0.004953	Canal 57
240	12832.75	4062.247	21.70734	12833.12	4062.112	21.70574	2.29E-05	7.55E-06	Canal 65
272	12611.61	4000.205	22.06734	12611.5	3999.812	22.07219	4.5E-07	2.49E-06	Canal 84
159	12514.88	3839.469	21.36859	12515.22	3840.397	21.36522	0.000376	7.01E-05	Canal 95
136	12513.03	3840.152	21.00388	12513.37	3841.08	21.01054	1.4E-07	1.97E-06	Canal 95
169	12627.01	3846.049	21.09016	12625.44	3846.37	21.09291	4.15E-05	1.31E-06	Canal 99

149

The hazard to water distribution pipes resulting from pollution sources is classified into five groups ranging from very high to very low, as shown in Figure 6.14. The percentage of water distribution pipes falling in each group is given in Table 6.13. It is seen that over 50 per cent of water distribution pipes are under very low hazard. As few as 11.4 per cent of water distribution pipes (57 pipes) are classified as under very high to high hazards. It is necessary to investigate the vulnerability of these pipes and, if these are vulnerable to hazards, immediate actions are required for these 57 pipes to avoid potential water quality deterioration that may cause related disease outbreaks. The possible remedial actions are to replace and rehabilitate water distribution pipes (if vulnerable to hazards) and clear up and reinforce pollution sources which are responsible for hazard. Thus the hazard map aids engineers to prioritize a maintenance programme for risk mitigation in order to meet tight budget constraints.

Table 6.13. Hazard group classification		
Groups	**Number of pipes**	**Percentage (%)**
Very high	34	4.10
High	23	2.75
Medium	80	9.56
Low	54	6.45
Very low	309	36.92

6.5.2 Pipe condition assessment model

6.5.2.1 Inputs for model

<u>Water pipe indicators</u> Among the 20 water pipe indicators for the pipe condition assessment model (shown in Sections 3.1 and 3.3 of Chapter 3), only nine indicators were used (due to availability) for the Guntur study area. These are listed in Table 6.14 and Figure 6.15.

Indicators	Weightings	Balance factors
Table 6.14. Pipe condition assessment indicators used for the study		
First level indicators		
Diameter	0.3	1
Length	0.2	1
Material	0.5	1
Joint method	0.4	1
Number of connections	0.6	1
Bury depth	0.3	1
Traffic density	0.7	1
Pipe age	0.7	1
Surface permeability	0.3	1
Second level indicators		
Pipe indicators	0.4	2
Installation indicators	0.6	2
Corrosion indicators	0.5	2
Strength indicators	0.5	2
Breakage	1.0	2
Third level indicators		
Physical indicators	0.6	3
Environmental indicators	0.4	3

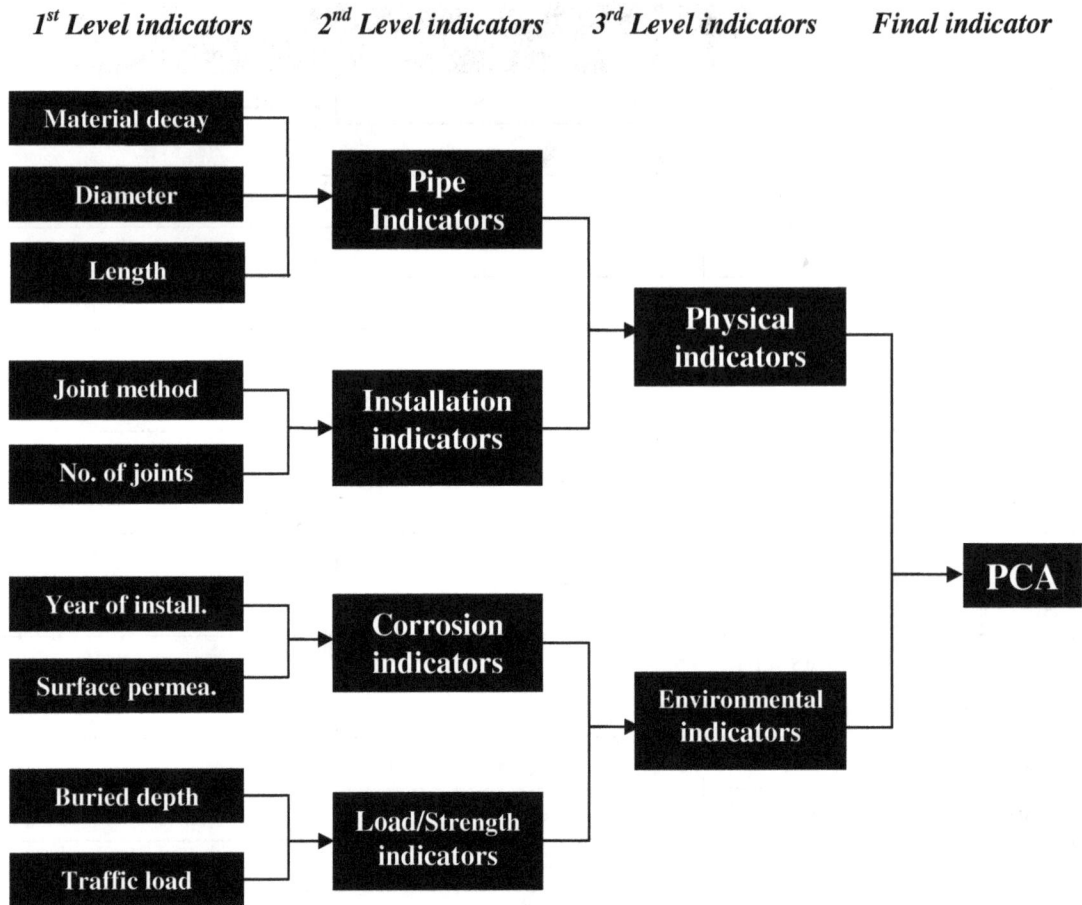

Figure 6.15. Composite structure of pipe condition assessment indicators for case study area

Weighting and balance factors

- For the case study, the weightings for pipe indicators were obtained from interviews with experienced engineers in the field. The engineers were asked to respond to the questionnaires shown in Appendix D, to give their opinion on the relative importance of each indicator. The analytical hierarchy process (AHP – see Section 3.4.4 of Chapter 3) was then used to derive the weights for each indicator in each group. The weights used for Guntur are shown in Column 2 of Table 6.14.

- For the case study, the balance factors used were established using engineering judgement. As explained in Section 3.4.3, balance factors indicate the degree of compromise among the pipe indicators in the same group. The balance factors used in the Guntur study are shown in Column 3 of Table 6.14.

Membership functions There are three fuzzy indicators used in the pipe condition assessment model for the Guntur study area, i.e. pipe material corrosion index, traffic load and surface permeability. The membership functions used are shown in Figure 6.16.

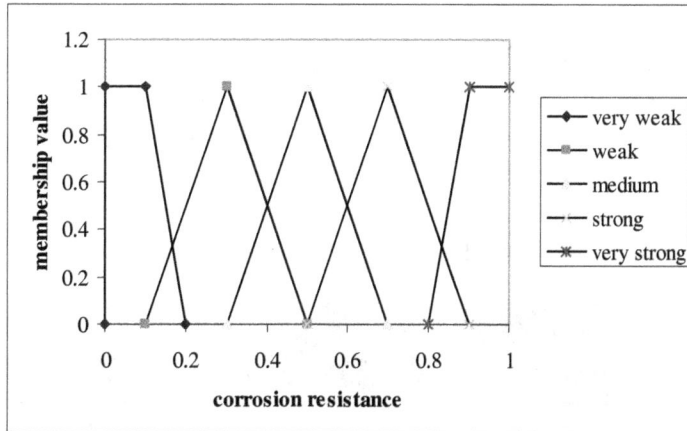

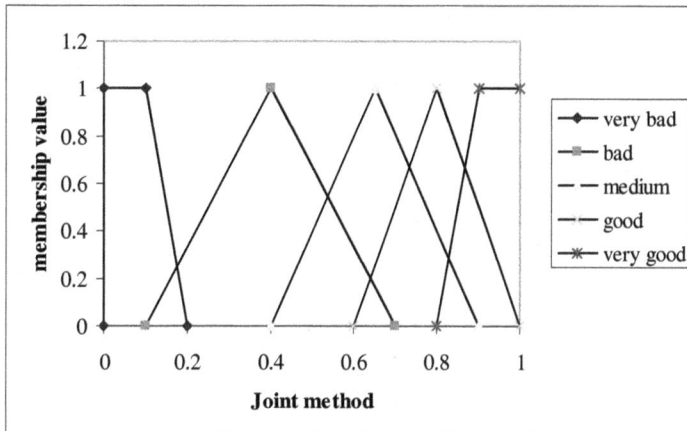

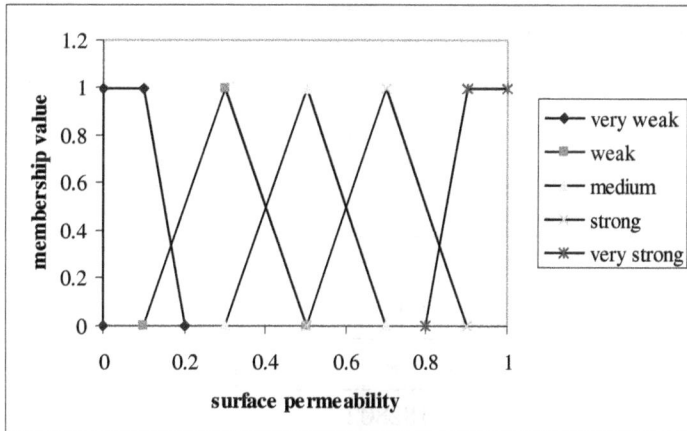

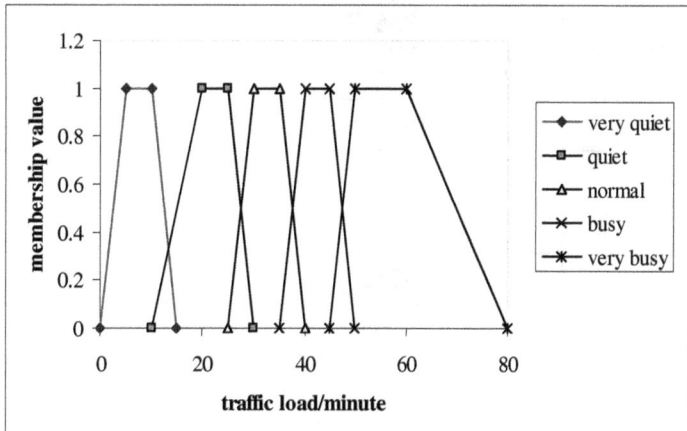

Figure 6.16. Membership functions used for the study

153

6.5.2.2 Model output

The output from the pipe condition assessment model gives details of the pipe condition index for each pipe and a respective pipe condition group. Typical outputs from the pipe condition assessment model are shown in Table 6.15. It can be noted from Table 6.16 that the pipe conditions for the case study area are divided into five groups described as very bad to very good (see Figure 6.17). Table 6.16 shows the number of pipes falling into each pipe condition group.

Table 6.15. Typical output from the pipe condition assessment model for Guntur (Zone VIII)		
Pipe ID	**Pipe condition index**	**Pipe condition groups**
779	0.043009	1
598	0.123034	1
674	0.127655	1
791	0.157856	2
470	0.157925	2
594	0.160561	2
722	0.160912	2
683	0.161229	2
652	0.165564	2
464	0.168525	2
675	0.172551	2
593	0.173336	2
468	0.177353	2
474	0.178039	2
473	0.179092	2
649	0.179634	2
588	0.182802	2
656	0.183607	2
734	0.183849	2
785	0.184558	2
795	0.18582	2
361	0.186374	2
467	0.187123	2
650	0.188046	2

154

Table 6.16. Water pipe condition groups		
Pipe condition groups	**Number of pipes**	**Percentage (%)**
Very bad	2	0.24
Bad	44	5.26
Medium	394	47.07
Good	389	46.48
Very good	8	0.95

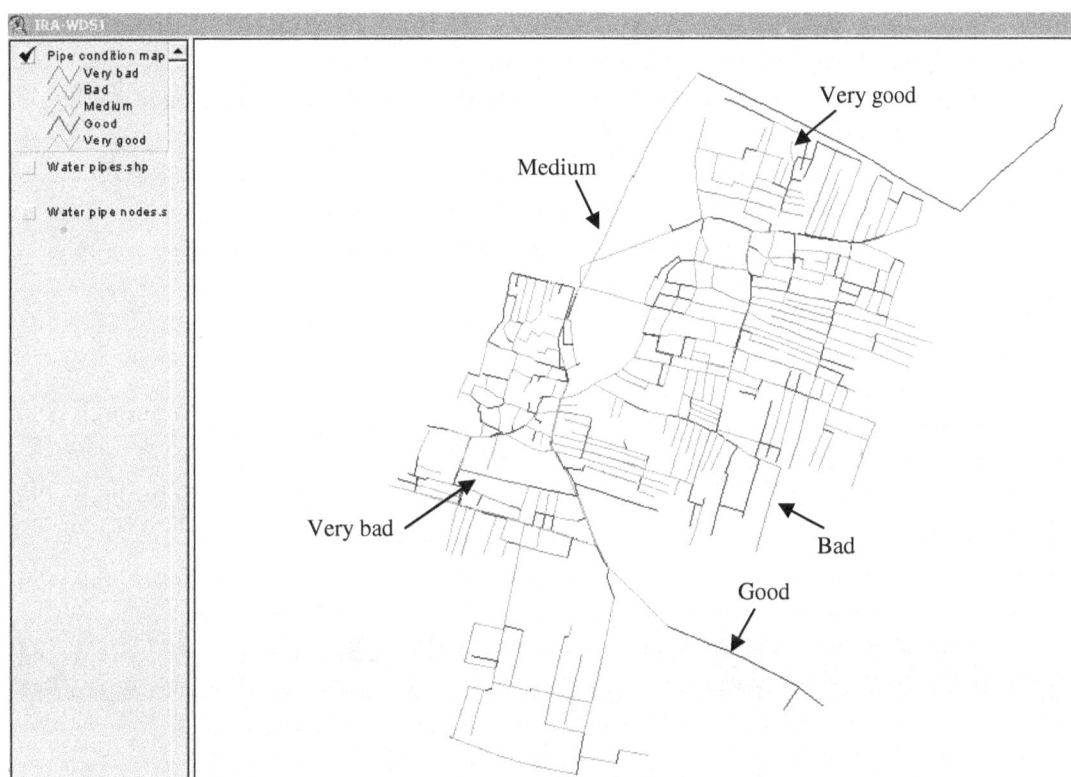

Figure 6.17. Results obtained from the pipe condition assessment model for Guntur (Zone VIII)

Table 6.16 shows that about 94 per cent of the pipes are classified as medium to very good. The percentage of pipes that are classified as bad to very bad is only 5.5 per cent. There is a negligible percentage of pipes (0.24 per cent) that are marked as very bad, indicating that there is no alarming situation for the pipe rehabilitation. On the other hand, almost half of the pipes are classified as very good to good. The results indicate that although the current situation is not bad because 50 per cent of the pipes subjected to medium risk, of these 5.26 per cent are bad and only 0.24 per cent are marked very bad indicating that the authorities need to be prepared for a rehabilitation programme.

There is often a limited budget for a water municipality to rehabilitate its water distribution system. Therefore, there is a need to prioritize the limited budget for the rehabilitation of the worst pipe. The results from this model will enable decision-makers to prioritize their investments in terms of rehabilitation. For example, the model predicts that currently two pipes are in very bad condition. These pipes need to be rehabilitated immediately; otherwise there will be a risk to health because of contaminant intrusion. Both are RCC pipes of 100 mm diameter and are over 20 years old. Due to the weak strength of RCC pipe, lining or slip lining is not appropriate. Therefore replacement of these two pipes is recommended. The results also indicate that 44 pipes are in bad condition. The municipal authority can prepare rehabilitation programme for these pipes. This may include:

- Lining 20 AC pipes: these AC pipes are less than 15 years old, but due to the traffic and soil condition, these pipes deteriorate very fast. Lining would reduce internal deterioration especially chemical attack.
- Replace 14 RCC pipes: these RCC pipes are older than 20 years with smaller diameter and weak in physical strength. Therefore replacement of these pipes is appropriate.
- Slip lining 10 CI pipes: this would improve the physical strength and hydraulic capacity of these pipes.

6.5.3 Risk assessment model

6.5.3.1 Model outputs

Weightings

For the case study area, the weightings for the risk factors were obtained from interviews with experienced engineers in the field. The engineers were asked to respond to the questionnaires shown in Appendix E, to give their opinion on the relative pipe condition in relation to contamination. Table 6.17 shows the risk factors obtained.

Table 6.17. Risk factors for risk assessment	
Risk factors	**Weightings**
Section of pipe in contaminant zone and contaminant concentration (hazard)	0.4
Pipe condition (vulnerability)	0.6

6.5.3.2 Model outputs

The output from applying the risk assessment model to the case study are shown in Figure 6.18 and Table 6.18. The risk of contaminant intrusion for the case study area is divided into five groups, i.e. very high, high medium, low and very low (as shown in the risk map of Figure 6.18). Table 6.19 shows the number of pipes falling into each risk group and it is observed that a majority of water pipes (52.2 per cent) are in medium to low risk areas. However, 7.6 per cent of water pipes are in high risk areas and need action to mitigate against the risk of intrusion of contaminated water.

The risk is an interaction between the hazard of pollution sources and the vulnerability of water distribution system. Table 6.20 selects a few pipes from the risk map given in Figure 6.18 to show the derivation of risk from hazard and vulnerability. From the contaminant ingress model, pipe no. 98 has a very high hazard ranking (grade 1) due to its proximity to canal no. 248 and results in a high contaminant concentration. From the pipe condition assessment model, the pipe no. 98 is also assigned a high vulnerability (grade 2) as it is a small diameter AC pipe with a number of service connections and joints. In addition, it is located under a busy road which increases its traffic loadings. The combination of the very high hazard and the high vulnerability of pipe no. 98 gives a high risk for contaminant intrusion. In a similar way, other pipes are assigned risk grades based on the hazard and vulnerability derived from contaminant ingress model and pipe condition assessment model respectively.

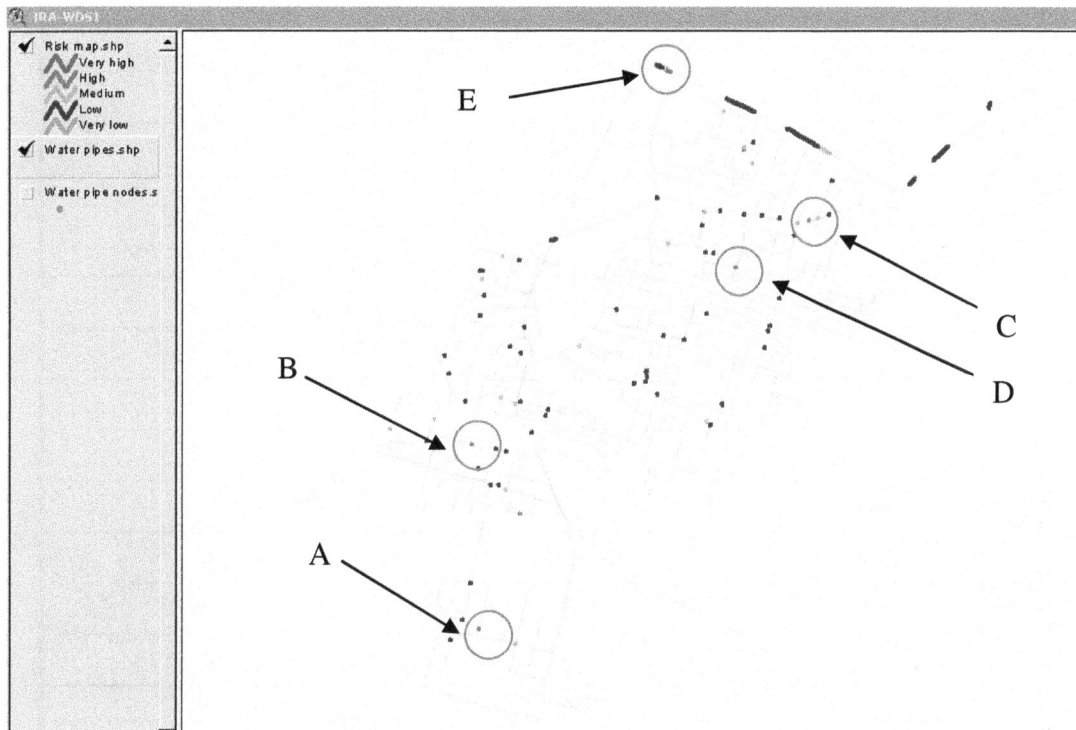

Figure 6.18. Results obtained from the risk assessment model for Guntur (Zone VIII)

Table 6.18. Typical output from the risk assessment model for Guntur (Zone VIII)

Pipe ID	Risk Index	Risk groups
779	0.483939	3
674	0.526132	3
791	0.541186	3
594	0.542534	3
683	0.542867	3
675	0.548511	3
686	0.602601	4
466	0.603477	4
604	0.603488	4
544	0.604466	4
740	0.604844	4
360	0.60511	4
357	0.606963	4
440	0.60763	4
525	0.607685	4
601	0.608237	4
602	0.608401	4
820	0.608807	4
673	0.609064	4
682	0.609359	4
592	0.611511	4
493	0.611668	4
796	0.611992	4
769	0.612234	4
732	0.612291	4
766	0.612311	4
487	0.612323	4
669	0.612385	4
358	0.612472	4
451	0.612513	4
449	0.612549	4

Table 6.19. Risk assessment groups		
Risk group	**Number of pipes**	**Percentage (%)**
Very high	2	0.23
High	62	7.40
Medium	82	9.80
Low	347	41.50
Very low	7	0.84

Table 6.20. A comparison among risk, hazard and vulnerability			
Pipe ID	**Hazard**	**Vulnerability**	**Risk**
98	1	2	1
576	3	1	2
395	4	2	3
508	5	4	4
765	5	4	5

The main factors that contribute to the 7.6 per cent of pipes subjected to high and very high risk are the open drains in the study areas and pipes with many joints and connections (high hazard with high vulnerability). Also, high risk is observed in areas where there are surface foul water bodies coupled with poor condition pipes (high hazard with medium vulnerability). From the risk map in Figure 6.18, several recommendations can be made to reduce the risk of contaminant intrusion. These include:

- Replace/rehabilitate one AC pipe which is found to be in bad condition and has very high susceptibility to contaminant intrusion (e.g. risk area A).
- Undertake a leakage detection and repair programme in areas that have pipes with many joints and connections (e.g. risk area B);
- Inspect open drains and reline where necessary (e.g. risk area C);
- Provide protection to water pipes in areas where they are close to the open drains (risk areas D);
- De-water and fill foul water bodies in the north-east (e.g. risk area E).

6.6 Concluding Remarks

One of the major benefits of using the developed methodology in the form of IRA-WDS is that it is possible for the decision-makers to gauge the impacts of the above recommendations on the risk index. This can be achieved by simply modifying the database appropriately and re-running the model.

It should be noted that the outputs from this model can than be coupled with a water network quality model (EPANET (Rossman 1994)) to show the movement of contamination within the distribution system. This will enable the decision-makers to identify areas and consumers most at risk to contaminated water. This can be achieved by first adding dummy input pollutant nodes to areas where the risk assessment model shows a high risk of contamination. Then by adding pollutant loads at these nodes it is possible to simulate their propagation in the network to identify areas and consumers most at risk. An example of such an application to the case study area is shown in Appendix F.

References

Akcakaya, H.R. (1994). 'GIS enhances endangered species conservation efforts.' *GIS World*, 7, 36-40.

Andrews, J.D., and Moss, T.J. (2002). *Reliability and Risk Assessment*, Professional Engineering Publishing Ltd. London and Bury St. Edmunds, UK.

AWWARF. (1989). 'Economics of Internal Corrosion Control.'

AWWARF/DVGW. (1986). 'Internal Corrosion of Water Distribution Systems.'

AWWSC. (2002). 'Deteriorating buried infrastructure management challenges and strategies.' White Paper prepared for US Environmental Protection Agency workshop on Distribution System Issues, March 7-8, Voorhees, NJ.

Ballantyne, D., and Moore, D. (1995). 'Relative earthquake vulnerability of water pipes.' Annual Conference Engineering and Operation, Anaheim, California.

Bardossy, A., and Duckstein, L. (1992). 'Analysis of a karstic aquifer management problem by fuzzy composite programming.' *Water Resources Bulletin*, 28(1), 63-73.

Bardossy, A., Bogardi, I., and Duckstein, L. (1985). 'Composite programming as an extension of compromise programming.' Mathematics of multiple objective optimization, P. Serfini, ed., Springer Verlag, Vienna, Austria, 375-408.

Bear, J. (1972). *Dynamics of fluids in porous media*, American Elsevier Publishing Company, Inc., New York.

Besner, M.C., Gauthier, V., Barbeau, B., Millette, R., Chapleau, R., and Prevost, M. (2001). 'Understanding distribution system water quality.' *Journal American Water Works Association*, 93(7), 101-+.

Biggar, J.W., and Nielsen, D.R. (1976). 'Spatial variability of the leaching characteristics of a field soil.' *Water Resources Research*, 12(1), 78-84.

Bonds, W.R. (1989). 'Cement-Mortar Linings for Ductile Iron Pipe.' Ductile Iron Pipe Research Association, 245 Riverchase Parkway East, Suite O Birmingham, Alabama 35244-1856.

Brakensiek, D.L., and Onstad, C.A. (1977). 'Parameter estimation of the Green and Ampt infiltration equation.' *Water Resources Research*, 13, 1009-1012.

Chen, S.H. (1985). 'Ranking fuzzy numbers with maximizing set and minimizing set.' *Fuzzy sets and systems*, 17, 113-129.

Choe, K., and Varley, R. (1997). 'Conservation and Pricing-Does Raising Tariffs to an Economic Price for Water Make the People Worse Off?' Prepared for the 'Best Management Practice for Water Conservation' Workshop, South Africa.

Cooper, N.R., Blakey, G., Sherwin, C., Ta, T., Whiter, J.T., and Woodward, C.A. (2000). 'The use of GIS to develop a probability-based trunk mains burst risk model.' *Urban Water*, 2(2), 97-103.

Craun, G.F., and Calderon, R.L. (2001). 'Waterborne disease outbreaks caused by distribution system deficiencies.' *Journal American Water Works Association*, 93(9), 64-75.

Cunat, P.J. (2001). 'Corrosion Resistance of Stainless Steels in Soils and in Concrete.' Paper presented at the Plenary Days of the Committee on the Study of Pipe Corrosion and Protection, October 2001, Ceocor, Biarritz.

Danon-Schaffer, M.N. (2001). 'Walkerton's contaminated water supply system: a forensic approach to identify the source.' *Environmental Forensics*, 2, 197-200.

Davies, J.P., Clarke, B.A., Whiter, J.T., and Cunningham, R.J. (2001a). 'Factors influencing the structural deterioration and collapse of rigid sewer pipes.' *Urban Water,* 3(1-2), 73-89.

Davies, J. P., Clarke, B. A., Whiter, J. T., Cunningham, R. J., and Leidi, A. (2001b). 'The structural condition of rigid sewer pipes: a statistical investigation.' *Urban Water*, 3(4), 277-286.

Dubois, D., and Prade, H. (1988). *Possibility theory – An approach to computerized processing of uncertainty*, Harding, E.F., translator, Plenum Press, New York.

Eiswirth, M., and Hotzl, H. (1994). 'Groundwater conamination by leaky sewerage systems.' 25th International Conference IAH 'Water Down Under', 21-25 November 1994, Adelaide, Australia.

Enfield, C.G., Carsel, R.F., Cohen, S.E., Phan, T., and Walters, D.M. (1982). 'Approximating pollutant transport to ground water.' *Ground Water*, 20(6), 711-722.

Fedra, K. (1998). 'Integrated risk assessment and management: overview and state of the art.' *Journal of Hazardous Materials*, 61, 5-22.

Fipps, G., and Pope, C. (2004). 'Irrigation District Efficiencies and Potential Water Savings in the Lower Rio Grande Valley of Texas.' Department of Agricultural Engineering, Texas A&M University, Texas.

Galbraith, N.S., Barrett, N.J., and Stanwellsmith, R. (1987). 'Water and disease after Croydon - a review of water-borne and water-associated disease in the UK 1937-86.' *Journal of the Institution of Water and Environmental Management*, 1(1), 7-21.

Galbraith, N.S., Barrett, N., and Stanwell-Smith, R. (1992). 'A review of water-borne and waste-associated disease in the UK 1937-86.' *Journal of the New England Water Works Association*, 106(3), 169-185.

Geldreich, E.E. (1996). *Microbial quality of water supply in distribution systems*, Boca Raton, FL: Lewis Publisher.

Geter, W.F., Smith, P., Drungil, C., Shepherd, R. and Kuenstler, B. (1995). 'Hydrologic Unit Water Quality Model GIS Interface to Four ARS Water Quality Models for Use by Soil Conservation Service.' The International Symposium on Water Quality Modeling, Sponsored by ASAE – The Society for Engineering in Agricultural, Food, and Biological Systems, Orlando, Florida, 341-347.

Green, W.H., and Ampt, G.A. (1911). 'Studies in soil physics. I. The flow of air and water through soils.' *Journal of Agriculture Science*, 4, 1-24.

Guillermo, Y., Ringskog, K., and Shyamal, S. (2001). 'The High Cost of Intermittent Water Supplies.' Water and Sanitation Program, WSP Publications.

Hagemeister, M.E., Jones, D.D., and Woldt, W.E. (1996). 'Hazard ranking of landfills using fuzzy composite programming.' *Journal of Environmental Engineering*, ASCE, 122(4), 248-258.

Hardoy, J.E., Mitlin, D., and Satterthwaite, D. (2001). *Environmental Problems in an Urbanizing World*, Earthscan Publications Ltd, London.

Harr, M.E. (1962). *Groundwater and seepage*, McGraw-Hill Book Company, Inc., New York.

Harter, T., Wagner, S., and Atwill, E.R. (2000). 'Colloid transport and filtration of cryptosporidium parvum in sandy soils and aquifer sediments.' *Environmental Science & Technology*, 34(1), 62-70.

Harvey, R.W., and Garabedian, S.P. (1991). 'Use of colloid filtration theory in modeling movement of bacteria through a contaminated sandy aquifer.' *Environmental Science & Technology*, 25(1), 178-185.

Haverkamp, R., Parlange, J.Y., Starr, J.L., Schmitz, and Fuentes, C. (1990). 'Infiltration under ponded condition: 3. A predictive equation based on physical parameters.' *Soil Science*, 149, 292-300.

Haverkamp, R., Ross, P.J., and Parlange, J.Y. (1994). 'Three dimensional analysis of infiltration from the disc infiltrometer, 2. Physically based infiltration equation.' *Water Resources Research*, 30, 2931-2935.

Hillel, D. (1982). Introduction to soil physics, Academic Press, New York.

Hornung, M., Bull, K.R., Cresser, M., Ullyett, J., Hall, J.R., Langan, S., Loveland, P.J., and Wilson, M.J. (1994). 'The sensitivity of surface waters of Great Britain to acidification predicted from catchment characteristics.' *Environmental Pollution*, 87, 207-214.

How, C.F.H. (1998). 'Fugitive Emissions of VOCs from Industrial Sewer Networks: Integration of naUTilus and ArcView,' Master's Thesis, Univ. Texas, Austin.

Jones, D., and Barnes, E.M. (2000). 'Fuzzy composite programming to combine remote sensing and crop models for decision support in precision crop management.' *Agricultural Systems*, 65, 137-158.

Kaufmann, A., and Gupta, M.M. (1991). *Introduction to fuzzy arithmetic: Theory and applications*, Van Nostrand Reinhold, New York.

Kiene, L., Lu, W., and Levi, Y. (1998). 'Relative importance of the phenomena responsible for chlorine decay in drinking water distribution systems.' *Water Science and Technology*, 38(6), 219-227.

King, R.C. and Crocker, S.B. (1967). *Piping Handbook*. McGraw-Hill Book Company, London.

Kirmeyer, G.J., Friedman, M., Martel, K., Howie, D., LeChevallier, M., Abbzszadegan, M., Karim, M., Funk, J., and Harbour, J. (2001). 'Pathogen intrusion into the distribution system.' AWWA Research Foundation and the American Water Works Association, Denver, CO.

Kleiner, Y., and Rajani, B. (2001). 'Comprehensive review of structural deterioration of water mains: statistical models.' *Urban Water*, 3(3), 131-150.

Kramer, M.H., Herwaldt, B.L., Craun, G.F., Calderon, R.L., and Juranek, D.D. (1996). 'Waterborne disease: 1993 and 1994.' *Journal American Water Works Association*, 88(3), 66-80.

Kumar, L., Skidmore, A.K., and Knowles, E. (1997). 'Modeling topographic variation in solar radiation in a GIS environment.' *International Journal of Geographic Information Science*, 11, 475-497.

LeChevallier, M.W. (1999). 'The case for maintaining a disinfectant residual.' *Journal American Water Works Association*, 91(1), 86-94.

Lee, Y.W., Bogardi, I., and Stansbury, J. (1991). 'Fuzzy decision making in dredged-material management.' *Journal of Environmental Engineering*, ASCE, 117(5), 614-629.

Lee, Y.W., Dahab, M.F., and Bogardi, I. (1992). 'Nitrate risk management under uncertainty.' *Journal of Water Resources Planning and Management*, ASCE, 118(2), 151-165.

Lerner, D.N. (1994). *The impact of sewers on groundwater quality*, Thomas Telford, London.

Lindley, T.R., and Buchberger, S.G. (2002). 'Assessing intrusion susceptibility in distribution systems.' *Journal American Water Works Association*, 94(6), 66.

Lippy, E.C., and Waltrip, S.C. (1984). 'Waterborne Disease Outbreaks 1946-1980 - a 35-Year Perspective.' *Journal American Water Works Association*, 76(2), 60-67.

Loganathan, G.V., Park, S., and Sherali, H.D. (2002). 'Threshold break rate for pipeline replacement in water distribution systems.' *Journal of Water Resources Planning and Management*, ASCE, 128(4), 271-279.

Maidment, D.R. (1992). 'A Grid-Network Procedure for Hydrologic Modelling.', Report prepared for the Hydrologic Engineering Center, US Army Corps of Engineers, Davis, California.

McIntosh, A.C. (2003). 'Asian Water Supplies, Reaching the Urban Poor.', Asian Development Bank, Manila.

McIntosh, A., and Yniguez, C. (1997). *Second Water Utilities Data Book - Asia and Pacific Region*. Asian Development Bank.

McNeill, L.S., and Edwards, M. (2001). 'Iron pipe corrosion in distribution systems.' *Journal American Water Works Association*, 93(7), 88-100.

Meyer, P.D., Rockhold, M.L., and Gee, G.W. (1997). 'Uncertainty Analyses of Infiltration and Subsurface Flow and Transport for SDMP Sites.', Division of Regulatory Applications, Office of Nuclear Regulatory Research, U.S. Nuclear Regulatory Commission, Washington, DC 20555-0001, NRC Job Code W6503.

Mitchell, G.N., and McDonald, A.T. (1995). 'Catchment characterisation as a tool for upland water quality management.' *Journal of Environmental Management*, 43, 83-95.

Mizgalewicz, P. (1996). 'Agrichemical Transport in the Midwest Rivers: A GIS Approach.' Ph.D. Dissertation, University of Texas, Austin.

Moffa, P.E. (Ed.) (1990). *Control and Treatment of Combined Sewer Overflows*. Van Nostrand Reinhold, New York, NY.

Newell, C.J., Rifai, H.S. and Bedient, P.B. (1992). 'Characterization of Non-Point Sources and Loadings to Galveston Bay.' Publication GBNEP-15, Galveston Bay National Estuary Program, Webster, Texas.

Nofziger, D.L. (1979). 'The influence of canal seepage on groundwater in Lugert Lake irrigation area.' Oklahoma Water Resources Research Institute, OSU.

O'Loughlin, E.M., and Bowmer, K.H. (1975). 'Dilution and decay of aquatic herbicides in flowing changes.' *Journal of Hydrology*, 26.

Parlange, J.Y., Haverkamp, R., and Touma, J. (1985). 'Infiltration under ponded conditions. 1. Optimal analytical solution and comparison with experimental observations.' *Soil Science*, 139, 305-311.

Payment, P., Richardson, L., Siemiatycki, J., Dewar, R., Edwardes, M., and Franco, E. (1991). 'Randomized trial to evaluate the risk of gastrointestinal disease due to consumption of drinking water meeting microbiological standards.' *American Journal of Public Health*, 81(6), 703-708.

Payment, P., Siemiatycki, J., Richardson, L., Renaud, G., Franco, E., and Prevost, M. (1997). 'A prospective epidemiological study of gastrointestinal health effects due to the consumption of drinking water.' *International Journal of Environmental Health Research*, 7, 5-31.

Prodanovic, P., and Simonovic, S.P. (2002). 'Comparison of fuzzy set ranking methods for implementation in water resources decision-making.' *Canadian Journal of Civil Engineering*, 29, 692-701.

Roberge, P.R. (2000). *Handbook of Corrosion Engineering*. McGraw-Hill; ISBN 007-076516-2; 1140 pages

Rossman, L.A. (1994). 'EPANET users manual.' Risk Reduction Engineering Laboratory, US EPA, Cincinnati, Ohio.

Runkel, R.L. (1996). 'Solution of the advection-dispersion equation: Continuous load of finite duration.' *Journal of Environmental Engineering*-Asce, 122(9), 830-832.

Saaty, T.L. (1977). 'A scaling method for priorities in hierarchical structures.' *Journal of Mathematical Psychology*, 15, 57-68.

Saaty, T.L. (1980). The analytic hierachy process, McGraw-Hill International, New York.

Saaty, T.L. (1994). Fundamentals of decision making and priority theory with the AHP, RWS Publications, Pittsburgh, PA.

Sægrov, S., Baptista, J.F.M., Conroy, P., Herz, R.K., LeGauffre, P., Moss, G., Oddevald, J.E., Rajani, B., and Schiatti, M. (1999). 'Rehabilitation of water networks - Survey of research needs and on-going efforts.' *Urban Water*, 1(1), 15-22.

Salvucci, G.D., and Entekhabi, D. (1994). 'Explicit expressions for Green-Ampt (Delta function diffusivity) infiltration rate and cumulative storage.' *Water Resources Research*, 30, 2661-2663.

Saunders, K., W., and Maidment, D.R. (1996). 'A GIS Assessment of Nonpoint Source Pollution in the San Antonio-Nueces Coastal Basin.', CRWR Online Report 96-1, University of Texas, Austin.

Shamir, U., and Howard, C. D. D. (1979). 'An analytic approach to scheduling pipe replacement.' *Journal American Water Works Association*, 71(5), 248-258.

Smith, L.A., Fields, K.A., Chen, A.S.C., and Trafuri, A.N. (2000). *Options for leak and break detection and repair of drinking water systems*, Battelle Press, Columbus, Ohio.

Steele, A., G.P. Wealthall, G. Harrold, N. Tait, Leharne, S.A., and Lerner, D.N. (1999). 'Groundwater contamination by chlorinated solvent DNAPLs in the UK.' *Ground Engineering*, 32(5), 20-21.

Stephenson, D. (1979). 'Pipeline Design for Water Engineers'. *Development in Water Science*, 6, Elsevier Scientific Publishing Company, Oxford.

Summers, P. (2001). 'Finding your way.' *Journal American Water Works Association*, 93(11), 58-61.

Texas Board of Water Engineers. (1946). 'Seepage Losses from Canals.' Austin, Texas.

Thill, J.C. e. (1999). *Spatial multicriteria decision making and analysis: a geographic information science approach*, Ashgate Publishing Company, Brookfield, Vermont.

Tim, U.S., and Jolly, R. (1994). 'Evaluating Agricultural Nonpoint-Source Pollution Using Integrated Geographic Information Systems and Hydrologic/Water Quality Model.' *Journal of Environmental Quality*, 23, 25-35.

United Nations (2005) 'The millennium development goals report 2005', United Nations, New York.

US Bureau of Reclamation (USBR). (1963). 'Linings for Irrigation Canals.' Bureau of Reclamation Report, Washington DC.

USEPA. (1994). 'PESTAN - Pesticide analytical model, version 4.0.' Centre for Subsurface Modeling Support, US Environmental Protection Agency, Ada, Oklahoma.

USEPA. (1998a). 'Estimation of infiltration rate in the vadose zone: Application of selected mathematical models Volume 2.' EPA/600/R-97/128b. Subsurface Protection and Remediation Division, National Risk Management Research Laboratory, United Sates Environmental Protection Agency, Washington, DC.

USEPA. (1998b). 'Estimation of infiltration rate in the vadose zone: Compliation of simple mathematical models Volume 1.' EPA/600/R-97/128a. Subsurface Protection and Remediation Division, National Risk Management Research Laboratory, United Sates Environmental Protection Agency, Washington, DC.

USEPA. (2002). 'Potential contamination due to cross-connections and backflow and the associated health risks.' White Paper prepared for US Environmental Protection Agency Workshop on Distribution System Issues, March 7-8, EPA's Office of Groundwater and Drinking Water, Washington.

Vairavamoorthy, K. (1994). 'Water Distribution Networks: Design and Control for Intermittent Supply.' Thesis Presented to the Imperial college of Science, Technology and Medicine, London UK in partial fulfilment of the requirement for the degree of Doctor of Philosophy.

van Genuchten, M.T. (1980). 'A closed-form equation for predicting the hydraulic conductivity of unsaturated soil.' *Soil Science Society of America Journal*, 44, 892-898.

Wallingford Software (2004). 'Inforworks WS software version 5.52'. Wallingford Software Ltd, UK.

Woldt, W., and Bogardi, I. (1992). 'Groundwater monitoring network design using multiple criteria decision making and geostatistics.' *Water Resources Bulletin*, 28(1), 45-61.

Wyatt, C.J., Fimbres, C., Romo, L., Mendez, R.O., and Grijalva, M. (1998). 'Incidence of heavy metal contamination in water supplies in North Mexico.' Environmental Research Section A, 76, 114-119.

Yan, J.M., and Vairavamoorthy, K. (2003a). 'Fuzzy approach for pipe condition assessment.' Proc. ASCE International Conference on Pipeline Engineering and Construction, July 13-16, 2003, Baltimore, Maryland.

Yan, J.M., and Vairavamoorthy, K. (2003b). 'Prioritising water mains rehabilitation under uncertainty.' Proc. International Conference on Computing and Control for the Water Industry (CCWI), 15-18 September 2003, Imperial College, London.

Yates, P., and Bishop, I. (1997). 'A method for the integration of existing GIS and Modelling system.' Proc. Geo computing 97 & SIRC 97, 26-29 Aug., 1997, Univ. of Otego, New Zealand, 191-197.

Zadeh, L.A. (1965). 'Fuzzy sets.' *Information and Control*, 8(3), 338-353.

Zeleny, M. (1973). 'Compromise programming.' *Multiple criteria decision making*, Cochrane J.L. and Zeleny, M., eds., University of South Carolina Press, Columbia, South Carolina, 263-301.

Appendix A

Contaminant Seepage Examples

This appendix provides an example of contaminant seepage from different pollution sources. These pollution sources are: lined canal/ditch, unlined canal/drain and surface foul water bodies. Figures A.1 and A.2 show water distribution pipes that lie below a canal/drain (lined/unlined) and a surface foul water body respectively. For each of these pollution sources (lined canal/ditch, unlined canal/drain, and surface foul water body), the required input data are presented (Tables A.1, A.3 and A.5 for lined canal/drain, unlined canal/drain and surface foul water body respectively), along with output of relative contaminant concentration (Table A.2 and Figure A.3 for lined canal/ditch, Table A.4 and Figure A.4 for unlined canal/ditch and Table A.6 and Figure A.5 for surface foul water body). The outputs of relative contaminant concentration are obtained by using the procedure described in Chapter 2 of this book.

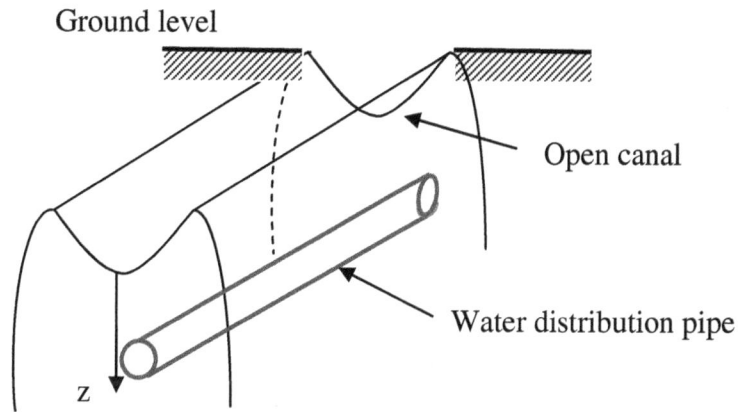

Figure A.1. Contaminant seepage from open canal

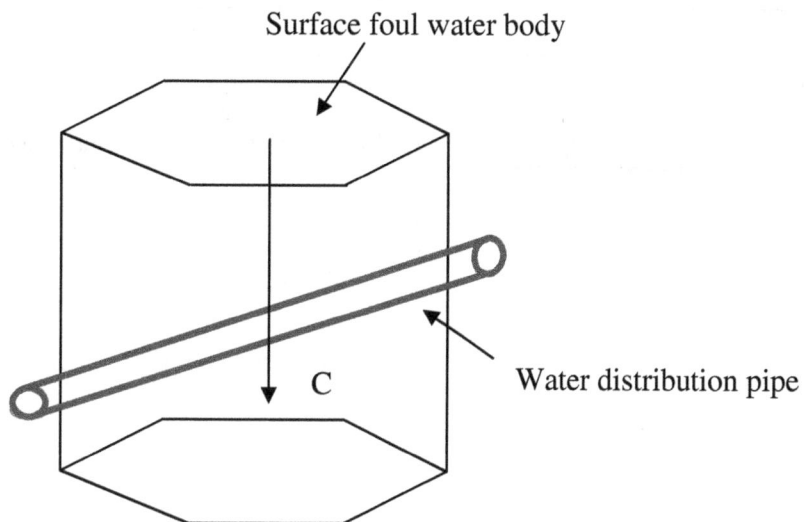

Figure A.2. Contaminant seepage from surface foul water body

169

Table A.1. Example to demonstrate the estimation of contaminant concentration at water distribution pipe due to lined canal/ditch

Known parameters

Sewer pipe

Property	Symbol	Value	Units
Material	Brick		
Seepage rate	r	0.05	*m/day*
Depth of water	h_s	10	*cm*

Soil

Property	Symbol	Value	Units
Saturated volumetric content	θ_s	0.43	cm^3/cm^3
Initial volumetric water content	θ_0	0.0776	cm^3/cm^3
Saturated hydraulic conductivity	K_s	1.05	*cm/hour*
Soil characteristic curve coefficient	b	3.07	-
Soil porosity	n	0.43	cm^3/cm^3
Air entry head	ψ_b	-38.9	*cm*
Pore size index	λ_b	0.56	-
Bulk density	ρ_b	1.4	*g/cc*
Sorption constant	K_d	7.3×10^{-2}	*cc/g*

Contaminant

Property	Symbol	Value	Units
Liquid phase decay	λ	2.22×10^{-4}	*/hour*
Diffusion coefficient	D_p	0.72	cm^2/day

Procedure used

See Sections 2.3.1.2 and 2.4.1

Results

See Table A.2 and Figure A.3 for profile of relative contaminant concentration

Table A.2. Relative contaminant concentration in soil due to lined canal/ditch (for data presented in Table A.1)	
Depth z (m)	Relative concentration C/C_0
0.0	1.000
0.5	0.940
1.0	0.883
1.5	0.829
2.0	0.779
2.5	0.732
3.0	0.688
3.5	0.646
4.0	0.607
4.5	0.570
5.0	0.536
5.5	0.504
6.0	0.473
6.5	0.445
7.0	0.418
7.5	0.392
8.0	0.369
8.5	0.346
9.0	0.325
9.5	0.306
10.0	0.287

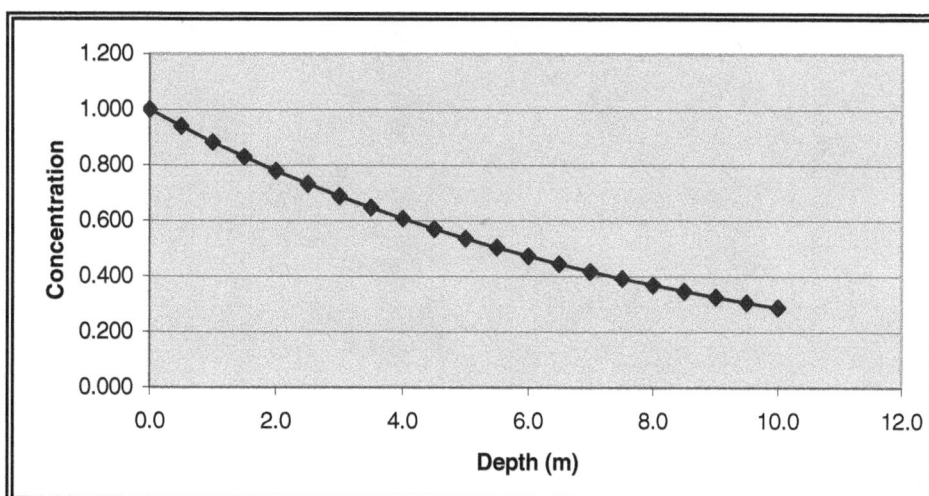

Figure A.3. Relative contaminant concentration in soil due to lined canal/ditch (for data presented in Table A.1)

171

Table A.3. Example to demonstrate the estimation of contaminant concentration at water distribution pipe due to unlined canal/drain

Known parameters

Sewer pipe

Property	Symbol	Value	Units
Soil type	Silty clay		
Water depth	H	5	cm
Width	B	10	cm

Soil

Saturated volumetric content	θ_s	0.36	cm^3/cm^3
Saturated hydraulic conductivity	K_s	0.0079	$cm/hour$
Soil porosity	n	0.36	cm^3/cm^3

Contaminant

Liquid phase decay	λ	2.22×10^{-4}	$/hour$
Diffusion coefficient	D_p	0.0006	$cm^2/day.$

Procedure used

See Sections 2.3.1.1 and 2.4.2

Results

See Table A.4 and Figure A.4 for profile of relative contaminant concentration

Table A.4. Relative contaminant concentration in soil due to unlined canal/drain (for data presented in Table A.3)	
Depth z (m)	Relative concentration C/C_0
0.0	1.000
0.5	0.586
1.0	0.312
1.5	0.166
2.0	0.100
2.5	0.053
3.0	0.028
3.5	0.015
4.0	0.009
4.5	0.005
5.0	0.003

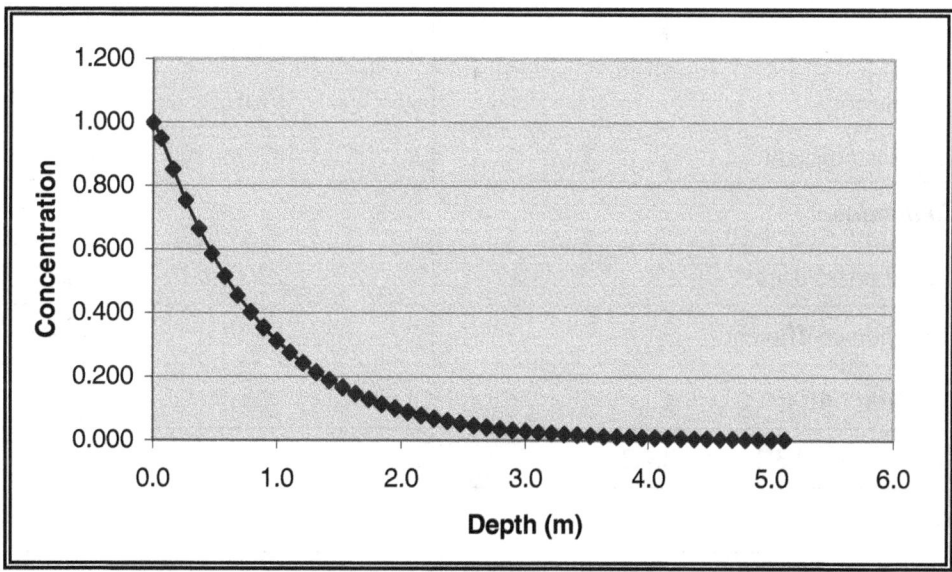

Figure A.4. Relative contaminant concentration in soil due to unlined canal/drain (for data presented in Table A.3)

Table A.5. Example to demonstrate the estimation of contaminant concentration at water distribution pipe due to surface foul water body

Known parameters

Sewer pipe

Property	Symbol	Value	Units
Soil type	Loam		
Water depth	h_s	10	*cm*

Soil

Property	Symbol	Value	Units
Saturated volumetric content	θ_s	0.43	cm^3/cm^3
Initial volumetric water content	θ_0	0.0776	cm^3/cm^3
Saturated hydraulic conductivity	K_s	1.05	*cm/hour*
Soil characteristic curve coefficient	b	3.07	-
Soil porosity	n	0.43	cm^3/cm^3
Air entry head	ψ_b	-38.9	*cm*
Pore size index	λ_b	0.56	-
Bulk density	ρ_b	1.4	*g/cc*
Sorption constant	K_d	7.3×10^{-2}	*cc/g*

Contaminant

Property	Symbol	Value	Units
Liquid phase decay	λ	2.22×10^{-4}	*/hour*
Diffusion coefficient	D_p	0.72	cm^2/day

Procedure used

See Sections 2.3.1.3 and 2.4.2

Results

See Table A.6 and FigureA.5 for profile of relative contaminant concentration

Table A.6. Relative contaminant concentration in soil due to surface foul water body (for data presented in Table A.5)	
Depth z (m)	Relative concentration C/C_0
0.0	1.000
0.5	0.930
1.0	0.865
1.5	0.805
2.0	0.749
2.5	0.697
3.0	0.648
3.5	0.603
4.0	0.561
4.5	0.522
5.0	0.486
5.5	0.452
6.0	0.420
6.5	0.391
7.0	0.364
7.5	0.338
8.0	0.315
8.5	0.293
9.0	0.272
9.5	0.253
10.0	0.236

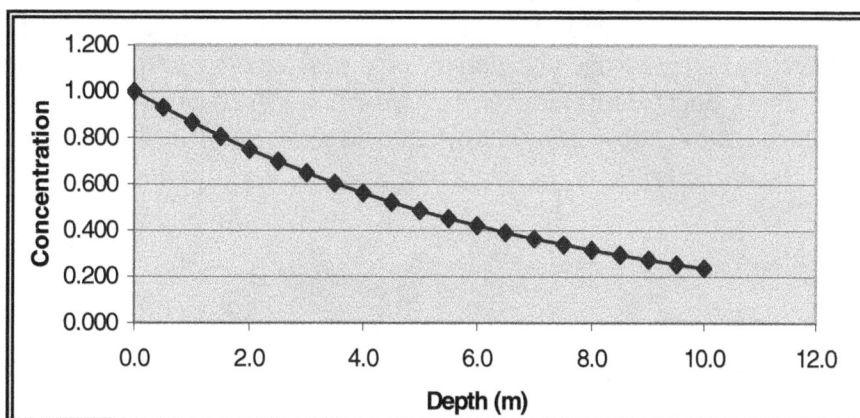

Figure A.5. Relative contaminant concentration in soil due to surface foul water body (for data presented in Table A.5)

Appendix B

Analytical Hierarchy Process

In the Pipe Condition Assessment (PCA) and Risk Assessment (RA) models, it is extremely important to evaluate the possible alternatives carefully. For example, in the PCA model it is necessary to know the relative influence of each of the factors of Group 1 at Level 1 (material decay, diameter, length, internal protection and external protection) on the pipe indicators, which eventually influences the physical indicators. Similarly it is necessary to know the relative influence of corrosion indicators and load/strength indicators of Group 2 at Level 2 on environmental indicators which eventually influences the pipe condition. In the Risk Assessment model, the relative influence of the factors such as hazard (contaminant concentration and section of pipe in contaminant zone) and vulnerability (pipe condition) on the risk needs to be known. This makes decision-making difficult and thus there is a need for an approach which allows the decision-maker to break the evaluation process down into a series of assessments of the different factors involved. The Analytical Hierarchy Process (AHP), which is a mathematical technique for multi-criteria decision-making (Saaty 1977; Saaty 1980; Saaty 1994), allows the policy analyst to do this by structuring the problem hierarchically and guiding him/her through a sequence of pair-wise comparison judgements.

AHP is conducted using the following steps:
1. Set up the hierarchy (goal, factors and alternatives)
2. Perform pair-wise comparisons for factors
3. Prepare a matrix (judgement matrix) for factors
4. Compute the priority vector for factors
5. Comparison of alternatives
6. Compute the priority vector for alternatives
7. Assess consistency of pair-wise judgements
8. Compute the relative weights/ranks.

In both PCA and RA models, the relative influence of different factors (for example, the relative influence of material decay, diameter, length, internal protection and external protection) on only one alternative (pipe indicators) is required to be assessed, and hence Steps 5 and 6 are skipped. The procedure used in obtaining the relative weights for each factor is described below and shown in the flowchart of Figure B.1.

176

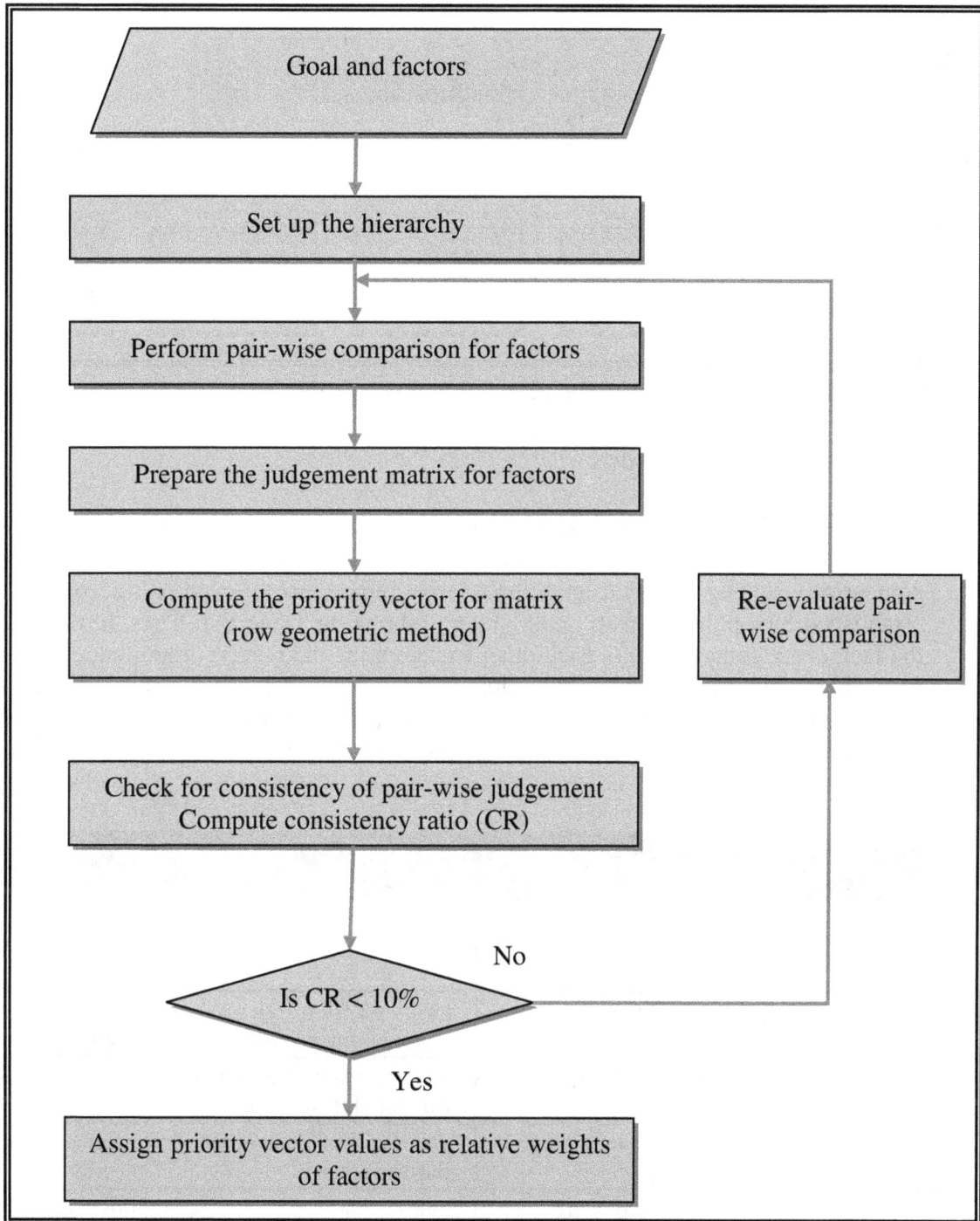

Figure B1. The procedure for obtaining the relative weights for each factor

1. Setting up the hierarchy

The problem needs to be structured into a hierarchy (see Figure B.2). The first level denotes the overall goal of the decision-maker. For example, this is to find out the best estimate of the pipe indicator. The second level consists of several different factors that contribute to this goal. The number of factors involved can vary from case to case, for example in Group 1 of Level 1 there are five, whereas in Group 2 of Level 2 there are two.

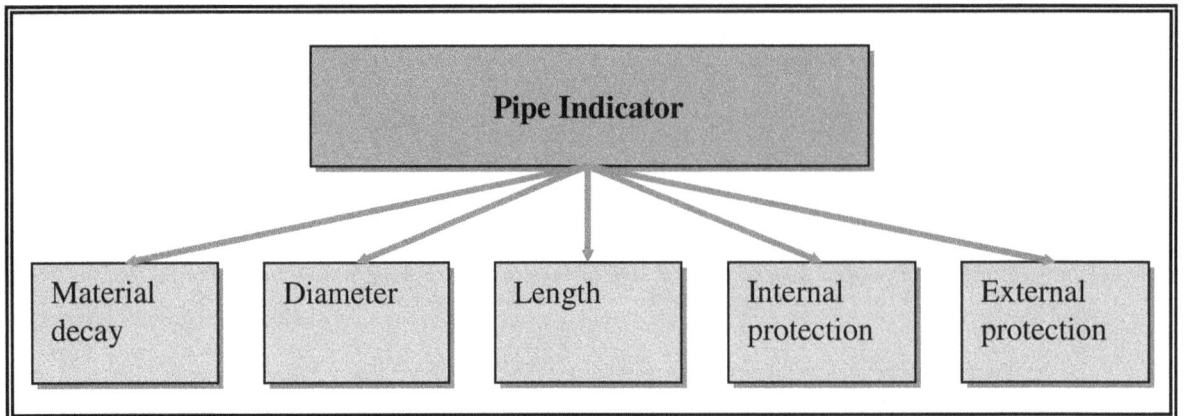

Figure B.2. Establishing the hierarchy of the problem in PCA/RA models

2. Pair-wise comparisons

The Analytic Hierarchy Process (AHP) method does not require decision-makers to quantify precisely the level of importance, but they are required to carry out pair-wise comparisons among factors to give the relative importance of each pair according to established nine-point intensity scale systems shown in Table B.1. Thus, in this step, the factors are compared with each other to determine the relative importance of each factor in the accomplishing the overall goal. The structure of the questionnaire to aid decision-makers to determine the relative importance of each factor over another according to scale system (modified to a 5-point scale) is presented in Appendix D for some cases.

Table B.1. Scales for pair-wise comparisons		
Comparative importance	**Definition**	**Explanation**
1	Equally important	Two decision elements (e.g. indicators) equally influence the parent decision element
3	Moderately more important	One decision element is moderately more influential than the other
5	Strongly more important	One decision element has a stronger influence than the other
7	Very strongly more important	One decision element has significantly more influence than the other
9	Extremely more important	The difference between influences of the two decision elements is extremely significant
2, 4, 6, 8	Intermediate judgement values	Judgment values between equally, moderately, strongly, very strongly, and extremely
Reciprocals		If v is the judgement value when i is compared to j, then 1/v is the judgement value when j is compared to i.

3. Matrix for factors

A matrix is prepared with the factors (in our example material decay, diameter, length, internal protection and external protection) listed at the top and on the left. Based on individually surveyed information and the resulting informed judgement of the decision-maker (Step 2), the matrix is then filled in with numerical values denoting the importance of the factor on the left relative to the importance of the factor on the top. A high value means that the factor on the left is relatively more important than the factor at the top. In Table B.2, for example, material decay is considered to be three times as important as diameter, whereas length is only one third as important as the internal protection. When a factor is compared with itself the ratio of importance is obviously one, resulting in a diagonal line across the matrix. The resulting matrix is known as the judgement matrix.

Table B.2. The judgement matrix for the factors					
	Material Decay	**Diameter**	**Length**	**Internal Protection**	**External Protection**
Material Decay	1	3	4	2	2
Diameter	1/3	1	2	2	2
Length	1/4	1/2	1	1/3	1/3
Internal Protection	1/2	1/2	3	1	1
External Protection	1/2	1/2	3	1	1

In this example the priorities are clear. Material decay is considered to be the factor which influences the pipe indicator most (the pipe indicator in turn influences the pipe condition), followed by internal and external protection. Diameter is considered more important than length.

4. Priority vector for factors

In this step the decision-maker uses the matrix (Table B.2) to get an overall priority value for each factor. AHP computes an overall priority value or weight for each decision element based on the pair-wise comparisons using mathematical techniques such as

- Eigenvalue
- Mean Transformation and
- Row Geometric Mean

In the present study (Pipe Condition Assessment model and Risk Assessment model) the 'Row Geometric Mean' technique for computing the weights under AHP has been employed.

Row Geometric Mean: In this method, the geometric mean of each row is calculated (i.e. the elements in each row are multiplied with each other and then the nth root is taken, where n is the number of elements in the row). This forms the vector of geometric mean. The elements of this vector are then normalized by dividing them with the sum. The resulting normalized vector is an approximated maximum eigenvector, herein named as the priority vector. The calculations for the example are presented below:

The vector of geometric mean

Material Decay	$: (1*3*4*2*2)^{1/5}$	$= 2.17$
Diameter	$: (0.333*1*2*282)^{1/5}$	$= 1.21$
Length	$: (0.25*0.50*1*0.333*0.333)^{1/5}$	$= 0.42$
Internal Protection	$: (0.50*0.50*3.0*181)^{1/5}$	$= 0.94$
External Protection	$(0.50*0.50*3.0*1*1)^{1/5}$	$= 0.94$
Total		$= 5.70$

The Priority vector

Material Decay	: 2.17/5.70	$= 0.38$
Diameter	: 1.21/5.70	$= 0.21$
Length	: 0.42/5.70	$= 0.07$
Internal Protection	: 0.94/5.70	$= 0.17$
External Protection	: 0.94/5.70	$= 0.17$
Total		$= 1.00$

5. Consistency of pair-wise judgements

One of the most practical issues in AHP is the non-consistency in pair-wise comparisons. If all the comparisons are perfectly consistent, then the following expression should hold true for any combination of comparisons of the judgement matrix.

$$a_{ij} = a_{ik} \times a_{kj} \tag{B.1}$$

where
a_{ij} - relative importance factor (tabulated values in Table B2) of decision criteria i to j.

Table B.2 is reproduced below with values of i and j (Table B.3).

		Material Decay	Diameter	Length	Internal Protection	External Protection
Table B.3. The judgement matrix for the factors						
	i j	1	2	3	4	5
Material Decay	1	1 a_{11}	3 a_{12}	4 a_{13}	2 a_{14}	2 a_{15}
Diameter	2	1/3 a_{21}	1 a_{22}	2 a_{23}	2 a_{24}	2 a_{25}
Length	3	¼ a_{31}	½ a_{32}	1 a_{33}	1/3 a_{34}	1/3 a_{35}
Internal Protection	4	½ a_{41}	½ a_{41}	3 a_{41}	1 a_{41}	1 a_{41}
External Protection	5	½ a_{51}	½ a_{51}	3 a_{51}	1 a_{51}	1 a_{51}

If   i=1; j=2; k=3
$a_{12} = 3$
$a_{13} = 4$
$a_{32} = ½$

According to equation (B.1), a_{12} should be equal to a_{13} x a_{32}

However, perfect consistency rarely occurs in practice. Consistency ratio (CR) is commonly used to reflect the degree of consistency of the judgement matrix. The CR is calculated as follow:

$$CI = \frac{\lambda_{max} - n}{(n-1)} \qquad \text{(B.2)}$$

$$CR = \frac{CI}{RCI} \qquad \text{(B.3)}$$

where
CI - consistency index
λ_{max} - maximum eigenvalue of judgement matrix
RCI - Random consistency index as given in Table B.4
n - the number of factors

Table B.4. RCI values for different values of n								
n	1	2	3	4	5	6	7	8	9
RCI	0	0	0.58	0.90	1.12	1.24	1.32	1.41	1.45

Maximum eigenvalue (λ_{max}) is obtained by adding the columns in the judgement matrix and multiplying the resulting vector by the vector of priorities (i.e. the approximated eigenvector) obtained earlier. The procedure is explained below.

Adding the columns in the judgement matrix

Material Decay	Diameter	Length	Internal Protection	External Protection
2.58	5.50	13.00	6.33	6.33

Vector of priorities

Material Decay	0.38
Diameter	0.21
Length	0.07
Internal Protection	0.17
External Protection	0.17

Multiplication and addition

Material Decay	2.58 x 0.38	0.98
Diameter	5.50 x 0.21	1.15
Length	13.0 x 0.07	0.91
Internal Protection	6.33 x 0.17	1.07
External Protection	6.33 x 0.17	1.07
Total	λ_{max}	5.18

$$CI = \frac{5.18 - 5}{(4-1)} = 0.045$$

$$CR = \frac{0.045}{1.12} = 0.04$$

The pair-wise comparisons in a judgement matrix in AHP are considered to be adequately consistent if the CR is less than 10 per cent (Saaty 1980). If CR is greater than 10 per cent, there is a need for further evaluation of the pair-wise comparison in the judgement matrix. In the example above, CR is 4 per cent, indicating that the pair-wise comparison is consistent.

6. Computing the relative weights

If the CR of the judgement matrix is satisfactory (less than 10 per cent, for example), the priority vector values will be assigned as relative weights of factors. Thus, in this example, the relative weights for each factor are:

Material Decay	0.38
Diameter	0.21
Length	0.07
Internal Protection	0.17
External Protection	0.17

Appendix C

Pipe Condition Assessment Indicators

The different pipe condition assessment indicators are presented in Chapter 3 of this book. This Appendix provides the details of how these indicators influence the pipe condition.

1. Pipe Indicators

These indicators are related to physical properties of pipe. Pipes deteriorate in different ways due to their physical properties.

Material decay: This indicator is used to manifest the effect of the current condition of different pipe materials on pipe failure. Pipes made from different materials and of different age fail in different ways. The Hazen-William coefficient of friction (C), which varies according to the pipe material and age, is considered to characterize this influence. The 'C' values proposed for different pipe materials of different ages are presented in Table C.1.

Table C.1. Typical values of the Hazen-William coefficient of friction (C) for different types of pipe material									
Pipe Material	Age in years								
	New	10	20	30	40	50	60	70	80
DI	140	130	130	120	120	120	110	100	-
PVC	150	140	140	140	140	140	130	-	-
HDPE	140	130	130	130	130	130	120		
AC	150	130	130	120	120	120	100	-	-
PE	130	120	120	120	120	120	110		
PC/RCC	130	120	110	95	70	70	70	-	-
Steel/GI	150	130	130	100	100	100	60	60	60
CI	150	110	100	90	80	70	70	60	-

(Stephenson 1979; Wallingford Software 2004; King and Crocker 1967; Bonds 1989).

Diameter:

Research into the relationship between pipe diameter and pipe failure reveals that larger diameter pipes (i.e. trunk mains greater than 300 mm) are less prone to failure than smaller diameter pipes. These is due to following three reasons:

- *Pipe wall thickness* increases with pipe diameter. Larger pipes are therefore less susceptible to failure than smaller diameter pipes (Cooper et al. 2000).

- *Ground movement* Larger pipes are less susceptible to ground movement from traffic than smaller pipes as they have a greater cementing surface area (Cooper et al. 2000).
- *Chlorine decay* Studies of chlorine decay in pipes note that chlorine decay profiles are most pronounced in small diameter pipes. This is due to increased absorption of chlorine through contact with biomass. Kiene et al (1998) estimates that this is most pronounced in pipes with a diameter of less than 75 mm.

Typical minimum and maximum diameters for different types of pipe material are presented in Table C.2.

Table C.2. Typical minimum and maximum diameters for different types of pipe material		
Pipe material	Diameter in mm	
	Minimum	Maximum
DI	75	1600
PVC	100	1200
HDPE	100	1600
AC	50	2500
PE	63	1000
PC/RCC	400	1200
Steel/GI	60	2235
CI	75	2000

Pipe length: The vulnerability of a pipe is directly related to its length. Larger length pipes are more prone to failure than smaller length pipes.

Studies reveal two principal reasons for this:

- *Pipe stress* Over-stressing of pipes is more likely in longer segments of pipe resulting in potential longitudinal breaks (e.g. hoop stress – longitudinal breaks caused by transverse stresses). Studies of vulnerability of varied pipe lengths to failure from earthquake hazards have further reinforced the theory that pipe failures increased with pipe length (Ballantyne and Moore 1995).
- *Pipe jointing* The number of pipe joints increases with pipe length. Studies of pipe jointing have identified it as a high risk point for potential contaminant ingress. The materials used to join the water pipes, e.g. seal threaded pipe, should also be considered as possible sites for microbial colonization (Geldreich 1996). The latter would be of concern as this promotes biofilm formation and consequent chlorine consumption.

Internal protection: The pipes with internal protection by lining and/or coating are less susceptible to corrosion. Modern metallic pipes are mostly manufactured with internal linings to prevent internal corrosion from soft or aggressive waters. However, older metallic pipes may be unlined and would therefore be susceptible to internal corrosion. The AWWA Research Foundation has published two manuals that provide a detailed description of internal corrosion processes and control (AWWARF 1989; AWWARF/DVGW 1986). Internal corrosion can manifest itself in different ways. They are commonly grouped as follows:

- Pipe degradation (e.g. pitting), which can result in leakage or vulnerability to mechanical failure;
- Tuberculation and scale formation can reduce hydraulic capacity and impair water quality; and
- Corrosion by-product release (e.g. rusty or red water), which can impair water quality.

External protection: The pipes with external protection by lining and/or coating are less susceptible to deterioration. Several types of external corrosion can occur in water mains, including galvanic, electrolytic, pitting, crevice, uniform, localized and microbiologically induced. Galvanic and electrolytic corrosion are the most common types of external corrosion in water distribution systems.

2. Installation indicators

These indicators are related to the pipe and other conditions at the time of installation of pipe. Improper installation conditions will fail the pipe structurally.

Bedding condition: All pipes require proper bedding so as to have adequate structural support. Proper bedding also facilitates the laying of pipes to the required line and level. Improper bedding may result in premature pipe failure.

Workmanship: Workmanship deals with the human factor of quality control of construction work. In many developing countries, pipework does not follow standard codes of construction. This may be because the codes do not exist, are not enforced or logistically/financially are simply not feasible. As a result, poor workmanship may deteriorate the pipes and cause more risk regardless of pipe age and other factors.

Joint method: The main functions of the joints (Davies et al. 2001a) are:

- To be watertight
- To be durable
- To be resistant to root intrusion.

It was reported that improper selection of joint type was the major cause of joint-related structural defects and hence pipe deterioration. Some types of joints experience premature failure (e.g. leadite joints).

Number of joints: Studies of pipe jointing have revealed that pipes at joints are more susceptible to failure. Hence the greater the number of joints a pipe has, the greater the risk of it getting structurally worse.

3. Corrosion indicators

The pipes deteriorate due to corrosion and these indicators are related to the different causes of corrosion.

Year of installation: The year of installation reflects the age of the pipe. More structural defects have been reported in older pipe than in newer pipes. Thus the effects of pipe degradation become more apparent over time.

Soil corrosivity: Generally, buried pipelines suffer from soil corrosion due to (Cunat 2001):

- High moisture content
- A pH value less than 4.5
- A resistivity less than 1000 ohm-cm
- Presence of chlorides, sulphides and bacteria
- Presence of stray currents.

Some soils are corrosive; sandy soils are high up on the resistivity scale and therefore considered the least corrosive while clayey soils are more corrosive. Underground pipes deteriorate due to soil corrosivity. Pipes deteriorate quicker in more corrosive soil and the degree of deterioration depends on the pipe material. The corrosion performance of stainless steel pipes in soil is generally poorer than PVC pipes.

The soil corrosivity of different soils and the range of soil resistivity for different degrees of soil corrosivity are presented in Tables C3 (a) and C3 (b) respectively.

Surface permeability: Surface permeability reflects the ground condition. A more permeable surface allows more moisture to percolate to the pipe. The surface salts will be carried to the pipe with the moisture. The soils around the pipe are also subjected to wetting and drying. This will deteriorate the pipe.

Table C.3 (a). Soil corrosivity for different types of soils	
Soil type	**Corrosivity**
Sand	Essentially non-corrosive
Loamy sand	Mildly corrosive
Sandy loam	Mildly corrosive
Sandy clay loam	Mildly corrosive
Loam	Moderately corrosive
Silt loam	Corrosive
Silt	Highly corrosive
Clay loam	Highly corrosive
Silty clay loam	Highly corrosive
Sandy clay	Corrosive
Silty clay	Extremely corrosive
Clay	Extremely corrosive

Table C.3 (b). Typical range of soil resistivity for different degree of soil corrosivity	
Soil resistivity Ohm-m	**Degree of soil corrosivity**
>20,000	Essentially non-corrosive
10,000 to 20,000	Mildly corrosive
5,000 to 10,000	Moderately corrosive
3,000 to 5,000	Corrosive
1,000 to 3,000	Highly corrosive
<1,000	Extremely corrosive

(Roberge 2000)

Groundwater condition: The following three types of situation exist for water pipes laid underground in relation to the groundwater table.

- Water pipes permanently above the groundwater table
- Water pipes permanently below the groundwater table
- Water pipes intermittently above and below the groundwater table.

Water pipes are deteriorated by the groundwater table through the following effects:

- Water with minerals may corrode pipes. Some groundwater is aggressive toward certain pipe materials.

- Water flowing through the bedding material may cause ground loss and a subsequent lack of support around the water pipes.
- Intermittent wetting and drying will make the bedding material unstable.

4. Load/strength indicators

The pipes deteriorate as a result of the load/pressure exerted on them. These indicators relate to the different types of loads.

Buried depth: The buried depth has an influence on the structural failure of the pipe. It is widely reported that there is steady decreasing defect rate up to a certain depth and after this depth the defect rate increases (Davies et al. 2001b). The first occurrence probably reflects road traffic and second occurrence reflects the effect of backfill soil, frost load, overburden pressure and soil moisture with buried depth. In this study the effect of traffic load on the pipe failure has been considered separately. Hence the pipes buried at higher depth have more possibility of failure than those buried at shallower depths.

Traffic load: The traffic load influences the pipe conditions. Pipes situated below roads are subjected to the traffic load. Pipe failure rate increases with traffic loads. However, the traffic load depends on the location of pipe. The traffic load is normally more on the principal roads. At the same time these roads are stronger and greater care is taken in the design and construction of these roads and hence the effect of traffic load on the failure of pipes laid below these roads may be minimum.

Hydraulic pressure: Changes to internal water pressure will change stresses acting on the pipe. If the internal pressure is more than the rated pressure, the chances of pipe failure are more.

5. Intermittency indicators

Water supply systems in developing countries have inherent problems due to their intermittent operation (Vairavamoorthy 1994), which cause the pipes to deteriorate. These indicators are related to pipe deterioration due to intermittency in operation.

Number of valves: Different types of valves are necessary for discharge and pressure control. However, it is considered that the pipes installed with valves deteriorate faster than the pipes without valves, mainly due to poor quality, improper installation and frequent operation of valves. Thus the greater the number of valves, the greater the deterioration of the pipe.

Number of water supply periods per day: Water supply systems in developing countries are normally operated intermittently. The frequency of water delivery in the pipe may vary (for example, from twice a day to once in two days). The intermittent water supply deteriorates the pipe due to existence of zero or no pressure and contaminant ingress during the periods of no pressure and variation of pressure from maximum to zero. Hence it is considered that the greater the number of water supply periods, the more the pipes will deteriorate.

Duration of water supply/day: When water supply systems operate intermittently, the duration for which water is present in the system varies. The chances of a pipe deteriorating are more when there is no water in the pipe. Hence the longer the duration of water supply, the smaller the chances of pipe failure.

6. Failure indicators

These indicators relate to disruptions to the system such as breakage, leakage, water quality etc. At this stage only one failure indicator, i.e. breakage history, is considered. Current leakage data indicates the actual condition of the pipe and hence is considered at the next level. No water quality indicator is considered directly, but the contaminant ingress model simulates the contaminant concentration at the pipe and is included in risk assessment.

Breakage history: This is the important indicator in assessing pipe condition. If the pipe breaks frequently at a particular location, then it has the combined effect of all the parameters explained above and the chances of pipe failing again are also more.

Appendix D

Questionnaires for Pipe Condition Assessment

Instructions

The purpose of questionnaires of this kind is to generate the weights for factors of each group at each level by using the analytical hierchy process (AHP). This method requires the degree of preference of one factor over another factor. Therefore there is a need to carry out comparisons for two factors at one time.

Generation of weights for different factors are necessary at the following two stages. These are:
1. Pipe condition assessment (PCA) model
2. Risk assessment (RA) model

The PCA model requires weights for factors of each six groups at level 1; three groups at level 2 and one group at level 3. The pipe condition indicators are the factors in this case. Thus the weights are to be generated for 10 groups. In this Appendix, we take only one group as an example for each hierarchical level (as shown in Figure B.1). Other groups shall follow the same procedure.

The RA model requires the weight to be generated for the two factors at one level.

The questionnaire consists of two columns for each comparison. The respondent is required to tick the preference in **column 1** and tick the degree of preference in **column 2** of each comparison.

For example, in the case of Questionnaire 1, to compare the two indicators of *diameter* and *length* in the *pipe* indicators group, if a respondent feels diameter is a greater contributory factor for deterioration than length, the respondent should tick 'diameter' in **column 1** of the table and then go to column 2. If the respondent thinks that 'diameter' is 'strongly contributory' over the 'length' for pipe deterioration, then 'strongly preferred' should be ticked in **column 2** of the table. In this way the respondent is required to complete all the pair-wise comparisons for each group. At the beginning of the Questionnaire there might be notes describing how each factor contributes to the final output.

Pipe Condition Assessment

Interviewee:

Organization: ....

Address: ....

....

....

Profession: ....

Position ....

Experience ....(years)

Date: ..../.........../...................................

Time: ....

Level 1 - Pipe Indicators Group

> **Notes**
>
> *Material decay:* This indicator is used for manifesting the effect of the current condition of different pipe materials on pipe failure. Pipes made from different materials and of different age fail in different ways.
>
> *Pipe diameter:* Research into the relationship between pipe diameter and pipe failure reveals that larger diameter pipes (i.e. trunk mains greater than 300 mm) are less prone to failure than smaller diameter pipes.
>
> *Pipe length:* The vulnerability of a pipe is directly related to its length. Larger length pipes are more prone to failure than smaller length pipes.
>
> *Internal protection:* Pipes with internal protection by lining and/or coating are less susceptible to corrosion.
>
> *External protection:* Pipes with external protection by lining and/or coating are less susceptible to deterioration.
>
> **For details refer to Appendix C**

1. Material decay – Diameter

Column 1	Column 2	
❑ Material decay ❑ Diameter	❑ Equally preferred ❑ Moderately preferred ❑ Strongly preferred	❑ Very strongly preferred ❑ Extremely preferred
Reasons for preference if any		

2. Material decay – Length

Column 1	Column 2	
❑ Material decay ❑ Length	❑ Equally preferred ❑ Moderately preferred ❑ Strongly preferred	❑ Very strongly preferred ❑ Extremely preferred
Reasons for preference if any		

3. Material decay – Internal protection

Column 1	Column 2	
☐ Material decay ☐ Internal protection	☐ Equally preferred ☐ Moderately preferred ☐ Strongly preferred	☐ Very strongly preferred ☐ Extremely preferred
Reasons for preference if any		

4. Material decay – External protection

Column 1	Column 2	
☐ Material decay ☐ External protection	☐ Equally preferred ☐ Moderately preferred ☐ Strongly preferred	☐ Very strongly preferred ☐ Extremely preferred
Reasons for preference if any		

5. Diameter – Length

Column 1	Column 2	
☐ Diameter ☐ Length	☐ Equally preferred ☐ Moderately preferred ☐ Strongly preferred	☐ Very strongly preferred ☐ Extremely preferred
Reasons for preference if any		

6. Diameter – Internal protection

Column 1	Column 2	
☐ Diameter ☐ Internal protection	☐ Equally preferred ☐ Moderately preferred ☐ Strongly preferred	☐ Very strongly preferred ☐ Extremely preferred
Reasons for preference if any		

7. Diameter – External protection

Column 1	Column 2	
☐ Diameter ☐ External protection	☐ Equally preferred ☐ Moderately preferred ☐ Strongly preferred	☐ Very strongly preferred ☐ Extremely preferred
Reasons for preference if any		

8. Length – Internal protection

Column 1	Column 2	
☐ Length ☐ Internal protection	☐ Equally preferred ☐ Moderately preferred ☐ Strongly preferred	☐ Very strongly preferred ☐ Extremely preferred
Reasons for preference if any		

9. Length – External protection

Column 1	Column 2	
☐ Length ☐ External protection	☐ Equally preferred ☐ Moderately preferred ☐ Strongly preferred	☐ Very strongly preferred ☐ Extremely preferred
Reasons for preference if any		

10. Internal protection – External protection

Column 1	Column 2	
☐ Internal protection ☐ External protection	☐ Equally preferred ☐ Moderately preferred ☐ Strongly preferred	☐ Very strongly preferred ☐ Extremely preferred
Reasons for preference if any		

Level 2 – Physical Indicators Group

> **Notes**
>
> **Pipe indicators: The pipe indicators consist of the combined influence of the indicators such as Material decay, Diameter, Length, Internal protection and External protection on pipe condition.**
>
> **Installation indicator: the installation indicator is the combined influence of indicators such as Bedding condition, Workmanship, Joint method and Number of joints on pipe condition.**
>
> **For details refer to Appendix C**

1. Pipe indicators – Installation indicators

Column 1	Column 2	
❏ Pipe indicators ❏ Installation indicators	❏ Equally preferred ❏ Moderately preferred ❏ Strongly preferred	❏ Very strongly preferred ❏ Extremely preferred
Reasons for preference if any		

Level 3 – Pipe Condition Group

> **Notes**
>
> **Physical indicators: Pipe indicators and Installation indicators**
>
> **Environmental indicators: Environmental indicators are the combined effect of Corrosion indicators and Load/strength indicators on pipe condition.**
>
> **Operational indicators: Operational indicators are the combined effect of Intermittency indicators and Failure indicators on pipe condition.**
>
> **For details refer to Appendix C**

1. Physical indicators – Environmental indicators

Column 1	Column 2	
☐ Physical indicators ☐ Environmental indicators	☐ Equally preferred ☐ Moderately preferred ☐ Strongly preferred	☐ Very strongly preferred ☐ Extremely preferred
Reasons for preference if any		

2. Physical indicators – Operational indicators

Column 1	Column 2	
☐ Physical indicators ☐ Operational indicators	☐ Equally preferred ☐ Moderately preferred ☐ Strongly preferred	☐ Very strongly preferred ☐ Extremely preferred
Reasons for preference if any		

3. Environmental indicators – Operational indicators

Column 1	Column 2	
☐ Environmental indicators ☐ Operational indicators	☐ Equally preferred ☐ Moderately preferred ☐ Strongly preferred	☐ Very strongly preferred ☐ Extremely preferred
Reasons for preference if any		

Appendix E

Questionnaires for Risk Assessment

Problem

Water distribution pipes can be subject to contamination for several reasons, such as seepage from sewer pipes, open drains or surface foul water bodies. The contaminant load is obtained by combining the contaminant concentration and the length of contamination along water distribution pipe. These pipes are therefore subject to risk because of the level of contaminant load (hazard) and condition of water distribution pipes (vulnerability). The risk may vary depending on the contaminant load and condition of deteriorated pipe subjected to the contaminants. Thus there are the following two risk factors:

1. Contaminant load (hazard)
2. Water pipe condition (vulnerability).

These factors are shown below schematically:

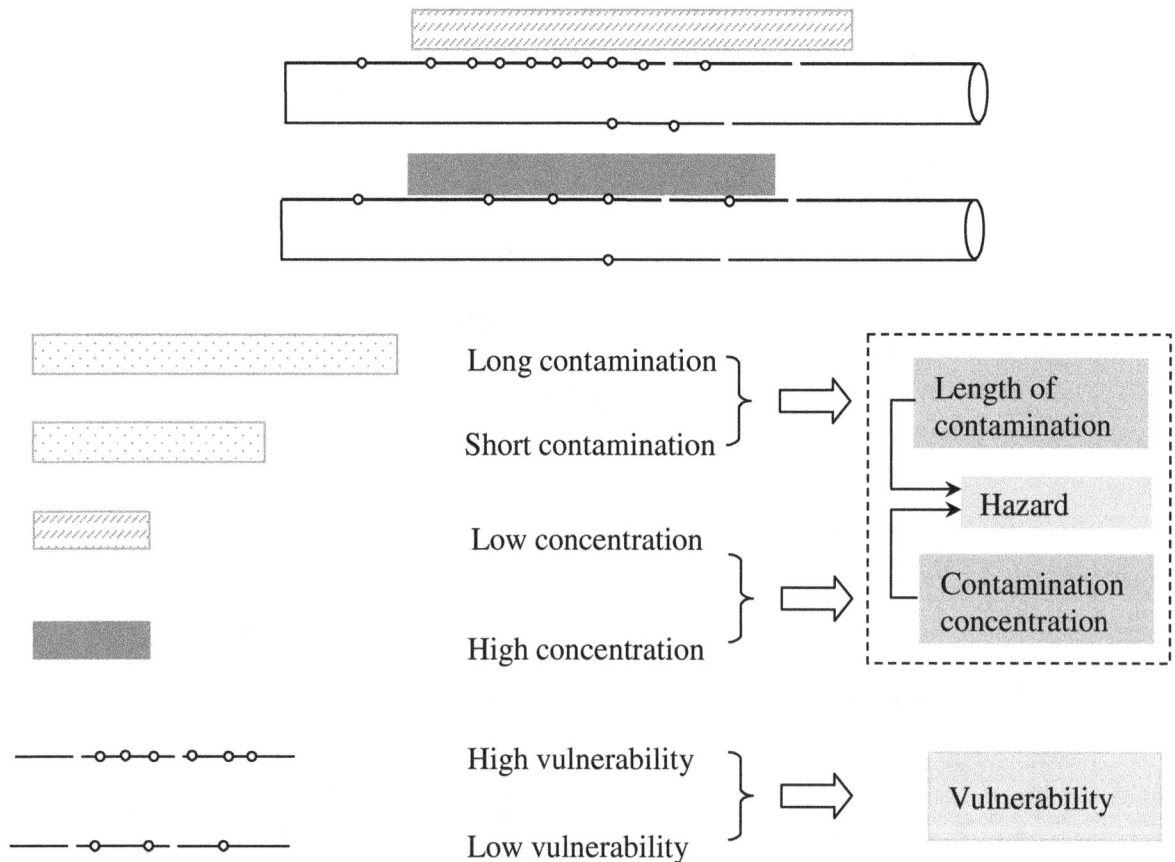

Questionnaire 2

Risk Assessment for Contaminant Intrusion

Interviewee: _____

Organization: _____

Address: _____

_____

_____

Profession: _____

Position _____

Experience _____ (years)

Date: _____ / _____ / _____

Time: _____

Objectives

The objective of this questionnaire is to assess the risk according to the relative contribution of two factors: hazard and vulnerability. Your assessment regarding the relative importance of each of these factors will be helpful for the risk assessment.

Pair-wise comparisons

> Pair-wise comparisons are given below. You are requested to tick the preference in the left column and tick your degree of preference in the right column.
>
> ***Just for example***, if you feel 'vulnerability' is a greater contributory factor than 'hazard', you should tick 'vulnerability' in **column 1** of the table and then go to column 2. If you think that 'vulnerability' is 'Strongly preferred' over the 'Hazard' for risk, then tick 'Strongly preferred' in **column 2** of the table. In this way, please complete these pair-wise comparisons.

Vulnerability (pipe condition) vs Hazard (contaminant load)

Column 1	Column 2			
❑ Vulnerability ❑ Hazard	❑ Equally preferred ❑ Moderately preferred ❑ Strongly preferred		❑ Very strongly preferred ❑ Extremely preferred	
Reasons for preference if any				

200

Appendix F

Water Quality Model

Introduction

Safe drinking water is essential to sustain life, and a reliable and adequate supply is to be ensured by governments. The water supply system has a close association with the health of the people in urban societies, as it is the major source of water for them. The rising population has exerted a very large demand on the public water supply system. The quantity of water supplied depends upon the availability of water at the sources. To have some control over the quantity of water being supplied, most of the cities and towns in developing countries with less available water have adopted an intermittent water supply system. The quality of water supplied is the issue of top priority as contaminated water is a potential hazard to public health. Most water supply networks have water treatment plants for purifying water before it is supplied, but there exists no means of purification if water is contaminated in transit. Intermittent water supply systems are highly prone to contamination while in transit. Hence, assessment of the risk involved in water distribution networks is essential.

The quality of water supplied is an issue inherent with water supply networks or schemes. Water quality may deteriorate either at the source or in the pipelines. Quality deterioration at the source can be averted to a great extent by appropriate and ample treatment processes. However, quality relapse in transit needs to be addressed properly.

Intermittent systems of water supply fulfil to a great extent the water demands of the public, especially when the available water is inadequate. Even though the water supplied may be less than the demand, it ensures a sustainable supply of water. But this solution is not free from flaws. Intermittent supplies are prone to contamination in distribution pipes that are often under no or negative pressure. The situation is serious in cities with unsanitary excreta disposal where sewage flows in open ditches close to distribution pipes. In Delhi, an intermittent supply and the proximity of water and sewage pipelines were the prime suspects of a paratyphoid fever outbreak in 1996 (Guillermo et al. 2001). The bacteriological quality of an intermittent water supply is substantially lower than that of a continuous service. In four districts in Indian towns between 27 per cent and 76 per cent of samples under intermittent water supply tested positive for fecal coli-forms, whereas the figure was only 10 per cent for the samples under continuous water supply. In-house storage tanks to cope with an intermittent supply also risk bacteriological deterioration of water.

Water quality deterioration in the pipelines can occur for many reasons, the major one being contamination due to seepage from drainage networks and foul water bodies. In many places, sewer pipelines are normally positioned above the water pipelines. This is quite common in the development process. Initially the water pipelines are laid, and later sewer pipes are laid. Most of the water supply systems in the country are designed with an assumption of continuous supply, whereas the systems actually operate intermittently. This means that there are many occasions when the pressure in the pipeline is zero or negative. A low pressure inside the water supply pipeline favours the entry of sewage into the pipeline. When the water supply resumes, the contaminants get mixed with water, resulting in the deterioration of the quality of water supplied. Thus leakages in the drinking water pipelines and close proximity of sewer lines, foul water bodies and garbage disposal areas to pipelines pose a serious risk of contamination of the drinking water and hence the health of the people.

Once a potentially hazardous situation has been recognized, however, the risk to health, the availability of alternative sources, and the availability of suitable remedial measures must be considered so that a decision can be made about the acceptability of the supply. Failure to provide adequate protection and effective treatment will expose the community to the risk of outbreaks of diseases. Those at greatest risk of waterborne disease are infants and young children, people who are debilitated or living under unsanitary conditions, the sick, and the elderly.

The quality of water supplied is of utmost importance in all water distribution systems. However, the system cannot be made 100 per cent foolproof, avoiding all possible quality deterioration. Constant watch on the system and routine maintenance works are required for the proper functioning of the system. In developing countries, the funds available for maintenance or renovation works will often be too little. Thus it becomes essential to have a trade-off between the works to be undertaken. The assessment of risk involved in water supply systems is essential for the adoption of better management policies for averting hazards. The fault that is likely to affect the maximum number of population and also those that have serious impacts on the health of the general public are to be attended to with immediate priority. This decision-making is crucial in protecting the health of the public and the management of available funds. Such decision support systems require handling a large amount of data, for which geographic information systems (GIS) will be the best tool. GIS technology is applied in a variety of problems in water distribution networks. GIS gives a visual model of the field conditions and hence can be used with ease, even by a layman. A Water Quality model can be integrated with the GIS tool to simulate the hydraulic and water quality analysis at various points in the pipe networks. Then, using the GIS tool, the area and number of families affected by deterioration in water quality can be determined. A decision support system with GIS interface will be an effective tool in the proper management of the water supply system.

The aim is to assess the risk involved in intermittent water supply systems and to determine the area affected and decide alternative routes for water supply using GIS tools. Risk is defined as the product of probability of occurrence of an event and the loss associated with it. In case of water supply networks the event of concern is the occurrence of a leakage in the pipeline and water getting contaminated due to the presence of sewer lines or other sources of contamination nearby. The failure probability analysis can be done using a fault tree analysis. Then, using the data obtained by spatial analysis, the loss involved in the particular event can be determined. Thus the risk of contamination in pipe networks can be determined.

Integration of water supply network analysis models and GIS can be a feasible and affordable tool for many municipalities and engineering firms for analysing the system as well as for assessment of risk and adopting suitable alternatives. It can serve as an efficient tool in water distribution system management. The applicability of the developed models has been demonstrated with a case study of the Guntur water supply system.

Methodology

The procedure adopted for development of an integrated water quality risk assessment model consists of three phases. The first phase consists of integrating the pipe network analysis model with GIS. A network analysis model is used to simulate the propagation of contaminant through the network and locating the affected sections of the network. The integrated model is then applied to the water supply network of zone VIII in Guntur city. Assessment of risk is done in the second phase. This includes quantification of risk involved in various components of the network and health risk to the customers. Third phase consists of formulating the decision support system. The various phases of the methodology are shown in the block diagram (Figure F.1).

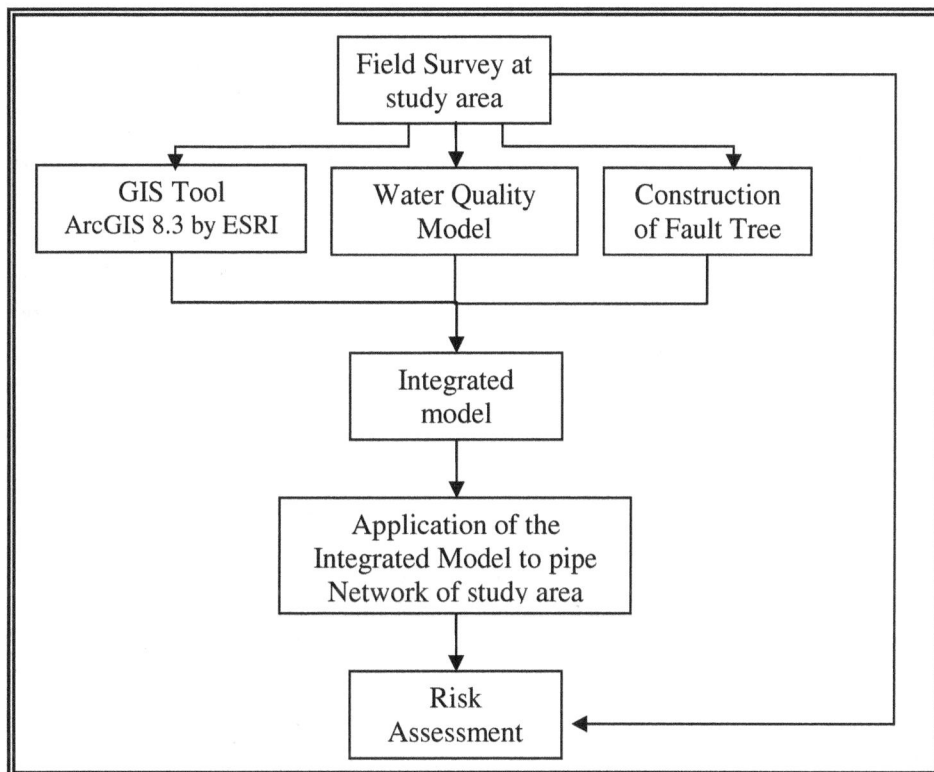

Figure F.1. Various Phases of Methodology

ArcGIS Desktop 8.3 software package by ESRI (Environmental Systems Research Institute, Inc.) was used to map the network and other geographic features of zone VIII. The water supply network analysis model was integrated to ArcGIS using the macro editor provided for visual basic application. This retrieves required data from the attribute tables of features of the map and creates the input for the network analysis model. After successful simulation of the model, it loads the results to the attribute table of appropriate features in the map. Then using the spatial analysis tool provided in ArcGIS, the contamination prone areas are identified. The results are displayed in the GIS interface.

A field survey was done for gathering information on the frequency of failure of network components, frequency of contamination events, number of people affected by a particular event of contamination etc. From this data, the probability of failure of network components was determined. Information on the routine maintenance works and replacements, and the expected expenditure on medical treatments on occurrence of contamination was also collected. A risk table was created, to facilitate comparison of risk involved in various network components and to identify the locations that require immediate attention.

Creating Thematic Maps

Thematic maps were created for different features of the study area. In GIS all thematic maps are associated with an attribute table, which contains the properties of every element of the feature class (thematic maps). Each field in the attribute table represents a particular property. GIS will automatically create the attribute table and adds certain default fields to it. Many more fields are required to fully describe the network as required by EPANET. These fields can be added to the table by a procedure similar to that in other database management tools.

Features are represented in GIS by means of points, lines and polygons. In the case of a water supply network, the nodes are mapped as points and links as lines. The ward map, soil-types map etc. are created using polygons. The fields required in the attribute table for the nodes and links are given in Tables F1 and F2 respectively. There are certain fields that are essentially required for the simulation of network analysis model. These fields are to be populated for the creation of the proper input file. Certain fields are required for loading the results. The units of the values entered in the fields depend upon the unit system chosen for the analysis. There are two main types of units for EPANET, viz. US customary units and SI Metric units. The unit of parameters based on the unit type selected is given in Table F.3. There is an option to choose the unit system while creating the input file, which sets the unit for all the parameters. Details on the input file format and other information for running the simulation are available at the help section in the EPANET 2.0 software package.

Table F.1. Fields to be added in the GIS Attribute table for Network Analysis using EPANET (for the feature class for Nodes)		
Field	**Field Type**	**Remarks**
Object ID	Number	Added automatically by GIS
Shape	Text	Added automatically by GIS
* Node ID	Text	ID of the node
* Node type	Text	Type of node (Junction, Tank or Reservoir)
* Elevation	Number	For tank, it is the bottom level of the tank and for reservoir it is the total head available
Initial quality	Number	Initial concentration of chemicals at the nodes
Demand	Number	Demand at the nodes. No demand for tank and reservoir nodes Demand may be zero for head dependent flow analysis
Pattern	Text	ID of the time pattern for the node
Source type	Text	Type of source (detailed in EPANET Help)
Source strength	Number	Concentration at the source
Source pattern	Text	ID of the time pattern for source concentration
* Flow coefficient	Number	Flow coefficient value, in case of head dependent flow
+ Actual demand	Number (single)	Demand or outflow calculated during the run
+ Hydraulic head	Number (single)	Total hydraulic head at the node
+ Pressure	Number (single)	Pressure at the node
+ Actual quality	Number (single)	Concentration of chemical species at the node
+ Mass flow rate of chemical source	Number (single)	Flow rate of chemical at the node
# No. of house connections	Number (integer)	No. of house connections from the node
# No. of standpipes	Number (integer)	No. of standpipes connected to the node
* Essential fields for pipe network analysis + Essential fields for loading results # Essential fields determining no. of outlets affected by contamination.		

Table F.2. Fields to be added in the GIS Attribute table for Network Analysis using EPANET(for the feature class for Links)		
Field	**Field Type**	**Remarks**
ObjectID	Number	Added automatically by GIS
Shape	Text	Added automatically by GIS
* Link ID	Text	ID of the link
* Link type	Text	Type of link (Pipe, Valve or Pump)
* Start node	Text	ID of Start node for the link
* End node	Text	ID of end node for the link
* Length	Number	Length of the link (only for pipes)
* Diameter	Number	Diameter of link
* Roughness coefficient	Number	Roughness coefficient for the pipe material (only for pipes)
Minor loss coefficient	Number	Minor loss coefficient for links
Valve type	Text	Type of valve, as defined by EPANET
Valve setting	Number	Pressure/flow settings for valves
Reaction type	Text	Reaction type in the link (Bulk/Wall)
Reaction coefficient	Number	Reaction coefficient for the link
* Link status	Text	'Open' or 'Closed'
[+] Flow rate	Number (single)	Flow rate in the link
[+] Velocity	Number (single)	Velocity of flow in the link
[+] Head loss	Number (single)	Total head loss during flow in the link
[+] Status	Text (Open/Closed)	Status of the link during simulation
[+] Settings	Number (single)	Pipe roughness/ valve setting during simulation
* Essential fields for pipe network analysis [+] Essential fields for loading results		

Table F.3. Unit System used in EPANET 2.0		
Parameter	US customary units	SI Metric units
Concentration	mg/L or ug/L	Mg/L or ug/L
Demand	(same as Flow)	(same as Flow)
Diameter (Pipes)	inches	mm
Diameter (Tanks)	feet	m
Efficiency	%	%
Elevation	Feet	m
Flow coefficient	Flow units / /psi	Flow units / /meter
Flow	CFS(Cubic feet/sec) GPM (gallons/min) MGD (million gallons/day) IMGD (Imperial MGD) AFD (acre-feet/day)	LPS(litres/sec) LPM (litres/min) MLD (mega litres/day) CMH (cubic-metres/hr) CMD (cubic-metres/day)
Roughness coefficient	Unitless (Millifeet for Darcy Weisbach equation)	Unitless (Millimetres for Darcy Weisbach equation)
Hydraulic head	feet	m
Length	feet	m
Minor loss coefficient	Unitless	Unitless
Pressure	Pounds per square inch	m
Reaction coefficient (Bulk)	1/days (1st order)	1/days (1st order)
Reaction coefficient (Wall)	Mass/L/day (0 order) Feet/day (1st order)	Mass/L/day (0 order) Metres/day (1st order)
Source mass injection	Mass/minute	Mass/minute
Velocity	Feet per second	m/s
Volume	Cubic feet	Cubic metres
Water age	hours	hours

Integrating Network Analysis Model (EPANET) with GIS

The software package used for GIS application was ArcGIS Desktop 8.3, which is composed of three modules called ArcMap, ArcCatalog and ArcToolbox. ArcGIS provides for changing or creating toolbars and menus in the work environment. Custom commands can be created with VBA (Visual Basic Application) in ArcMap using the extensive object library. New objects are created and codes are attached to them to accomplish a particular set of actions. Custom-made toolbars and menus can be saved to a template (*.mxt in ArcMap). All maps made in a particular template will have all the custom-made commands saved to the template and will be available every time the map is opened.

A template (Pipe_Network_Analysis.mxt) was created to save the new toolbars and menus for integrating the water supply network analysis tool. All the maps created for analysis of water supply networks were made in this template. The template consisted of the menus and commands as explained below.

The menu for water quality analysis is depicted in Figure F.2. It consists of four commands, namely, *'Create Input File'*, *'View Input File'*, *'Run Model'* and *'Load Output'*. The command, *'Create Input File'*, will create a text file in the format for input to the network analysis model, EPANET 2.0. Clicking on to the command will open up a dialog for retrieving specific data from the themes (Figure F.3). The data required are derived from the related shape files (representing the themes or layers in ArcMap) from appropriate fields in the attribute tables. The fields contained in the attribute tables of the selected theme are listed in the combo box next to each parameter. The field, which contains the value corresponding to the parameter required, is to be selected for each combo box in the dialog. There are two options for hydraulic analysis viz. Pressurized flow analysis and the Head dependent flow analysis (Figure F.4). For head dependent flow analysis, the flow coefficient values are to be added to the attribute tables as required by EPANET.

After choosing the necessary options, clicking to the *'ADD Network Components'* button starts adding the network parameters to the default input file. After adding the network components, another dialog as shown in Figure F.5 opens up automatically for choosing the analysis options. This is similar to the normal EPANET interface. For each tab in the dialog, short notes are given at the bottom of the dialog. Clicking the *'Create Input File'* button completes the input file and a message box is displayed (Figure F.6).

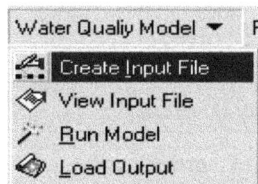

Figure F.2. Menu for simulating water quality model (network analysis model EPANET 2.0)

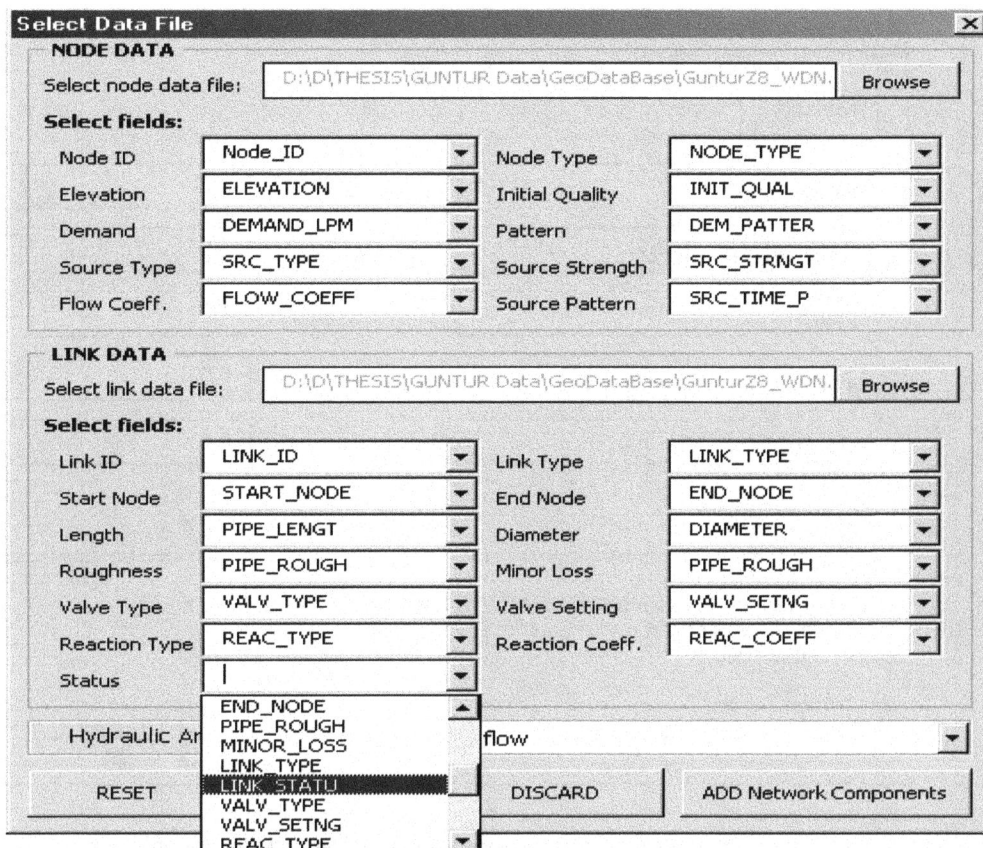

Figure F.3. Dialog for retrieving data from appropriate fields of selected themes

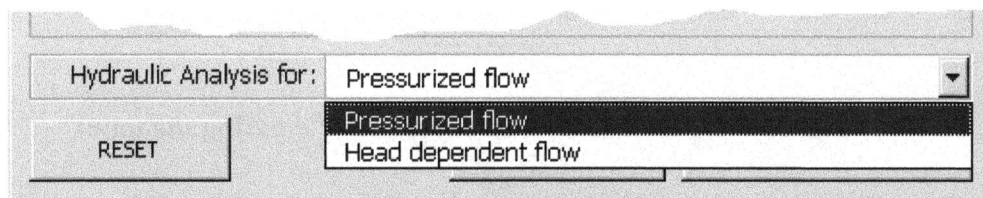

Figure F.4. Dialog box for choosing the type of analysis

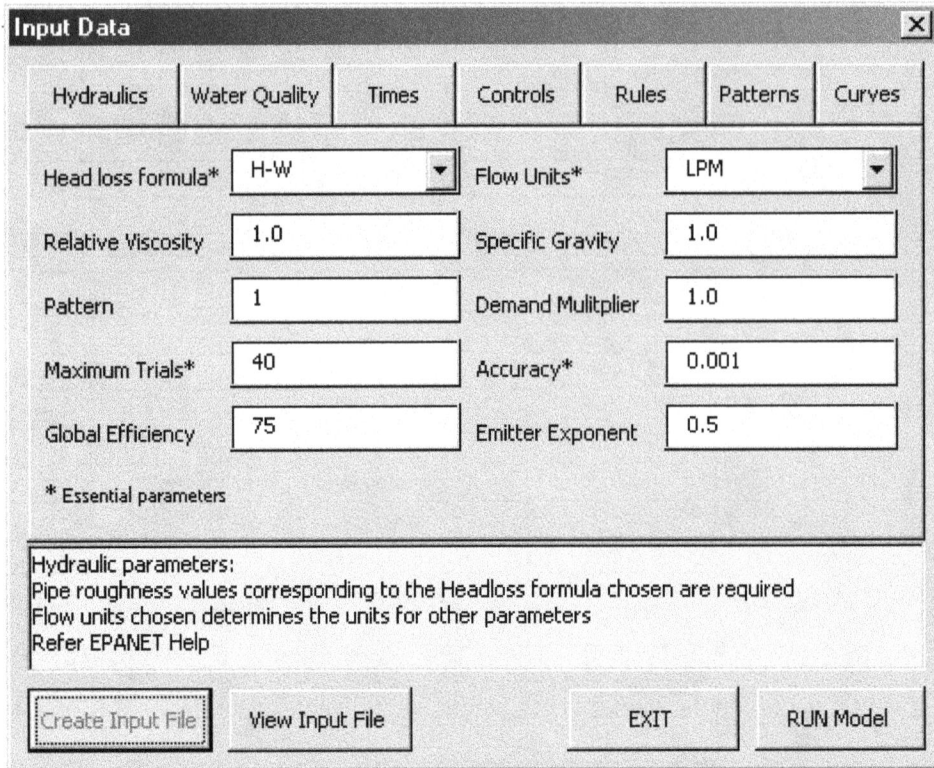

Figure F.5. Dialog for choosing the analysis options

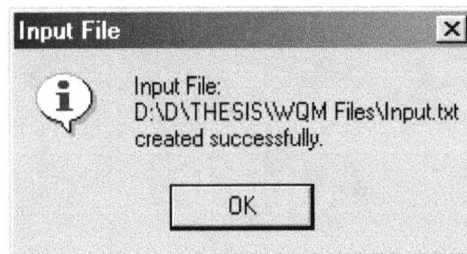

Figure F.6. Message box, on successfully creating the input

The input file created can be viewed using the '*View Input File*' command from the *Water Quality Analysis* menu (Figure F.7). The default input file can also be saved in a different filename.

Once the input file is created, the network can be simulated using the '*Run Model*' command from the menu. An input file other than the default input file can be chosen in the dialog that appears. A different name may be given for the report file. The simulation is triggered by the '*RUN*' button in the dialog. It generates a message, whether the run was successful or not. If the run was unsuccessful, the report file can be viewed for error checking in the input file. The errors should be corrected before any further simulation or loading of results.

```
View File                                                                    ×

[TIMES]                                                                        ▲
Duration                  24:00
Hydraulic Timestep        1:00
Quality Timestep          0:05
Pattern Timestep          1:00
Pattern Start             0:00
Report Timestep                      1:00
Report Start              0:00
Start ClockTime           12:00 am
Statistic        NONE


[REPORT]
Status   Full
Summary          No
Page     0


[ENERGY]
Global Efficiency         75
Global Price              0
Demand Charge                    0

[OPTIONS]
Units                     LPM
Headloss                  H-W
Specific Gravity 1.0
Viscosity                 1.0
Trials                    40
Accuracy                  0.001
Unbalanced                Continue 10
Pattern                   1
Demand Multiplier         1.0
Emitter Exponent          0.5
Quality                   None    mg/l
Diffusivity               1.0
Tolerance                 0.01

[END]                                                                          ▼

                                   SAVE AS            OK
```

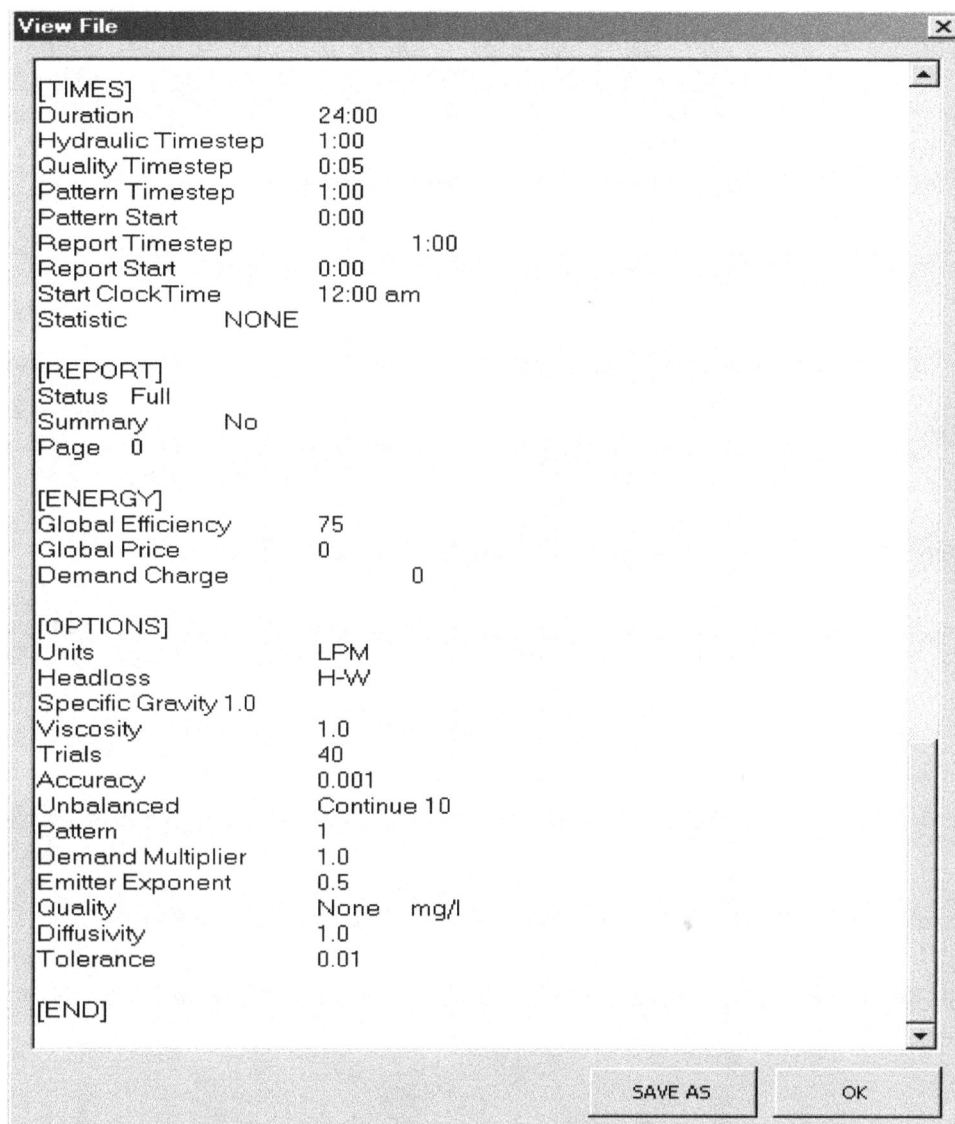

Figure F.7. Dialog box for viewing the input file created

Once the input file is successfully run, the outputs can be loaded to the attribute tables. The output tables should have fields for loading the results as described in Appendices 1 and 2. The results can be loaded to the attribute table of the thematic maps in the current map document in ArcMap. This implies that the maps should be added as layers to the current map document. Activating the '*Load Output*' command from the menu brings up the dialog for choosing the fields to which the results are to be loaded.

The dialog lists the themes already loaded into the map. The combo boxes list the fields available in the tables. Respective fields may be chosen for both node and link results. The time period for which the results are to be loaded should also be chosen from the lowermost combo box in the dialog. After loading the results, the symbology of the layer is changed to show the variation in chemical concentration.

211

Water Quality Simulation

The water supply network of the study area was simulated so that the water quality condition for four cases could be analysed. The menus and commands developed as explained above were used for the analysis. The four cases are:

Case 1: Contamination at a single node – Instantaneous intrusion
Case 2: Contamination at a single node – Continuous intrusion
Case 3: Contamination at multiple nodes – Instantaneous intrusion
Case 4: Contamination at multiple nodes – Continuous intrusion.

Node no. 534 was chosen as the contaminated node for cases 1 and 2. This is one of the nodes at which the sewer line crosses pipelines. The scenario in case 1 is that a particular amount of contaminant has entered into the pipeline through a leak at this point. This is assumed to result in a contaminant concentration of 100mg/l in water at this node for the first five minutes after resuming water supply. The contaminant intrusion will be absent once water supply resumes because of higher pressure within the pipeline.

For case 2, the node 534 is assumed to have continuous intrusion into the pipeline, resulting in the contaminant concentration of 100mg/l in water for the first five minutes after resuming water supply and 10mg/l for the rest of the time for which water is supplied. This is the case when the pressure inside the water pipeline is not sufficient to push the contaminant outside the pipe. But since the pipe is not empty, the intrusion rate will not be as high as when there was no water in the pipe. Thus it was taken as about 10 per cent of the initial intrusion rate.

Cases 3 and 4 consider similar situations, but with the contaminant intrusion occurring at two different nodes. Node no. 589, which is close to a foul water body, and node no. 487, which is crossed by a sewer line, were chosen for these two cases. The resulting contaminant concentration in water and the pattern of variation in the intrusion rate was considered the same as that of the previous cases.

Assessment of Risk due to Contamination

A field survey was conducted in zone VIII of Guntur City, for gathering information on failures of water supply and drainage network components and occurrence of contamination events. The aim was to meet the technical people as well as the general public and collect data on failure frequencies, time taken to repair, maintenance/replacement expenses, frequency of occurrence of epidemics due to contaminated water and the population affected. A questionnaire was prepared for the survey (Table F.4). The survey yielded valuable information on the major causes of failures in the water supply system as well as the drainage network, the frequency and severity of such failures and the cost of repair or replacement. Information was obtained on the impact of a contamination event on the general public and GMC (Guntur Municipal Corporation). The expenditure on medical treatment in the case of an intake of contaminated water was also obtained from the public. The fault tree approach was used to assess the overall probability of failure due to contamination. Information obtained from the survey was compiled to develop a fault tree for determining the probability of occurrence of contamination in the water supply network. The probability of occurrence of each of the base events in the fault tree was calculated from the data obtained from the field survey. The data on expenses incurred in each failure or contamination event were used to evaluate the risk involved in the system.

Table F.4. Questionnaire for field survey of Study area – zone VIII of Guntur City

Risk Assessment of Water Supply Pipe Networks in Guntur

General

Date: .... February 2004 Interviewer: _____	
LOCATION:	

Respondent Details

Respondent Name:	
Age:	
Duration of stay in the region: [Years]	
Address:	
Number of members in Family:	Adult Children
Educational qualification:	
Source of water:	Pipe Connection Street Pipe Others [specify]:
Water consumption per day: [Approximate]	

Vulnerable Locations

Area:				Number of locations:		
Location/Land mark	**Sewer**			**Water Pipe**		
	Type [Open/Closed]	Diameter [cm]	Burial Depth [m]	Type [Major/ Distributory/Domestic]	Diameter [cm]	Burial Depth [m]
1.						

Failure of Water Supply Pipes

Number of failures [Leakage/Break]:				
Location	Failure point [Valve/Joint/Pipe]	Type of failure [Major/Minor]	Causes of failure [E.g.: age, heavy traffic, corrosion, material defect...]	Time taken to restore water supply or for maintenance [Days/Hours]
1.				

Failure of Sewer Lines

Number of failures [Leakage/Break]:		Time span [Years]:	
Location of failure	**Type of failure [Lining failure/ Pipe-Break/Unlined]**	**Causes of failure [E.g.: age, heavy traffic, corrosion, material defect…]**	**Time taken to restore or for maintenance work [Days/Hours]**
1.			

Consequences*

Work location [pipe/joint/valve/sewer]	Work type	Cost per unit work [Rs]	Other expenses
1.		Pre:	
		Res:	

Pre: Maintenance before failure, Res: Restoration work after failure.

* To be obtained from Authorities

Additional information

In case of water supply failure, what are the alternative sources available	

Lorry load	Cost: Rs……… per……….	Quantity: ………………………………
Stand pipe		Quantity: ………………………………
…………….	Cost: Rs……… per……….	Quantity: ………………………………

Other expenditure due to failure	

Whether contamination has occurred at any time	☐ Yes ☐ No

If YES,
        How many times contamination has occurred:
                                 Disease:
                Duration of persist:
        Number of members of family affected:	

Survey done by
Signature…………………………
Name……………………………..

Risk is defined as the product of probability of occurrence of an event and its consequences. One additional menu – *Risk Assessment* – was added in the template (Pipe_Network_Analysis.mxt) for fault tree analysis and to retrieve data from attribute tables about the number of house connections and standpipes affected by contamination (Figure F.8). The dialog for fault tree analysis contains a fault tree as shown in Figure F.9 and was developed based on the information gathered from the field survey. The probabilities for failure of various components are to be entered in the corresponding enabled text boxes, and the probability of contamination is automatically calculated. The text box for probabilities that are automatically calculated, are disabled.

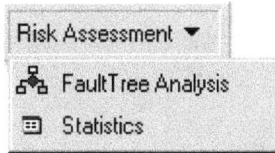

Figure F.8. Menu for Risk Assessment

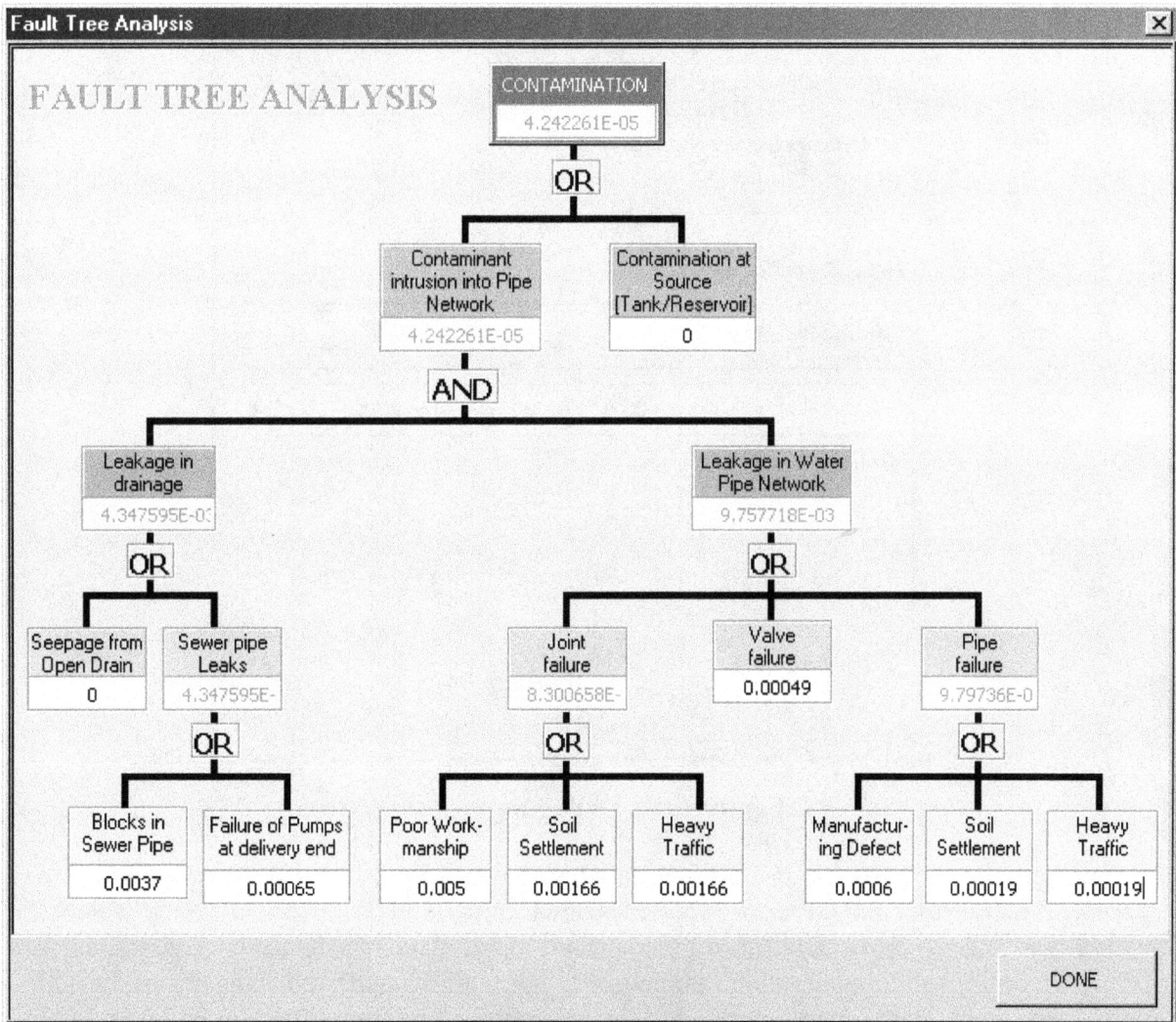

Figure F.9. Dialog for fault tree analysis

The 'Statistics' command in the menu activates the statistics dialog shown in Figure F.10. The purpose of this is to retrieve the data from the attribute tables, the number of house connections and standpipes in the network affected by contamination. Similar to earlier cases, the appropriate feature class and corresponding fields are to be selected from the lists given in the dialog window. Probability of contamination can be either typed in or obtained from the fault tree. On clicking the 'CALCULATE' button, the total number of house connections and standpipes at which the chemical concentration is greater than zero is calculated and displayed in the space below.

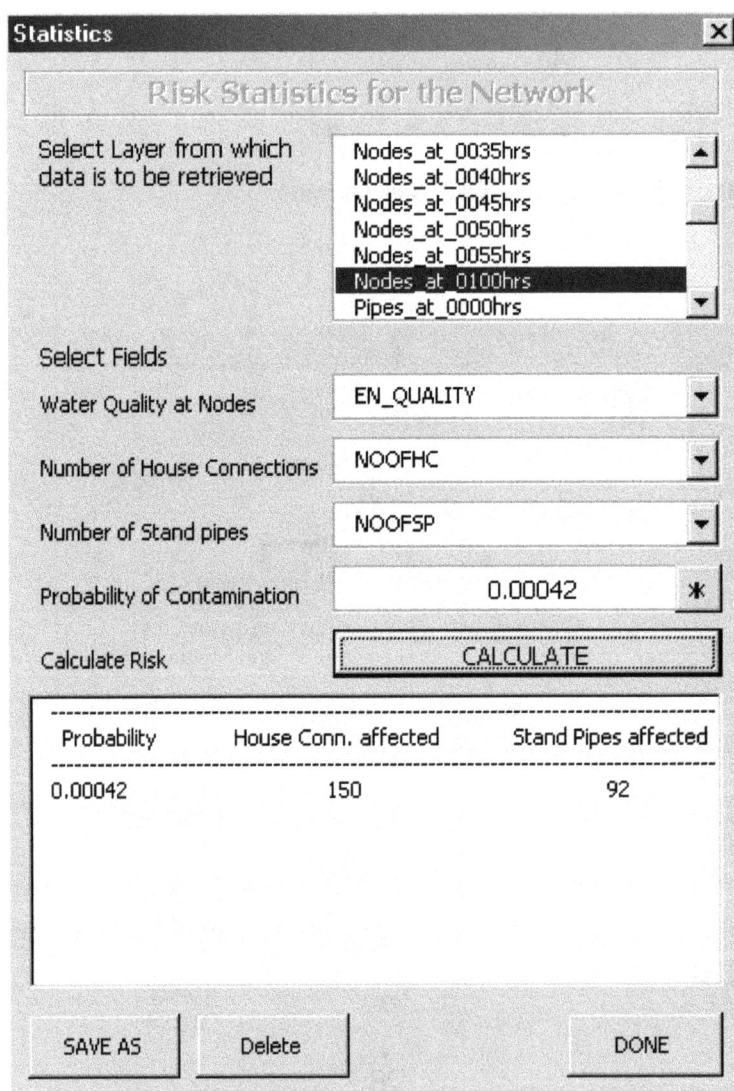

Figure F.10. Dialog for risk statistics

Various options are available in GIS for spatial analysis of the results. ArcMap provides the 'Spatial Analyst' tool for different types of spatial analysis. The inverse distance weighted method was used to create a buffer region surrounding the nodes affected by contamination. This is according to the assumption that people living within a certain distance from the node will use the water from a particular node. The area covered by the buffer can be measured to understand the extent of contamination. From the population density map, the approximate

216

population at risk of being affected by a particular event of contamination could be found out. The probability of occurrence of the event of contamination is determined from the fault tree analysis. The consequence is evaluated in monetary terms. Contamination essentially occurs with a failure in the water supply network and drainage network as depicted in the fault tree. This implies that one of the consequences is the cost of repair or replacement of the failed network component. A repair or replacement activity requires 1 to 5 days to complete, depending on the type of failure. During this time period, alternative arrangements are to be made for water supply. The expense incurred in this provision adds to the consequences of the failure event. These are the consequences affecting the authorities responsible for water supply or drainage networks. There are also consequences which affect the consumers. Contaminated water is hazardous to health and in most cases it requires that medical treatments are to be sought. This is yet another consequence of contamination. Thus the total consequence is the sum of costs incurred by the authorities in restoration of water supply and temporary alternative arrangements, and to consumers who are in the affected area.

The product of contamination probability and consequences gives the risk involved in a particular failure event. A risk table was created to evaluate the total consequence of various failure events and risk engrossed in that. The risk table helps to compare the risk in various components and to make decisions about the maintenance or replacement work that requires immediate attention. The expenses entailed with various consequences are obtained from the field survey of technical people who attend the failures in zone VIII and also from the Engineers-in-charge at GMC (Guntur Municipal Corporation).

The sensitivity of risk to various measures adopted for improving the system was also analysed with the risk table. For example, the risk was determined after reducing the probability of occurrence of failure of joints due to a particular cause, say improper maintenance. This gave the percentage reduction in risk produced by adoption of better maintenance methods. Similarly, the reduction in risk was determined for other measures. The percentage reduction in risk in each case was compared to determine the most sensitive measure. This helps to discard the measures which do not yield significant reduction in risk.

Since only limited funds are available for routine maintenance works, an intelligent fund allocation is required to use resources efficiently. Risk assessment gives handy information on activities to be undertaken immediately. The risk table gives both the event that requires immediate attention and the event that reduces risk significantly. A judicious combination of these two creates an excellent tool in decision-making processes.

Application of Model to Study Area

The development and application of a GIS-based risk assessment model following the procedure explained in the previous section are detailed below.

Field survey

The salient features of the water supply network of zone VIII of Guntur, as revealed from the field survey, are as follows.

- There are frequent occurrences of leaks in water supply network as well as the sewer networks. The failure frequency is about eight cases per day for water pipelines and two to three cases per day for sewer pipelines.

217

- The time taken for maintenance work ranges from one day to one week in certain cases. On average the leaks remain unattended for about three days.
- The majority of leaks in the water supply network occur at the joints. This is attributed to poor workmanship and the absence of soil bedding for the pipeline. A few cases of leakages were due to cracks in pipelines and wear and tear in valves.
- Leaks in the sewer line also occur at joints, but the main cause of leaks is the frequent blocks in the sewer lines. Sometimes it happens as a result of failure of the pumps at the delivery end of the sewer lines.
- Contamination of water supply has occurred many times. This lasts for some time after water supply resumes and also when people try to pump water from the pipes after the supply has stopped. The contamination was identified by changes in the colour and taste of water and the odour. This confirms the movement of sewage from the leaks in the sewer lines and its entry to the water pipeline through the leaks in it.
- The water is not used if contamination is identified by colour, odour or taste, but there were cases when the contamination could not be identified by these means. This resulted in consumption of polluted water, leading to severe health hazards.
- Outbreaks of disease due to consumption of contaminated water were reported to affect about 500 people per year.
- In the event of contamination or leaks in pipelines, GMC (Guntur Municipal Corporation) supplied drinking water to the people of affected area by tanker lorry.
- The expense involved in a leakage event includes the cost of components, replacement/maintenance charge, the cost of alternative arrangements for water supply and the cost of medical treatment for health probems caused by contamination. This information was collected from the general public and also from the technical people from GMC and Deputy Engineer in charge of water supply networks.

Thematic maps of the study area

Thematic maps of the study area were prepared in ArcGIS Desktop 8.3 and the attribute tables were modified by adding the fields required, as mentioned in Appendices 1 and 2. The maps concerning pipe network (Figure 6.2), sewer network (Figure 6.3), open drain network (Figure 6.4) along with foul water bodies (Figure 6.5), land cover (Figure 6.7) and population density (Figure F.11) were prepared and used for further analysis.

Integration of EPANET model with ArcGIS 8.3

The water supply network analysis model, EPANET 2.0, was integrated to the GIS environment using Visual Basic scripts as explained in the methodology. The input file for EPANET was successfully created from the interactive and user-friendly menus and commands developed. Also the model was simulated with the created input file. The results of water quality analysis for the different cases and various time intervals were loaded to the attribute table of the corresponding thematic maps. After loading to the attribute tables the results were displayed in a map using suitable colour ramp showing the variation of contaminant concentration at the affected nodes. This was achieved using the symbology property of the maps as given by ArcGIS.

population/sq.km

	7500 - 20000
	20000 - 30000
	30000 - 40000
	40000 - 50000
	50000 - 60000
	60000 - 70000
	70000 - 83000

N

0 125 250   500   750   1,000
Meters

Zone VIII, Guntur

Figure F.11. Population density map for zone VIII of Guntur (ward-based)

Water Quality Simulation for Pipe Network

Water quality simulation for the water supply network of zone VIII of Guntur was done with the following parameters.

- Analysis was done for head dependent flow at outlets (nodes). The flow coefficient value for the outlets was assumed on average to be 40, where the flow unit is LPM and head in metres. (Flow coefficient value of 40 corresponds to the orifice constant 0.82 and opening diameter of 15 mm.)

- The nodes assumed to be affected by contamination (node numbers 534, 589 and 487 in different cases as described in the methodology) is set to be contaminated by a non-reactive contaminant with resultant initial concentration of 100 mg/l. The node was set as a 'set-point' source with the contaminant being present at the node in the initial five minutes for plug flow cases (cases 1 and 3). For continuous intrusion cases (cases 2 and 4) the contaminant concentration was 100 mg/l for the initial five minutes and 10 mg/l for the rest of the time period.

- Extended period simulation was done for a time period of one hour with a time interval of 10 minutes.

- The results of water quality analysis for the last time interval (after one hour) for case 1 and case 2 are displayed in the GIS interface as shown in Figure F.12. Results of case 3 and case 4 are shown in Figure F.13.

- A buffer was created for the contaminated nodes for a distance of 100 m around the node. This is under the assumption that people within this distance from the node use water from those nodes. This was done using the spatial analyst tool in ArcGIS, with the Inverse Distance Weighted (IDW) method of interpolation. This gives the area surrounding a node that is likely to be affected by the contamination, as given in Figure F.14 and Figure F.15.

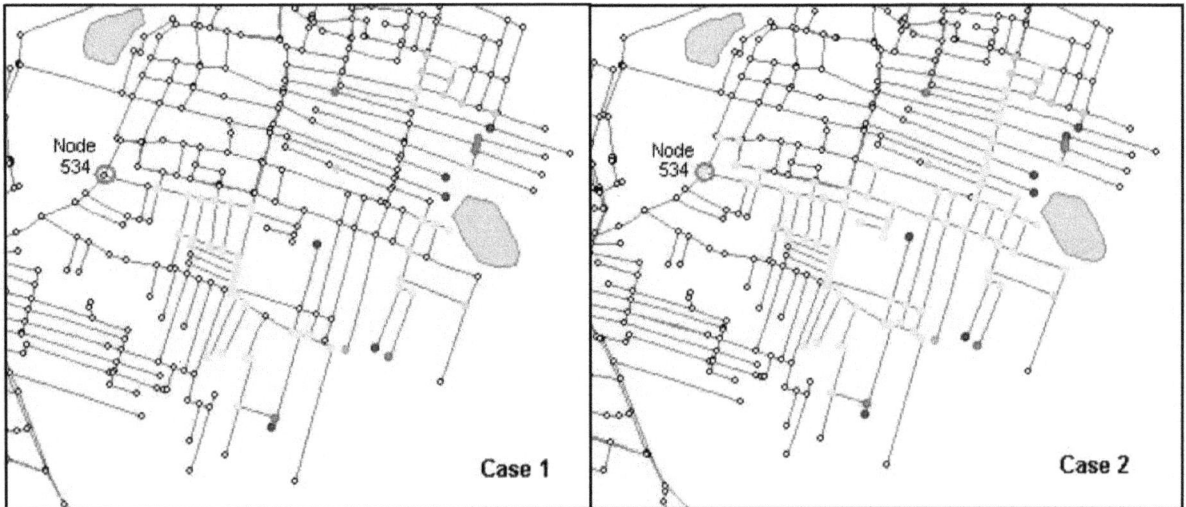

Figure F.12. Results of water quality simulations after one hour for node 534

Case 1: Single node – Plug flow intrusion
Case 2: Single node – Continuous intrusion

220

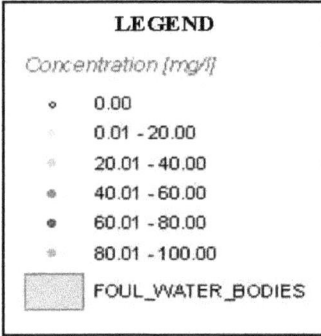

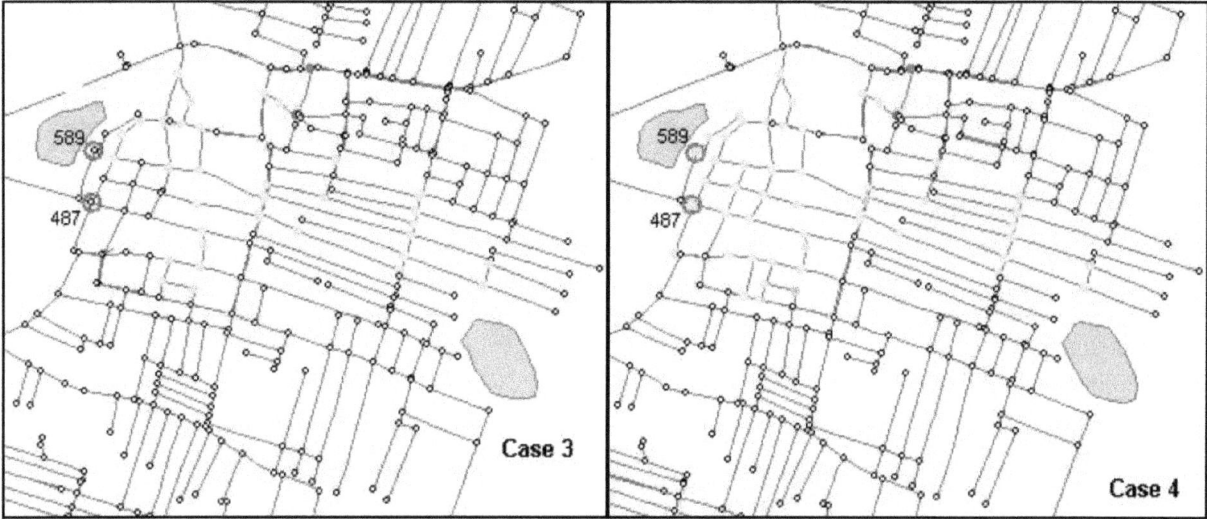

Figure F.13. Results of water quality simulations after one hour for nodes 589 and 487

Case 3: Multiple nodes – Plug flow intrusion
Case 4: Multiple nodes – Continuous intrusion

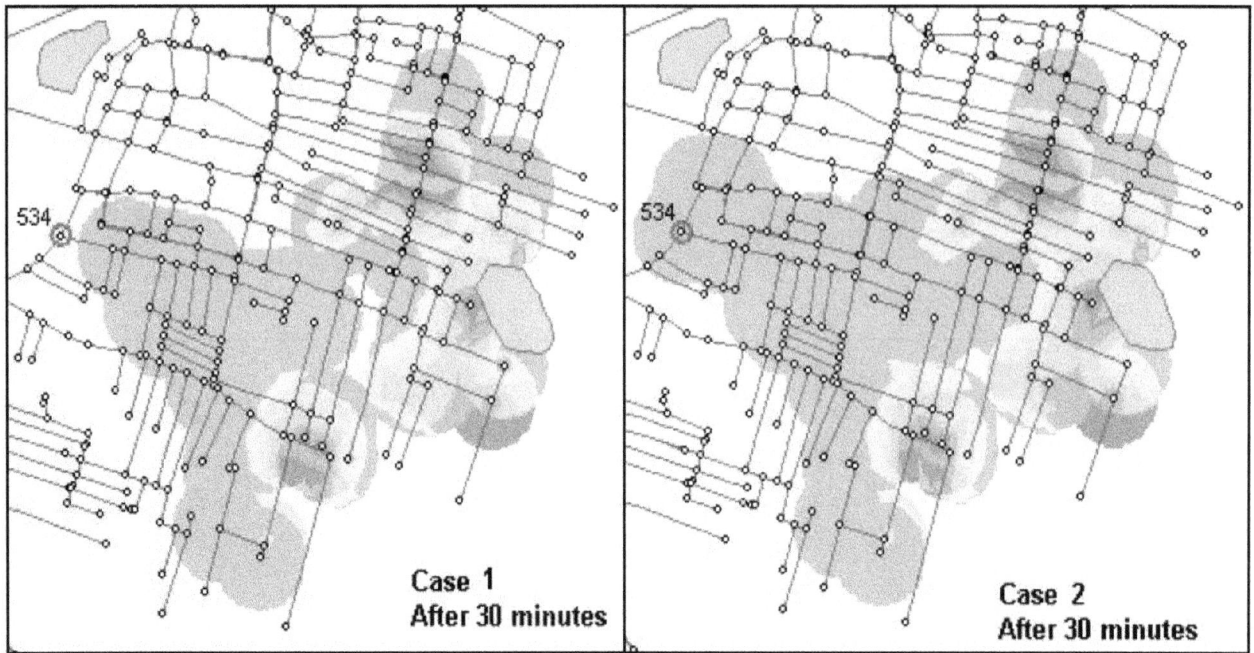

Contaminant
Concentration [mg/l]

▨	0 - 20
☐	20 - 30
☐	30 - 40
▨	40 - 50
▨	50 - 60
▨	60 - 70
☐	70 - 80
☐	80 - 100

Case 1: Single node – Plug flow intrusion
Case 2: Single node – Continuous intrusion

Figure F.14. Affected areas due to contamination at node 534

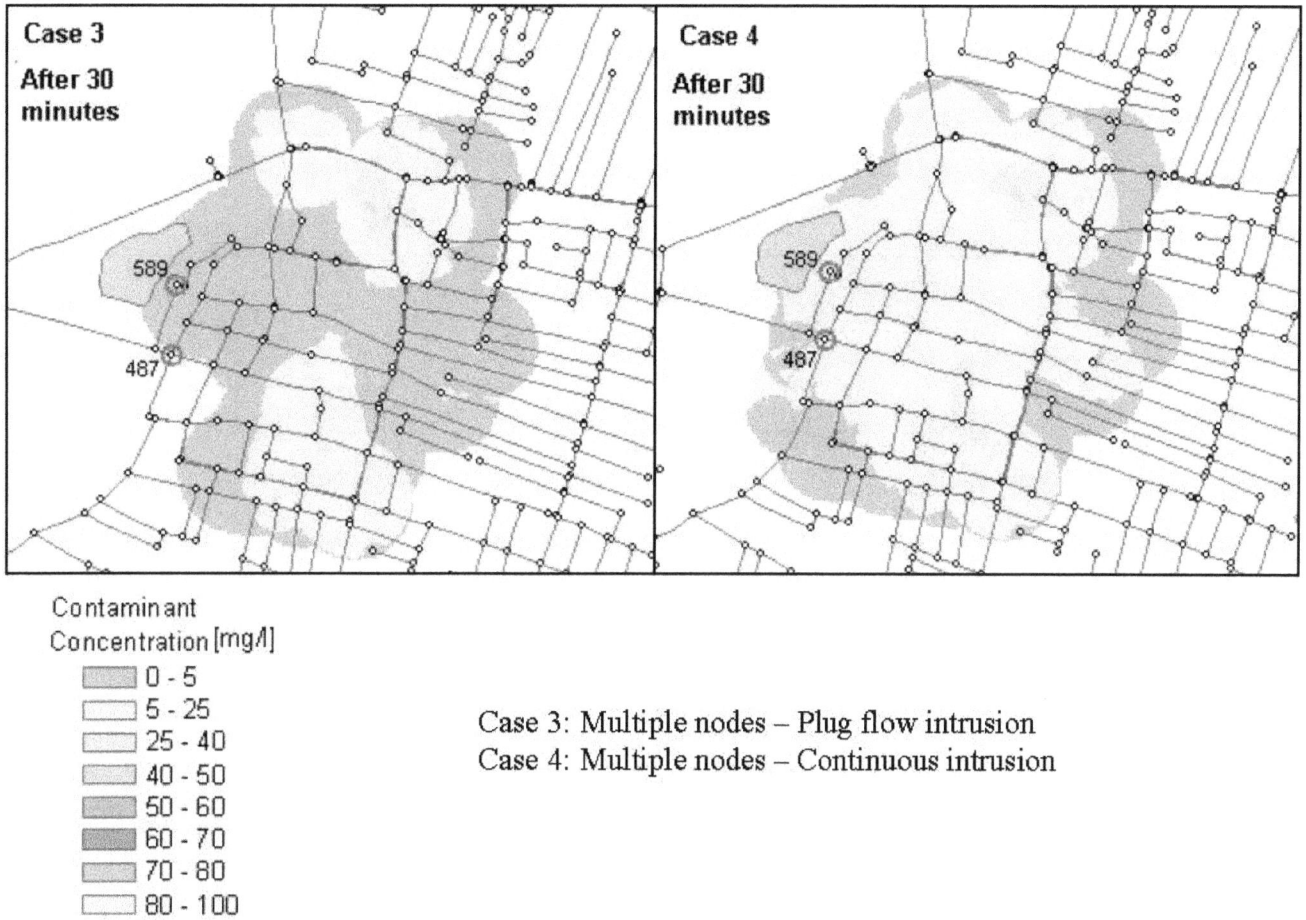

Figure F.15. Affected areas at due to contamination at nodes 589 and 487

Retrieving Statistics for Contaminated Nodes

After loading the results from the water quality simulation, the information on affected population could be obtained. The total number of household connections and standpipes to the nodes affected by contamination was retrieved from the GIS database. This includes all the connections from the nodes with contaminant concentration greater than zero.

The number of affected connections at different time intervals was obtained and is shown in Figure F.16, which gives the statistics for nodes affected by contamination during the one-hour simulation. From the figure it can be seen that continuous intrusion has affected a greater number of nodes compared with plug flow intrusion at any time interval. Also the location of the contaminated node has significant effect on the number of affected nodes. For example, in case 1, node no. 534, which supplied water to a large number of downstream nodes, was contaminated, resulting in more affected nodes than in case 3, where multiple nodes were affected. The results obtained for plug flow intrusions (cases 1 and 3) are to be closely analysed. The results displayed show affected nodes at each time intervals. In these cases the nodes affected earlier in the time period may not be considered as affected nodes later, as intrusion is stopped and fresh water starts flowing through those nodes after some time. But there are chances of health hazards during the time when the nodes were affected. Thus the actual number of affected nodes will be between the number of nodes affected in case of plug flow intrusion and continuous intrusion. Maps generated showing the area affected due to contamination also give insight to the extent of contamination. The maps are created by assuming that people within a radius of 100 m from a node have access to water from that node and interpolated using the Inverse Distance Weighted method of spatial analysis in ArcGIS. These results are important in the final decision-making. After determining the rankings based on risk analysis the final decision on management policy is to be made by considering the number of nodes, and hence the number of people affected by different events of contamination.

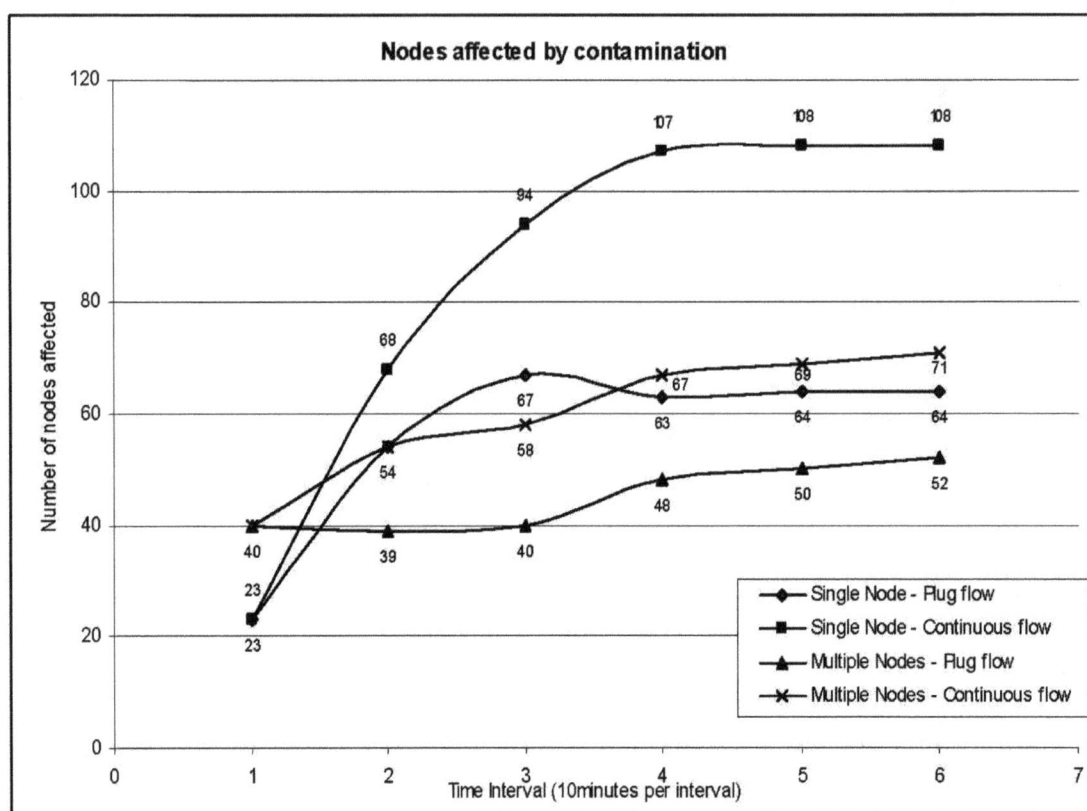

Figure F.16. Retrieving statistics for contaminated nodes

Determination of Alternative Connectivity for the Affected Nodes

Using the network analysis tool in ArcGIS, the connectivity to various nodes from the tank, in case of blocking of a part of the network, was traced out. Blocking of part of the water supply network is done to repair the leakage or eliminating the contamination occurred. It was checked whether there is an alternative route to supply water to the downstream nodes, in case a particular node was contaminated due to failure of the network component. This is essentially required if the maintenance work to be undertaken is of large volume and it takes more time to complete. Thus it may affect large number of people for longer time. Re-routing the water saves money spent on tankers and other alternative means of water supply.

Figure F.17. Contaminant intruded node and affected nodes after one hour of water flow

225

Figure F.18. A possible path of water from the tank to various nodes through the contaminant affected node

Figure F.19. Alternative path for water flow to various nodes, bypassing the contaminant affected node

In the trial simulation, node no. 534 was assumed to be having a leakage and contaminant intruded into the water supply pipes. Figure F.17 shows the spread of the contaminant within the water supply network after one hour of water flow as simulated by EPANET 2.0. Figure F.18 shows a possible pathway of water from the tank, through node no. 534, to various nodes. Node 534 has to be isolated to prevent contamination as well as to repair the leakage occurred. Thus three pipes that are connected to node 534 were blocked. Then again the network analysis tool was used to see whether the downstream nodes are connected to the tank through an alternative route. Figure F.19 depicts the results of this analysis.

These results are required to determine the cost of alternative arrangements in case of maintenance activity. The cost of alternative arrangement also adds to the total risk involved in the water supply network. Suitable planning before undertaking the maintenance work saves time and money. Determining the alternative routes for water supply and re-routing the water supply avoids the need for transport of water by tankers, and hence reduces the risk.

Fault Tree for Risk Analysis

The fault tree developed is shown in Figure F.20. The probabilities for the events shown in circles (basic events) are calculated from the field data and the probability of contamination is determined using the logical gates as shown in the fault tree.

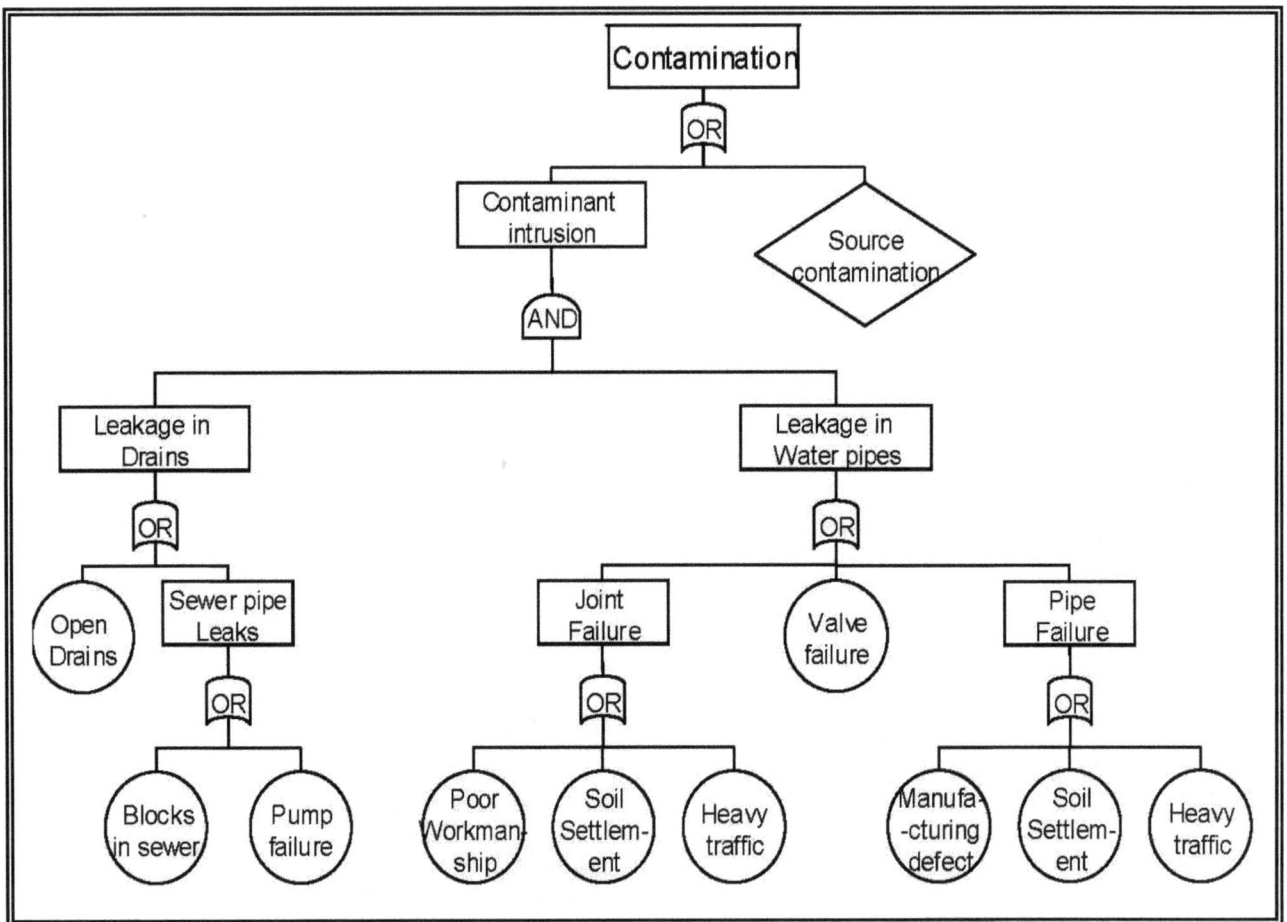

Figure F.20. Fault tree for contamination in water distribution system

Probability is determined as the ratio of the number of occurrences of failure of a component to the total number of the components in the network. For example, there are 821 pipes in the water supply network of zone VIII. The field survey revealed that an average of eight pipe leakages occur per day in the zone. Therefore there are 8 x 365 = 2920 cases of leakages per year. Of these 85 per cent of leakages are due to failure at joints; i.e. about 2503 cases. Also 60 per cent of the 2503 cases are due to poor workmanship. Thus the probability of occurrence of leakage in the network due by joint failure due to poor workmanship is

$$(2503 \times 0.60) \div (365 \times 821) = 0.00501$$

Other probabilities were also determined and are given in Table F.5.

Table F.5. Probabilities of base events		
Item	**Event**	**Probability**
Leaks from open drains		0.4000
Leak in sewer pipe	Block in sewer pipe	0.00278
	Pump failure at delivery end	0.10411
Joint failure in water distribution network	Poor workmanship	0.00501
	Soil settlement	0.00167
	Heavy traffic	0.00167
Pipe failure in water distribution network	Manufacturing defect	0.00059
	Soil settlement	0.00020
	Heavy traffic	0.00020
Valve failure in water distribution network		0.01007

Since the water is undergoing treatment at a water treatment plant before being supplied, the probability of contamination at the source is taken as zero. The probability of contamination calculated using the above values is 0.008949. From GIS, 512 locations were identified, where the water supply pipes cross (intersect) or are close to sewer lines or open drains. Thus from the fault tree results it is inferred that contamination is likely to occur four to five times per day (512 x 0.008949) at or near the intersections. This conforms to the results obtained from field survey, i.e. at least four events of contamination are reported in zone VIII of Guntur per day. Most of these events do not turn out to be a debacle, because the contamination is identified by the change in colour, odour and taste of water and so the water is abandoned.

Risk is defined as the product of probability and consequences. The consequences were evaluated in fiscal terms. The failures in zone VIII of Guntur remain unattended for about three days on average according to the information obtained from the field survey. Thus the probabilities of occurrence of failures in water supply networks and sewers increase to three times the actual value (Andrews and Moss 2002). This also increases the probability of contamination. Applying this concept in fault tree analysis, the resultant probability of contamination was obtained as 3.42×10^{-2}

Repair or maintenance activities necessitate provision of alternative arrangements for water supply to the area. GMC supplies water in tanker lorries to the affected areas, causing additional expense to authorities along with the cost of maintenance or replacements. There is also the expense of medical treatment for the general public if they consume contaminated water for medical treatment. All these constitute the consequences of failures in the water supply and drainage network.

For risk analysis the pipes were classified based on their diameters as major (diameter > 300 mm) and minor (diameter <=300 mm). Data collected for each group of failures showed that major failures occurred less frequently than minor failures. However, the consequences are large in the case of a major failure. A risk table (Table F.5) was created to calculate the total consequences, probability and hence the risk. Table F.7 shows the ranking of component failures based on risk. It can be seen that minor failures at the joints in the water supply network have significantly higher risk than other components. This indicates that utmost importance is to be given to the maintenance works for joints in a water supply network. Now the sensitivity of each component has to be considered as to how much the maintenance activity contributes in reducing the risk. The sensitivity analysis is done by reducing the probability of failures of each of the basic events and determining the resultant probability of contamination.

Table F.6. Calculation of risk involved in water distribution network of zone VIII of Guntur

Sl No	Failure event	Type of failure	Cost of maintenance [Rs/year]	Cost of replacement after failure [Rs/year]	Cost to GMC for alternative arrangements [Rs/year]	Probability of failure	No. of people affected [.../year]	Cost incurred in medical treatment [Rs/year]	Total consequences [Rs/year]	Failure risk [Rs/year]	Contamination risk [Rs/year]	Total risk [Rs/year]
a	b	c	d	E	f	g	h	i	j	k	L	m
			No. of failures x Cost of repair	No. of failures x Replacement cost	No. of failures x cost of alternative arrangement	from fault tree	field survey data	@ 500/head	e + f + i	g x (e + f)	Contamination Probability = 3.42E-02	k + l
1	Joint failure (WDN)	MINOR	2,482,000	3,723,000	2,482,000	0.0287	225	112,500	6,317,500	178,034	3,854.00	181,888
		MAJOR	42,000	105,000	31,500	0.0016	450	225,000	361,500	214	7,707.00	7,921
2	Pipe failure (WDN)	MINOR	350,400	876,000	438,000	0.00338	225	112,500	1,426,500	4,435	3,854.00	8,289
		MAJOR	6,000	30,000	6,000	0.00022	450	225,000	261,000	8	7,707.00	7,715
3	Valves (WDN)	MINOR	438,000	438,000	219,000	0.04000	225	112,500	769,500	26,280	3,854.00	30,134
		MAJOR	6,000	50,000	2,000	0.00082	450	225,000	277,000	43	7,707.00	7,750
4	Joint failure (Sewer)	MINOR	520,500	2,082,000	520,500	0.00972	225	112,500	2,715,000	25,290	3,854.00	29,144
		MAJOR	10,000	45,000	10,000	0.00077	450	225,000	280,000	42	7,707.00	7,749
5	Pipe failure (Sewer)	MINOR	55,500	111,000	27,750	0.00052	225	112,500	251,250	72	3,854.00	3,926
		MAJOR	2,000	10,000	1,000	0.00008	450	225,000	236,000	0.8	7,707.00	7,708

231

Table F.7. Ranking of component failures based on risk		
Rank	**Event**	**Risk [Rs]**
1	Minor joint failure in WDN	1,81,888
2	Minor valve failure in WDN	30,134
3	Minor joint failure in sewer line	29,144
4	Minor pipe failure in WDN	8,289
5	Major joint failure in WDN	7,921
6	Major valve failure in WDN	7,750
7	Major joint failure in sewer line	7,749
8	Major pipe failure in WDN	7,715
9	Major pipe failure in sewer line	7,708
10	Minor pipe failure in sewer line	3,926

By improving the quality of work and materials used, the probability of occurrence of basic events was decreased. For sensitivity analysis, it was assumed that by adopting suitable measures the probability of each basic event was reduced to 20 per cent of the actual value and the resulting probability of contamination could be determined. For example, the probability of a minor failure at joints in the water distribution network is 0.0287 (Table F.6). Adopting better maintenance methods and providing proper bedding at possible locations, it is assumed that the probability of failure is reduced to 0.0287 x 0.20 = 0.00574. Then using the fault tree it is determined that the reduced contamination probability is 0.02265. Thus there is a decrease of 33.87 per cent compared to the earlier value of contamination probability. Similarly, the probabilities of occurrence of other types of failures were also reduced and the percentage reduction in contamination probability was determined. The results are given in Table F.6.

From the results of sensitivity analysis it can be observed that the minor valve failures in water distribution network are the most sensitive event. This implies that a reduction in minor valve failures can significantly reduce the contamination probability. It can also be observed that minor joints failures in the water distribution network and sewer lines hold the second and third ranks respectively.

Table F.8. Results of sensitivity analysis for the failure events						
Failure	**Event type**	**Actual probability**	**Reduced probability**	**Resultant contamination probability**	**Percentage reduction**	**Rank**
Joint failure	MINOR	0.0287	0.00574	0.02265	33.87%	**2**
(WDN)	MAJOR	0.00157	0.00031	0.034162	0.25%	**5**
Pipe failure	MINOR	0.00338	0.00068	0.032878	4.00%	**4**
(WDN)	MAJOR	0.00022	0.00004	0.034247	0.01%	**6**
Valves	MINOR	0.04000	0.00800	0.02015	41.17%	**1**
(WDN)	MAJOR	0.00082	0.00016	0.034247	0.01%	**7**
Joint failure	MINOR	0.00972	0.00194	0.025484	25.59%	**3**
(Sewer)	MAJOR	0.00077	0.00015	0.034247	0.01%	**8**
Pipe failure	MINOR	0.00052	0.00010	0.034248	0.00%	**9**
(Sewer)	MAJOR	0.00008	0.00002	0.034248	0.00%	**10**

Table F.9. Combined results from risk and sensitivity analysis					
Failure	**Event type**	**Risk**	**Ranks based on risk**	**Sensitivity**	**Ranks for sensitivity analysis**
Joint failure	MINOR	**181888**	**1**	**33.87%**	**2**
(WDN)	MAJOR	**7921**	**5**	**0.25%**	**5**
Pipe failure	MINOR	**8289**	**4**	**4.00%**	**4**
(WDN)	MAJOR	**7715**	**8**	**0.01%**	**6**
Valves	MINOR	**30134**	**2**	**41.17%**	**1**
(WDN)	MAJOR	**7750**	**6**	**0.01%**	**7**
Joint failure	MINOR	**29144**	**3**	**25.59%**	**3**
(Sewer)	MAJOR	**7749**	**7**	**0.01%**	**8**
Pipe failure	MINOR	**3926**	**10**	**0.00%**	**9**
(Sewer)	MAJOR	**7708**	**9**	**0.00%**	**10**

For decision-making based on risk assessment, both the risk analysis results and the sensitivity analysis results are to be considered simultaneously. An extract from Tables F.6 and F.8 is given as Table F.9. It can be seen from the table that minor joint failure in the water supply network has the highest risk and is next to minor valve failure in sensitivity, whereas minor valve failure has the highest sensitivity and has a significantly lower value of risk than minor joint failures. Thus the decision can be to give more immediate attention to minor joint failures than to minor valve failures.

This is the case when the constraint is the fund availability for maintenance works. When more concern is given to public health and funding is not a constraint, however, the most sensitive event must be looked for, and in this case it is minor valve failure in water supply networks. This decision can also be taken when there is an outbreak of contagious diseases, especially those spread by water. In such cases, much care is to be given to prevent the spread of disease.

Often it requires case-specific decisions to be made. For example, which failure event to be given importance at any point of time? Such decisions cannot be easily made from the above results alone, as they are for the whole system. In such cases, the area affected by the particular event of contamination has to be considered, which is obtained earlier from the water quality analysis with GIS. This gives the area to which the contamination has spread. Then, depending upon the importance of the area, population density, presence of schools or hospitals etc. decisions can be made on events that require immediate attention.

Thus risk assessment proves to be an efficient decision support system. It provides an easy way of deciding upon the activity to be undertaken immediately, especially in situations of limited resource availability.

Conclusions

The integrated model was developed for water quality analysis within water distribution networks with the GIS environment. The network analysis model EPANET 2.0 was integrated into the GIS software package ArcGIS 8.3 by ESRI. The data required for analysis will be retrieved from the GIS tables and the results will be loaded back to the tables. Analysis was done for contamination occurring at a single node in the network and at multiple nodes in the network with varying rates of contaminant intrusion into the water supply pipeline. The results are displayed in the GIS interface and using the Spatial Analyst tool the area affected was mapped.

A field survey in the study area, i.e. zone VIII of Guntur City, revealed that around seven or eight failures occur in the water supply pipes per day and two or three in sewer lines. The average time taken for attending the failure by the authorities was about three days. The leakage in the water supply lines mostly occurs at the joints and this was attributed to the poor workmanship, soil settlement and heavy traffic. Leakages in sewer lines occur mainly due to blocks. Similarly the causes of failures of other components were also obtained and the fault tree was prepared from the information. Events of contamination in water supply were reported to occur many times a day at different locations. In many such cases the contamination was identified by changes in colour, odour and taste of water and so the water was discarded. There were cases when contamination was unidentified and resulted in health hazards to the public. The details of expenditure on maintenance and replacement activities, cost of alternative arrangements for water supply, and health care expenses were also obtained from the field survey.

The fault tree was constructed from information obtained from the field survey and the contamination probability was calculated as 0.034249. Sensitivity analysis of the failure events revealed that minor failures in the valve and joints in water supply networks have the highest sensitivity; i.e. reducing the probability of these failures significantly reduced the probability of contamination. A risk table was prepared to analyse the risk involved in each type of failure. This revealed that minor joint failure in water supply networks has a significantly higher risk than failure in the other components, implying the importance of attending to such failures with top priority.

The final decision depends upon other factors such as location of failure, importance of the affected area, presence of schools, hospitals etc. in the affected area (which are obtained from the GIS maps) and population density. In case of limited resource availability the priority may be given to reducing the risk and if resource availability is not the constraint then priority goes to reduction of probability of occurrence of contamination.

From the results the following conclusions are arrived at.

- Integration of the water quality model with GIS software helps as a decision-making tool for water supply management.
- Head dependent flow in intermittent water supply systems can be handled with EPANET 2.0 by imposing the emitter status to the nodes.
- Fault tree analysis not only helps to assess the probability of contamination in water distribution networks but also to prioritize the maintenance activities based on their sensitivity or impact on likely occurrence of contamination to the water supply.
- A risk table helps in deriving general management policies for the water supply system and along with GIS mapping it helps in arriving at location-specific decisions.

www.ingramcontent.com/pod-product-compliance
Lightning Source LLC
Chambersburg PA
CBHW080952050426
42334CB00057B/2602